CW01010955

STEVE WRAITH

STEVE WRAITH

EVERY BOY'S DREAM

Steve Wraith…

EVERY BOY'S
DREAM

& Jamie Boyle

Steve Wraith / Jamie Boyle ©
www.warcrypress.co.uk

Every Boy's Dream: Steve Wraith

ISBN: 978-1-912543-31-1

All rights reserved. No part of this publication may be reproduced or transmitted in any form or by any means, including photocopying and recording, without the written permission of the copyright holder, application for which should be addressed to the publisher via the dealing agent at warcypress@roobix.co.uk. Such written permission must also be obtained before any part of this publication is stored in a retrieval system of any nature. This book is sold subject to the Standard Terms and Conditions of Sale of New Books and may not be re-sold in the UK below the net price fixed by the Publisher / Agent.

Produced by Warcry Press (part of Roobix Ltd) on behalf of Steve Wraith /Jamie Boyle (c) 2020.

Printed and bound in Great Britain by P M M Group UK Ltd

Book Cover Design by David Stanyer (D S Creative)

Find out more at: facebook.com/warcrypublishing

I'd like to dedicate this book to:

Chris Heron, Bryan Williams, Ray Caan & Sam Booth.

CONTENTS

INTRODUCTION

A well-known chief executive of a football club, allegedly, once paid £2,000 to have me beaten up. I received a call from a good friend of mine down South to inform me of this. This fella runs a lot of the security down there and he went on to tell me he'd received contact from this chief executive and told me all about it. My mate said to me that I must be really annoying this person because he was now desperate to put me out of commission.

When I asked him what exactly did he mean he said, "He's offered me a couple of grand to come and rough you up". Well I was stunned, but he told me he had no intention of following it up but was happy to collect the money then his party would come up to Newcastle and we'd have a good drink on it. For legal reasons I can't name who it was or even the club, I will leave that to your imagination, but if he is reading this, we had a great night out....

Every Boy's Dream is a book I have been asked to do a few times over the last decade. It had come close but for one reason or another it didn't happen. When Jamie Boyle asked me, I thought he was the right choice and I am happy to say my gut instinct hasn't let me down.

This book gives you an insight into what I do, why I do it, who I have done it with and what I have felt like when I was doing it. I have been honest; I have told a few home truths and I have given my side of events in some fairly controversial moments in the recent history of the club I love and support, Newcastle United. The infamous 'coffin march', the fake sheikh, and the St James' Park gates, are all in here and some great stories about my time as the Fans' Liaison Officer. There is also a look inside the boxing world, unlicensed and pro-scene, and tales about some of the stars I have brought to Tyneside including Mayweather and

Tyson. I look ahead to the future and my acting journey and at some of the colourful characters I have met on the wrong side of the law.

I guess if you're reading this you either like me or hate me, there is no in-between with me. I am like marmite and I know that. Either way thanks for spending your money and your time on the book and I hope it helps you understand me a little more.

Steve Wraith, May 2020

1

To Begin at the Beginning

4.45pm May 5th 1973. A bright and breezy Spring Day in Wardley Gateshead. Elizabeth Wraith was pushing her first grandchild Steven along the disused railway tracks and taking in the fresh air. Without warning the one year old started to scream and cry and shake from side to side, his dummy dropping down into the confines of his pushchair. Elizabeth stopped abruptly and put the brake on the chair and tried to comfort her grandson. As she retrieved the dummy and placed it back in Stevens' mouth he bit her finger with such force that it startled her causing her to cry out loud...340 miles away Sunderland Football Club had just won the FA Cup Final..................

As far back as I can remember I always wanted to be a Newcastle United Supporter.

For anyone who doesn't understand the rivalry between Newcastle United and Sunderland then let me please enlighten you. The distance between the two Northern giants is ten miles and the hatred when the two meet in a football match is very real I can assure you. I don't hate people from Sunderland myself but there are the minority from both parties that do, and on match day derbies then that grows ten-fold. It's well known that I get a lot of real hatred on social media from their fans, especially on the Sunderland forums but I personally have never hated anybody, that can't be said for others though. At the end of the day it's easy to hate someone behind a computer screen but when people have actually met me in the flesh, and I'm talking about a lot of Sunderland fans here, we've always ended up getting on ok. In my opinion, apart from the match days, there isn't a real hatred between the two cities and if it happens its football related. That hatred only really built up in the 1970s/80s. In that era the British football hooligan scene was at its peak but thankfully it had ebbed away, that was until quite recently when a minority decided to cause trouble.

Everybody knows that Sunderland went on to beat us six times in a row and believe me that was painful to live through. Before they beat us in those games Sunderland hadn't beaten Newcastle for thirty-odd years so it was a huge achievement for them. After one defeat there was a mini riot outside of Newcastle's stadium with around two hundred people being involved, you may remember it being in the press that one man ended up trying to hit a police horse. That day wasn't good for Newcastle United and it certainly wasn't good for English football with the eyes of Britain looking upon us. Most of them weren't even fans just drunken bystanders who'd spent the day in the pub then come to hover around the ground for the frisk and that's exactly what happened that day. For the record it's not something I would ever encourage no matter how many we'd lost by and something I've never ever been involved with, that doesn't mean I don't understand the mentality of the people who do it because I've written a book on it, 'NME From The Bender Squad To The Gremlins'.

If you're asking me how much Newcastle United means to me? Well I've missed five home games since 1984. I missed those five, once because of work and the other times because of illness. Maybe this sounds a bit corny but I'm as black and white as a Magpie comes and sometimes I've taken it too seriously when in context there's more important things happening in the world than Newcastle United. I find that we're all like that from Newcastle about our football even though we've never won a domestic trophy since 1955 or a European trophy since 1969.

Our club is in the heart of the city and that's the difference between our club and the other 91 clubs. You can get off The Metro and you're literally five minutes from St James Park which is a unique experience. You can then come out of the ground and walk straight into bars and restaurants within 100 metres. Most other grounds are on the outskirts like Middlesbrough's and Manchester City's which are in the middle of industrial estates, so that's the difference and why its special. Newcastle is also the biggest city in the North-East and much publicised as the party capital. There's no getting away from it but the city of Newcastle is also a place that breeds tough people, I mean you just need to see what the women wear in the Winter in the Bigg Market to know that.

The people of Newcastle come from a working-class background and that comes from our proud history of mining and ship building industries and why there's an affinity between Geordies, Jocks and Scousers. We're all the same. We're just hardworking people who've never had anything handed to us. I'm extremely proud of where I come from and at times in my life it's been the most important thing. You know whoever I've met in the world no matter how famous I'll always talk about my city's heritage, the Tyne Bridge and of course Newcastle United. I'm proud that I come from the North-East and when I come back from my many trips away and I see the King George V Bridge and the Tyne Bridge on my right, I know I'm home and I still get goose bumps.

For the record I was brought up in Gateshead which is South of the Tyne but I was actually born in South Shields so yes, that makes me a 'sand dancer' not a 'real' Geordie. I had a brief spell in Washington when I was a baby but we never stopped there longer than a couple of months. I moved briefly to Wardley then Heworth where I grew up. They were happy times where I made some very good friends.

My parents John and Celia gave me the perfect start in life. Dad was a mortgage broker and mam worked as a nurse at The Queen Elizabeth Hospital in Gateshead so I was brought up by very hardworking parents. I have a younger brother Rob who's seven years younger than me. We have always been close. He's a college lecturer these days with his own family and I am immensely proud of him. We've both got brains but my little brother stuck at school and did well with his qualifications but I didn't. I didn't like school whatsoever.

2

An Entrepreneur is Born

My first memories of school are of me being 4 years old and going to the Drive Primary School which was in Felling, Gateshead. At the time I lived in Heworth so it was walking distance. Heworth and Felling are close together and nobody really knows where the boundary is that separates them.

I went to that School for two years but my parents were alarmed at my lack of progress. Two years in and I was still struggling to read, write or do basic maths and my test results were very poor. This was pre-Ofsted days and it was clear to my parents and others that the school was failing badly and nobody in my class was performing to the level that was required for the average six and seven-year-old. At the time the only thing the school was interested in was getting the numbers in and then sending you home. The whole school seemed to be happy with just letting all the kids mess about in class.

There was one boy in particular who was in my class called Graham and he was the class bully. Graham used to make everyone's life a misery on a daily basis including mine. I think it was around that time that my parents decided that they needed to take drastic action and they needed to get me out of the school so that's when they started hunting for a new school for me. On the last day of term which would be my very last day in that school I went into the toilets and bully boy Graham followed me in ready to set about me for no reason. It ended up very differently than any previous scenario, I turned around and just smacked him in the nose and blood poured like I'd turned on a tap. Just as I had hit him the Headmaster appeared and saw what had gone on and I thought that was me bang in trouble but to my surprise he told the pair of us to run along. Looking back now I think even the Headteacher must have thought that this kid Graham had it coming and it was his well-deserved.

From that day on my mam and dad decided that I needed to be put into private education. What I remember was my mam and dad taking me for various interviews at several schools before choosing St Ann's which was in South Shields around the time I was approaching my 8th birthday. To be honest this was far from ideal because it was eleven miles away from my home. Another bizarre fact about my new school was that it was an all-girls school who were starting to take in boys and I was going to be the first boy in the whole school. To cut a long story short I started the school and the teachers were told I had been struggling. The teachers promised my parents that they'd rectify my issues. Soon I was able to read and write although I was still playing catch up.

By the time I reached the age of 10 I was in a class of thirteen and I was still the only boy in the class although a few other boys had joined the school. I would go on to stay in that school for three years. In fact, this was where I put my first business plan into practise. How can I put this, well the girls in that school were more forward than the average girls and I became a novelty to them so they'd want to show me their 'bits' in exchange for me to show them mine! I would charge them 10p a look at mine and made a couple of quid to spend at the sweet shop at the weekend. I wonder if that's how Sir John Hall started out?

Eventually more boys did come to steal my limelight, if you like, but it was worth it because I met an extremely good friend there named Nigel Gibbs. Nigel was a year older than me but what we had in common was a similar love for music namely new wave band The Jam.

Sometimes in breaktime me and Nigel would do live gigs pretending to be Paul Weller and Bruce Foxton. The Jam was the first band I fell in love with. Nigel would pretend to be Bruce

Foxton and together we'd master the jumps that they did as well as the other mannerisms which would make all the girls in the school love us even more.

It wasn't all plain sailing in that school though, because I did have issues. I wouldn't say anger issues but because I suffered a lot in my early education, I was damaged. My scars came from being called, "Stupid" and "Thicko" etc…

When one girl who was winding us up called me thick from behind a door I punched my hand through the glass in the door to get her but managed to cut my hand in the process and was taken off to the hospital. That very same girl on another day was severely abusing me and that situation ended up with me kicking her between the legs, I got into serious trouble for that and rightly so. Looking back now on that early part of my life I'd been bullied quite badly and I think I was just rebelling and kicking out at anyone and anybody. Looking back, that short period at the Drive Primary School didn't teach me anything at all. My mam and dad were very aware of what was going on at St Anne's too and I think my dad more than my mam thought that if I stayed at this school, which was predominately made up of girls, that it might have an effect on my sexuality. My dad thought I might start being attracted to boys and in his head, he thought I'd grow up to be interested in flower arranging and stuff so again they started looking for another school for me in my last year of junior school.

Although I'd picked up a hell of a lot by then I still wasn't hitting the expected level that I was required to. Yes, I could now read, write and add up but I was still lagging. I think what made it easier for me to move schools in my last year was that my fellow band member Nigel Gibbs had left anyway to attend another school. For the last year of my primary I would again go to another private school but this time it would be in Sunderland (of all places eh!)

It would be a place called Argyle House which required an interview for me to even get a place, which I passed with flying colours.

Argyle House was an all-boys school. My entrepreneurial skills that earnt me 10p a time showing me bits in my old school wouldn't have seen me making any money in this new environment I found myself in. I didn't struggle to adjust and I quickly made friends. There were a lot of good lads in the class and I made friends with a couple of guys in particular named Neil Shotton and Thomas Collin who were both great lads. Neil supported Liverpool and Thomas supported Sunderland but I never held that against him. By that time, I was Newcastle daft so all our talk in the playground was about football. If I think of my years at that school with those lads then I think of varnished wooden floors, Bunsen burners, chalk and blackboards. It was just your typical old-fashioned school in the middle of Sunderland and it was next door to Thornhill Comprehensive as well as Tunstall School which was for disabled kids. What I found I struggled with was the discipline of Argyle School. The cane was still in use then. I received it twice for my sins.

In my new school there was a teacher named Mr Thompson who I still know today. Mr Thompson was a fabulous teacher and behind most classes i.e. English and R.E. etc...

Overall my last year went smoothly thanks to him and it put a bit of normality back into my school life compared to what had gone before.

3

School's Out for Steve

By the time I headed into the senior ranks at Argyle House I'd become easily distracted in class. If you want me to be honest, I became the class clown, the class idiot more than anything else. For example, I'd be throwing rubbers at kids' heads so I could make people laugh. Looking back, I was doing this because not only was I looking for attention but I think maybe I was looking for some kind of acceptance.

I'd say I came from a middle-class background and it's only now that I realise how hard both my parents worked to put me into private school. Then my little brother Robert was four and going into school too it must have been a costly experience for them both. I can honestly say that if both my parents had never done what they did for me there's a possibility that I could have ended up on a different path. I certainly wouldn't have been in the position I am now that's for sure.

We were usually in a class of around thirty and me and Geoff Pickering, a Sunderland lad from a wealthy family, would often start off a new term by sitting right at the back of the class and within half an hour to an hour of the first school day it was guaranteed that the teacher would have moved me and Geoff to the front to keep an eye on us because we were both so disruptive. If it was ever raining on a play time then me and Geoff would be instigating stupid things like, lets empty the filing cabinet and see if we can pass the cabinets to the front of the class then back again before the teacher checks in on his walk around.

We'd be throwing compasses out of the window and waiting for an unsuspecting victim's shrieks! If you would hear silly noises in the classroom it was us, if someone drew a cock on the board so the female teacher would get embarrassed then that was us. Me and Geoff quickly learnt which teachers were easy to wind up and the ones who just wouldn't tolerate our crap. At times me or Geoff would bring our ghetto blasters in which we smuggled in in those old Head bags, it just looked like our P.E kit but for whatever reason we would record the lessons. Then when the teacher said something else, we would play what he or she'd just said a few minutes previously to make her think she was hearing things. It was all really immature stuff from us but at the time we thought we were comedians and the classroom was our stage, we would play to our baying audience who thought we were side-splitting. Another one of our ideas was to take a polaroid camera in to see if we could get sneaky photos of innocent unsuspecting folks when the lessons were going on. At times the plan would be for Geoff to do something silly to get the teachers attention and when he was getting a grilling, I'd be doing my David Bailey impressions. That kind of rubbish I'm ashamed to say carried on for the next five years more or less in Argyle House School. To be brutally honest I just didn't have an interest in school and Geoff was the same.

I remember there being a maths' teacher, who will remain nameless, he is now a police officer, but he just didn't like me at all. He just couldn't stand me not to mention he was a staunch Sunderland fan and he knew I was a Mag, that didn't do me any favours at all with him. I know even to this day that he didn't like me because I supported Newcastle United but also because he thought I was cocky. He would say something to me, usually something negative, and I would just answer him back with attitude and he didn't like it. I had a similar relationship with the English teacher, he just didn't like me either. That English teacher would often grab me by the ear, of course that was at a time where you could get away with doing that to your students in the classroom. He eventually left to have an operation but never returned. Every cloud has a silver lining they say and when I was in 3rd year a new English teacher came in called Peter Yates and Mr Yates basically saw something in me that would change my life for the better but I'll come back to that later in the book. At that time, I wasn't that interested in doing sports myself. Yes, I liked football but I had two left feet when it came to playing it! I never liked doing any of the cross-country running that our P.E. sessions would provide. My dad at the time thought I should follow him in the sports, he liked golf and rugby, but that just wasn't for me.

I suppose my social dynamic changed when I got into drama. Now I'd always been into acting since I was 7 at St Anne's and I had been picked to play the lead part of King Canute in our school play. For the most part I was behind in my early years at school but I had always excelled in drama to the point that my parents started taking me to drama school and I had elocution lessons in Argyle House to help me speak better. I then began taking part in poetry competitions and even won a few against other schools in the North East. It would seem I had a natural flair for it and I still have the certificates I gained in school, to this day.

Through my secondary school years my parents enrolled me into The People's Theatre in Jesmond. At that time there was this scheme running called The Young People's Theatre which had been setup by a gentleman named Nick Whitfield. It was an amateur theatre group for beginners and I would go at 10 am on Saturday mornings and we'd start by doing warm-up games then we'd do improvisations and we'd finish at 12. I went on to do that every single week from aged 11 to 18 and that gave me the confidence I needed for my acting career. It was the same place that Neil Tennent from The Pet Shop Boys went to. Another guy called Tom Hill went but these days he's called Tom

Goodman Hill and has been in films with the likes of Sean Connery and was recently in ITV's hit four-part drama CHEAT. I would say it was in that place that I really learnt my craft for drama. Obviously, if I was involved in plays it would be more than just on a Saturday morning and I'd have to dedicate myself to rehearsals during the week. I played The Artful Dodger from Oliver Twist and I played Monks who was David Copperfield's eldest brother in David Copperfield among others. It got to a point where, because I was doing so well in the youth theatre, the adult theatre began to notice me and became interested in me for their roles. My first ever review in a newspaper came from playing the part of Lol, AKA Laurie Lee, in the play Cider With Rosie, it was also my first stage kiss when I was only thirteen. Not only did I get a review but that day it was the best review so can you imagine how big that was for the 13-year-old Steve Wraith, that his name had been in the paper.

You know all about the class idiot Steve Wraith but away from school I had this separate life and I was rapidly becoming a bit of a local star. I think that's why when I look back at all my years through school, I had this attitude of, 'oh well schools not important anyway because I'm well on my way to becoming a famous actor'. As soon as I walked in that theatre aged 11 I knew that was what I wanted to do in life and it became my tunnel vision. I think that's why I kept up with my elocution and poetry because I saw that as an extra part of my future which I may need. Drama was my soul focus. On the acting itself learning the lines came with ease.

The first part I got aged 11 at The People's Theatre was in A Midsummer Night's Dream by William Shakespeare. I would play Puck which was one of the main parts as a chief fairy and again I nailed it which again led me to getting rave reviews.

When I was in my early teens, I would get a massive opportunity because the youth theatre started doing trips abroad which led me to audition for a part in Under Milk Wood which was a very famous radio drama made in 1954 and has been made into a film etc. I went for this part and I got it meaning I would be touring in America! With that I did New York, Jersey and Philadelphia. It was in New Jersey that I was to have my first romance. I was only there for three weeks but I fell in love with an American girl. When we were over there, we didn't stay in hotels, we were staying in people's houses. I have to admit it was a life shattering moment in young Steve Wraith's life when I had to leave my newfound love because I was convinced that me and her would be together forever and I cried my eyes out on departure from the sleepy town of Herkimer. When I got back to Newcastle me and the love of my life were pen pals for a while but it quickly fizzled out. It wasn't only the U.S.A I got to travel to with my theatre school because when I was sixteen, I got the chance to go to Russia which was an amazing experience.

Shortly before I left school I had to go for my options. That day I went and had a chat with Mr. Johnson the headmaster and when he asked what I was going to do for my future I told him I was to become a famous actor, well Mr. Johnson laughed in my face! Mr Johnson ranted at me that there was no chance whatsoever of me becoming famous and that I should live in the real world. With that comment I just shrugged me shoulders and told him that's what my future held for me. Mr. Johnson was your typical headmaster who'd cane people for fun. Every single child in the school was frightened of him when he entered the room as he had a real presence about him. He'd always be seen with a cup of coffee and he carried Polos to take the edge off his breath. He also taught Maths which I hated! His favourite line when he'd point up at the blackboard was, "Chung Chung" but none of us knew what that meant. In his class I totally switched off, I had no interest and I used to just sit there copying everything from Thomas Collin who was the swot of the class and would produce 'A's for fun year in and year out. Every single week I'd ask Thomas for his homework and I'd copy it to the letter before we handed it in. I'll never forget the day that Thomas and I fell out and his idea of payback towards me was when he gave me his homework on 10 questions, he would do 8 right and two wrong. Thomas knew that the Headmaster had his suspicions that I was cheating my way through school but he couldn't work it out until now and Thomas provided him with the evidence he needed. When Mr. Johnson marked my homework, he saw that what I'd handed in was exactly the same as the lad I was close to so this was concrete evidence in his eyes. Like a police officer who'd been hunting bank robbers this was his jackpot moment. "Wraith yours and Thomas Collin's work are both wrong and they're identically wrong in the very same way" Mr. Johnson told me. "Wraith can you come up to the front of the class please." I got up and did the death march to the front with everyone's eyes burning into me. Glaring at me with his shirt half out, Mr. Johnson ranted, "Wraith can you enlighten us all how you got this wrong"? I just looked puzzled and I told him no. I said, "If I've got it wrong then how can I tell you how I've got it wrong that's your job". As I've said that he's immediately jumped out of the chair and got me by the neck and slammed me on top of the desk. At the time I was 14 but I was pinned against the desk gasping SIR...SIR... but I couldn't breathe. He then screamed at me, "YOU WRAITH YOU THINK YOU'RE CLEVER BOY, BUT YOU'RE GOING TO AMOUNT TO NOTHING IN LIFE". Then he screamed, "YOU DIDN'T DO THAT HOMEWORK BECAUSE YOU COPIED IT FROM THOMAS COLLIN DIDN'T YOU"? As soon as he shouted that my friend Thomas Collin said, "That's correct sir he did" like the proper swot he was and totally blew me in. By this point Mr. Johnson still had hold of me around the neck but somehow, I managed to say, SIR... SIR... and when he said, "What"? I

16

said, "Your breath stinks!" As soon as I muttered that there was an uproar as the whole class erupted in laughter and I was then dragged out by my ear to stand outside for the full lesson. The only other time something like that happened to me was during Religious Education. At the time the only religion I was interested in wore black & white stripes at St James' Park. I just found the whole thing boring so when I was told that I had to write an essay on Jesus, God and Mary I decided to beef it up a little bit and wrote a two page Western (I've actually still got it in the house) and I called the characters, Old Man God and Jesus the Kid and the pair of them worked in a Saloon. Don't ask me why I did it but at the time I thought it was a masterpiece but needless to say what followed was, '0/10 see me after school this is blasphemy'. That led to me getting a major detention and I got a few crossed words at home. Looking back at that time my mind was made up that I was going to become a famous actor and that was that.

Maybe my only proper success story during my school years was down to a couple of has-beens, Eastend villains named Ronnie & Reggie Kray. I remember as if it was yesterday seeing The Krays on television in 1982 stepping out of a green prison van at their mother Violet's funeral. I was a 10-year-old boy but something subliminal stuck in my head about those two. Now fast forward my life to when I was 15 years of age in 1987 and I was walking along Newcastle's Quayside Market. Now what was about to happen, I believe, was fate and it would shape my future forever although I didn't know it at the time. As I was walking through the indoor market an old orange copy of John Pearson's 1972 'The Profession of Violence' jumped out at me. I always had some money on me to spend so I walked over and picked up this tatty looking book which was 30p and straight away I turned the pages and went to the pictures. The first picture I saw was the twins in their sweaters as kids, then the next picture I saw was these two blokes getting out of the back of green vans and that's when the penny dropped and I could recall my first sighting from five years earlier. I took that book home and I read it twice in the same week and I was completely fascinated by it. The biggest attraction for me was their lifestyle. I loved the fact that they were sharp dressers and Reggie had a good-looking woman on his arm. I loved the fact that they were mixing with celebrities, that they were boxers and that they owned nightclubs and bars. At that point I was 15 so I was curious about these nightclubs and bars and the whole story bowled me over. I would say the writer John Pearson romanticised it to a degree so the murders they'd committed of George Cornell, Jack 'The Hat' McVitie and Frank 'The Mad Axeman' Mitchell were irrelevant as well as all their misdemeanours. I was only looking at all the positive stuff and the glamourised side to The Krays, if you like. As my fascination with the twins grew my mam encouraged it but my dad was the complete opposite. My dad, a lovely man that I'm lucky to have in my life and I love him, had a very hard upbringing with strict parents, he was an only child who would get punished quite severely by my Grandad for the slightest thing. This made My dad a disciplinarian and he would not think twice about hitting me if I did anything wrong. I certainly didn't come from an abusive home but if I needed a belt now and again, I would get it and rightly so. As I grew older, I did start to resent my dad for belting me and when I hit 21, we had a row. Dad and I had an infamous roll around on the living room floor. We can laugh about it now but I was an idiot that night, fuelled by the demon drink. My dad learned from that whole experience too. He never raised his hands to my brother because he felt guilty about what he had done to me.

Going back to those terrible twins, Peter Yates said to me that if I wanted to, I could study 'The Profession of Violence' book as part of my GCSE exams. The reason behind that was that I was currently studying no other books

18

under my previous English Teacher so this was his attempt in lighting my interest in something. I still had to follow the curriculum books such as Brave New World by Aldous Huxley, The Crucible by Arthur Miller and Twelfth Night by William Shakespeare I was also allowed to do two other books of my own choice for my GCSE English. I chose Day of the Triffids by John Wyndham and The Profession of Violence.

I sat all my exams at the cricket club in Sunderland but spent most of those days looking out of the window watching the groundsman cut the grass. My mind was focussed during my English Language, Literature and Geography exams though. I think I may have written my name on the top of the paper on the maths' exam and that's it because to me it was pointless.

Do I regret it? No of course not. I have still managed to achieve my life goals without these bits of paper. Would I advise youngsters or my kids to do the same? Of course not. I left school with a B and C in Language and Literature respectively and a C in Geography. I could have done better. The day I left I took my blazer off and set fire to it in the backstreets of Sunderland. I still meet Mr. Yates, along with Mr. Thompson, and Mr. Davies my Science teacher every year for lunch because it's only down to him that I got any qualifications and I'll always be eternally grateful to him. In fact, I dedicated my very first book to him 'The Krays The Geordie Connection' which was released in 2002 because he's a man who did so much for me when all the other teachers viewed me as a waste of time.

4

An Actor's Life for Me

I went to Newcastle College when I left school. The place had just started off a drama course there so I had no time to waste on my quest to become famous. I started in September 1988 and I was studying for a B-Tech diploma. You might laugh at this but the bloke who ran that course Gerard used to be Bungle in Rainbow. That was his claim to fame and he turned out to be a great guy. Although we were based at Newcastle College, we would rehearse at The Tyne Theatre on Westgate Road. Now I've got to be honest here, the only reason my early acting career didn't work was down to me. I went to college and met up with some great new friends. To be truthful nobody on my course went on to make it big in the acting game. My best mates from that period were Adrian Stones and Toby Cooper. Adrian went into the leisure industry and Toby continued to do a little bit of acting but then went into the retail industry.

Unfortunately, we became the first people to get suspended off the course. We were always doing silly things. On a morning before class we would hide amongst the boxes and rails of costumes and when someone walked in I'd throw a large blanket over the unsuspecting victim then the lads would grab them and put them in a wheelchair and push them into a lift that we had been told not to use. There was no badness in me at the time but I'd be constantly messing around and never took anything seriously. I was just a lad being a lad but I wasn't impressing anyone. The college suspended me and the lads for a full week but I didn't tell my parents I'd been suspended, I just continued to leave the house at my usual time and would just spend the days walking around the centre of Newcastle. At this time, I was 16 going on 17 and I'd started going out underage drinking, dabbling with recreational drugs and the female sex had become far more interesting to me than ever before. In regards to the drugs I was never a 'druggie' but I did dabble. Back in 1988 there wasn't a great deal of drugs around apart from E's and cannabis, certainly not as many as there is today in 2020. Luckily, I've never had an addictive personality, at the time I was mostly just drinking and it was all a learning curve. I was growing up.

Around the Christmas time of 1988 a local company were looking for people to star in a pantomime that would tour all the working men's clubs around the North East and it was a paid part. To get in there was an audition process that I had to go through. I went and cast for the pantomime Dame which was one of the main parts but I never got it. The guy who did get it was called Shaun Meechan but for some reason he pulled out so I got a call back asking if I'd now like to play the Dame? I had a chat with my mam and dad about it first. When I went back to the company, I was told that I would get an equity card which meant that I would be part of the actor's union. Basically, this card was meant to hold some magic powers if you were a young budding actor like myself and it would help to build up my profile. Another thing I was promised was 'x' amount of money for fifty shows over a 25-day period. With my earlier acting experience, learning the lines came easy to me and I got on well with the other actors but the harsh reality was that at the time I never took into consideration just how much hard work it was going to be doing a couple of shows a day. I'd get picked up at 6.30am to go to Ashington then we had to unload the van and do all the setup which was required for the play. Then before our play we'd do a dress rehearsal in full as well as make sure the lights and all our mics were spot on. We'd finish around midday then we'd have to pack up and do the same all again at the next venue. I'm not going to lie, all this new-found slave labour annoyed us and I was getting peanuts for it as well. As an actor I thought I would be doing drama not humping heavy set boxes around. The money I was getting for these long days was just ludicrous not to mention I got ripped off and nothing came of the promise to get me my equity card, it never materialised. For the fifty shows I received £500 which even by 1989 standards once you worked it out it amounted to next to nothing. I suppose I'd just wanted to become an actor for so long, but at the end of it all I felt totally disillusioned by the game.

I had left school with few qualifications and now I was scratching my head thinking what the hell do I do now?

5

The Post Office

With my acting dream in tatters I turned to my only option of work which was at my grandparents' post office. At the time I lived at home rent free which was good of my mam and dad. I was dipping in and out of college Monday to Friday and then working in the post office's newsagents Saturdays and Sundays with my Dad. I decided to broach the subject of working at the Post Office over a pint with my dad and grandparents in the Wheatsheaf pub on Carlisle Street. We used to go there on a Sunday night for a couple of hours. I knew my grandparents were looking to retire and I thought it made sense. The answer I got from my dad was, "You're joking aren't you"? I told him "Absolutely not" and that I was serious. My grandparents were more welcoming to the idea. They all agreed to speak about the idea and would get back to me.

I knew deep down my dad was thinking that I was hopeless at maths and that working in a post office I would need to add up day in, day out. After a discussion with my grandparents my dad came back with a suggestion. He told me that a friend of theirs, Mary McAvoy, had a post office and that she had agreed to take me on for four weeks but I would have to work for free and shadow her and learn the ropes. Mary in return would teach me how to run a Sub Post Office. I started the following week at Mary's post office in Burnopfield. Most of the customers that I would serve daily were the purple rinse brigade. I don't think I served one young person at all in my whole trial there but I think that was a blessing because I'd have only got distracted anyway. It became ideal for me and it was a great learning curve which I would take a lot from. Mary was tremendous, she showed me in great detail and with patience how to do all the transactions which were required. After four weeks I knew how to balance the books and she rang my grandparents up and said I was now capable and I could do everything. Yes, the post office didn't interest me as much as girls, Newcastle United or The Kray Twins but I knew if I wanted to subsidise my social life and hobbies that I needed to earn money. I didn't want to bum off my mam and dad for the rest of my life but I didn't have any options at that time. Yes, I could have gone and looked for a job elsewhere but as I didn't like hard work and my grandparents were looking to retire it made perfect sense. Another plus to the scenario was it also meant that my grandparents didn't have to move so I would be doing them a favour, not to mention my grandfather would be proud that I was following him in the family business. So, my dad did a deal with his dad and bought the post office from him. Dad then made me a 1% partner in the business and he took 99%. That meant dad was the Postmaster and I would be the Manager. I could not thank him enough.

Considering I struggled for much of my school years with maths I found dealing with and understanding money came naturally. I just found the whole process easy and I took to it like a duck to water. It was hard for the staff who had been there for such a long time. They didn't have John and Elizabeth as their bosses, it was now this young kid with a skinhead. Most of them were in their 60s and now they were taking orders from this 18-year-old kid. I wouldn't wear a shirt and tie, I'd go to work in my Newcastle United shirt, wearing jeans and Adidas Samba's which I've worn since the day I was born. I was the complete polar opposite of how my granddad John had been and it took a while for the staff to get used to having me around.

Dad let me wear what I wanted but my grandparents tried to get me to dress more appropriately but I wouldn't listen. I was 18 and I knew best. Another thing my grandad told me was that now I was running the post office it meant I wouldn't be able to drink in the local bars because I was now an upstanding figure in the community. This just made me do it even more. Grandad used to say that the bars were full of people who'd have the post office over in a heartbeat but it fell on deaf ears. Many times, I'd be serving lads and lasses who I'd grown up with but now I was on this side of the counter and they were on the other. It didn't make any difference to me and I'd still drink in The Black Bull (no longer there) where all the customers used to drink which didn't please my grandfather. That was the start of my life in a managerial role dealing with money.

The 5th of July 1995 was a dark day for the post office as there was an armed robbery. It was 2pm in the afternoon and we'd just opened after lunch. I was behind the post office counter when I just remember a car pulling up with a screech of smoke outside immediately after the big red post office van had just pulled up to drop the cash off so they'd obviously done their homework. I was serving a customer when I saw this person wearing a balaclava and boiler suit carrying a metal drain cover above his head running towards the door. If you've ever held one of these, you'll know just how heavy and damaging these things could be. As I saw him instinct made me hit the foot alarm. I then saw another man running in tight behind him also balaclavad up carrying this huge hunting knife. One of my female staff was on the newsagent's side also serving a customer and had seen the robbers too and turned around and ran through the connecting door to my grans house to safety. Everything was in slow motion. I gathered my senses and turned and ran into the back shop and hid in the toilet, luckily for me and the staff they didn't follow either of us. There was a crash as the security screen was put through and lots of shouting and then silence apart from the din of the foot alarm. That team of robbers struck lucky and stole around £20,000 as well as a load of stamps. To this day I don't know if those armed robbers got caught but what I do know was that I was the first suspect to be questioned. The reason behind that could only have been my relationship with The Kray Twins. I suppose the police would have been fools not to check me out. It didn't help that three days after that robbery I had Charlie Kray coming to Newcastle for some function. I was organising a sold-out event for Terry Moran a boy who suffered terrible burns from fireworks. I was actually finger-printed and questioned several times about my gangland connections and asked if I had told anybody any information that may have encouraged them to come and do it. I genuinely hadn't because that just wasn't me.

Yes, I was interested in studying criminals but as for being a criminal it was a no-no, but of course they had procedures to follow. Looking back, I found the whole experience of being treated like a criminal awful. For a start I didn't get the support from the post office. It was such a horrible experience to have to endure and humiliating in equal measures. Another thing about the actual robbery itself is it all seemed to happen in slow motion so I had to relive it in my mind time and time again for ages afterwards. One of the most bizarre situations was that after the robbery had just taken place, I went back out to serve the customer who I'd been serving before the robbers came in. This crazy customer hadn't moved and was still stood there waiting to be served. Another thing which really bugged me was one of the post office managers rang up and the first thing they said was, "How much did they get"? Not 'sorry to hear about this Steve and are you and the staff ok?' That was the beginning of the end for me with the post office. At that point I'd run the business for over five years and I felt like they did not like the way I did things. The post office managers were called inspectors and they'd just turn up unannounced at the drop of a hat like Darth Vader stepping off his spaceship to pick holes in what I was doing. I knew that I needed to find a way out but for the moment I would have to keep calm and carry on.

6

Falling in Love with Football

My grandfather on my mam's side George Davison Green was a football referee and a linesman in the top level. Grandad George was my hero who I looked up to and these days he's definitely my guardian angel. It was grandad George who first gave me my love for football. I wasn't really interested until he sparked my interest when I was around 10.

As a kid going into the post office my job would be to put the magazines in the Sunday papers and I remember in 1982 as a 10-year-old boy picking the paper up to discover Kevin Keegan had signed for Newcastle. The headline was, 'We're in heaven we've got Kevin!!!' I didn't know much about football then but I just remember that this Kevin bloke signing for Newcastle had made my dad over the moon. Before Keegan arrived, my dad hadn't gone to St James Park since the days after Malcom MacDonald AKA Supermac had been sold. To see my old man being excited over something like this grabbed my interest as a lad. As a boy you're looking for a connection with your father and that's where a connection with my dad came about.

Grandad George, who'd by now retired from reffing, had become a referee assessor. He'd often go to many games in the North East and judge the standard of refereeing and give them marks out of ten then he'd send his report back to the F.A.

In 1983 aged 11, my grandad George said he'd take me to a game so I went along and discovered my great passion for football. One thing about grandad George was he was never allowed to do Sunderland because he lived in Boldon. He often did Gateshead, Newcastle, Hartlepool and Darlington so he'd take me most weekends and I thought it was the best thing ever. I was lucky because at Gateshead I got to see Terry Hibbitt play who used to play with Supermac at Newcastle. They won the northern premier league and I got to see them lift the trophy. Grandad George once took me to a Hartlepool v Darlington game around 1984 and there was a pitch invasion. That all stemmed from this strange practise where fans from both sides could walk around the pitch into each end to visit one another, it inevitably led to this riot. I remember seeing this young guy trying to kung-fu kick the ref and then this old guy with a flat cap on in his 60s running up and punching the young karate expert in the head. I was just standing back gawping in amazement but my grandad George was trying to reassure me that this didn't normally happen at games. After going to a few of the lower league games with my grandad George he said that he had a special treat for me. He was going to take me to a Newcastle game. To suddenly get the opportunity to go to St James Park after only going to the likes of Gateshead, Darlington and Hartlepool's grounds was a dream come true for me.

It was the 1983/84 season and the likes of Kevin Keegan, Chris Waddle, Peter Beardsley and co. were playing and I was starstruck. The game was a friendly between Newcastle United and Liverpool dubbed 'Auf Wiedersehen Kev'. Newcastle had clinched promotion to Division One and Kevin had decided to bow out of the professional game. This was his farewell.

Instead of wearing my tracksuit and trainers, my mam made me dress smartly. I even had hair at the time so she'd comb it and style it perfectly. Unfortunately, I had to wear these horrible green flannel trousers, smart shoes with a shirt and jacket or I couldn't go. It was a small price to pay to be allowed into heaven on earth so I kept my mouth shut and let my mam do what she wanted, even though I looked like bloody Lord Snooty from the Beano Comic!

Walking up to the ground for the first time was special. The atmosphere was electric and getting into the old West Stand, which isn't there anymore, blew me away. We walked up a couple of flights of stairs and then into the directors' lounge where I saw all the old faces like Jackie Milburn aka 'Wor' Jackie, Joe Harvey and Bobby Cowell to name a few. All the major faces who had won The F.A. Cup three times through the 1950s were all there. These men were more or less gods to the people of Newcastle and here I was mixing with them and I couldn't take my eyes off them. I even saw some of the injured players who were currently in the first team like George Reilly. It was surreal. Cameras weren't as common back then so I have no photos from that day but my autograph book is full. That first visit to St James Park I was sat next to Peter Taylor who was commentating at the time for BBC radio and I knew from that day forward that this was going to be my club. This was a proper football club. The atmosphere of the crowd when the teams came out was like nothing I'd ever witnessed before. I was hooked. The game finished 2-2 with Keegan notching a generous penalty and he left St James' in a helicopter with the crowd singing 'Keegan, Keegan.' I felt a sense of loss and had a tear in my eye, and they wouldn't be the only tears that I would cry at this ground.

In 1985 hooliganism was a black stain on the beautiful game in England. It was at an all-time high and my dad didn't want me going to the games on my own which I was annoyed about.

I didn't have the same views as my father as all my mates were allowed to go to games so why couldn't I? At the time I was 13 and I could go into Newcastle town centre on my own and I was knocking around with kids from the theatre so in my head this was no big deal.

One of my best mates at the time was Matty Gregory. He was a bit older than me so I thought I'd be ok going with Matty but no meant no to my Dad. So, I had no choice but to sneak to the games without him knowing. I'd tell him I was going somewhere else. That's how much Newcastle United meant to me.

It did not take me long to realise that my new-found club was going to give me more pain than joy. Although we stayed up in our first season in the First Division, (we actually topped the league after 3 games) it was quite obvious that the board had little or no ambition and were simply happy with middle table obscurity. Over the next 2 years we sold our prize assets Chris Waddle to Spurs and then Peter Beardsley to Liverpool. We were a selling club and we, the fans, were not happy.

A young lad from Dunston had emerged on the scene. Paul Gascoigne also known as 'Gazza' had just led the youngsters to F.A. Youth Cup Glory alongside striker Joe Allon and now they were getting a chance to ply their trade at St James' Park in the first team. With Waddle and Beardsley now gone 'Gazza' took his chance and became the star of the show and was getting recognition from the pundits in the media. This would only lead to one thing, interest from other clubs, and inevitably Spurs came knocking again with their chequebook and our board of directors could not wait to cash in it seemed.

The following season saw Gazza return to Newcastle with his new club at the start of the new season. It was no secret that he had a sweet tooth and his favourite snack was a Mars Bar. So, I decided to try and make a few quid out of the situation. I took a box of 48 Mars Bars from the Newsagents and stuck them in the freezer overnight and the next day headed up to the ground early to sell them to fans going in. "Give Gazza a Mars Bar Only £1" was my sales pitch outside the turnstiles. I sold out in just under an hour. My pockets full of pound notes.

The game kicked off and when Gazza came over to take a corner there was a rainstorm of Mars Bars that I had sold outside the ground. Gazza saw the funny side and picked one up and started eating it. You can still see this on YouTube. The game itself finished 2 - 2 and Gazza set up one of the Spurs goals so I guess he had the last laugh.

7

A Brush with 'The Law'

I have only had a couple of brushes with the law and for the first one I need to take you back a few years. It was coming up to Christmas 1987. I was 15 years old and still at Argyle House School. Jason Nelson, who was in my class, lived with his parents and they ran a pub on Seaburn sea front. So, I suggested to the lads that we have a Christmas night out and try our luck in the bars of Seaburn. Geoff Pickering, Robert Atkinson, Neil Chamberlain and Jason all liked the idea. Jason said we could all stay at his house so all of us came up with different stories to tell our parents saying that we were just going to a sleepover. Jason knew about the pub scene through his dad and he told us all that if we all dressed up, we'd get into the bars. I didn't look old enough at all with my long dark Chrissy Waddle mullet perm (yes, I had hair once). To cut a long story short we put all our best gear on, hair gel and our dads' aftershaves.

Apart from underage discos this was our first venture out to have a drink, looking back it must have been like an episode of The Inbetweeners as none of us knew what we were doing. To our disbelief, we managed to pull it off in the first two bars. We all got served at 15 and we were all stood with pints in our hands like proper men who'd been to work all week. I think in reality with it being Christmas time all the bar staff in the pubs were just so busy that they never paid attention to The Inbetweeners crew, all the better for us, we were in and it felt great to play grownups sitting in the corner. Jason Nelson looked the oldest out of us all so he was our leader when it came to being served. The third bar we entered that night we all got knocked back and that brought us back down to earth but didn't knock our confidence until we realised that there was a call being put around the bars that there were underage drinkers doing the rounds so it was game over for us. With our thunder being stolen it was Jason who said, "Come on lads we'll head back to our house to continue the night." By then we'd all had maybe three or four pints and being kids we were all pissed as we walked along the Seaburn sea front. As we were toddling along the front there were cars going past with loud music, some of us had been playfully sticking the Vs up to passing vehicles as well as trying to push each other into the road. We were just daft young lads and the fresh air had well and truly hit us. We were young, innocent and stupid but that didn't wash with the occupants of the Silver BMW who passed us when one of us gave them the fingers, this car had three very angry blokes in it who were a lot older than us. It ended with the car full of men screeching to a halt, which was a very sobering sight. We continued to walk but a lot quicker and a lot quieter. Then they started revving their engine. This lot were looking for bother so all of us looked at each other, we didn't need to speak. We just scarpered. The five of us ran off in completely different directions. It wasn't the brightest of ideas. I didn't know the area of Seaburn at all. As I ran towards a set of houses, I could see Robert Atkinson and Neil Chamberlain going across this big grass field. I noticed a garden so I jumped in it and hid but as I was hiding, I could see this Silver BMW following Robert and Neil.

I took time to get my breath back. There was an eerie silence, you could have heard a pin drop. I laid still for another couple of minutes gathering my own thoughts and composure.

When I thought it was all safe, I left the garden and started walking in the direction that Robert and Neil had gone in. The further I walked up I could see over to a field in the distance and I could see the Silver car again. Then as I got closer, I could see Robert and Neil surrounded by two of the three men who'd gotten out of the car. I was still some distance away but I could just make out Robert Atkinson and it looked like he was getting punched by one of the men. Immediately I started running over towards my friends to help them and to try and stop this attack. By the time I had got there it was too late and the two men had got back in the car and left the scene. I turned to see my two friends and Neil was lifting Robert off the ground. I then asked Robert if he was alright and he told me he was fine and that he had just had a few punches in the back, everything was fine I thought, that was until I put my arm around Robert's back, it was saturated in blood. Robert had been stabbed! Now we all started to panic because we are only 15, in the middle of nowhere and one of our mates was dying. I said to the lads that we should head to Jason's house. They both had a puzzled look.

Christ none of us knew where he lived. There was no time to waste so me and Neil picked Robert up like soldiers of war carrying their fallen friend and we headed off down some streets. Luckily enough when we got to the first street, we saw Geoff Pickering and Jason Nelson chucking daggers into a tree and laughing in relief shouting, "We got away." Their joy was short lived though when I told them Robert had been stabbed.

We managed to drag Robert into Jason's house. Luckily his parents weren't in. We were all scared, we had all been drinking illegally and our friend's life was on the line. When we got Robert's top off, we could see he had a small incision in his back, it may have been small but the blood was just pissing out of him. We rang for an ambulance. It didn't take long to arrive.

The police arrived within minutes too. Robert was then taken away to the hospital and we were all held by the police to give our accounts of what had went on. We also had to admit we'd been out underage boozing so then the police rang all our parents to tell them what the situation was. Jason's parents arrived home to find blood all over the house and blue lights flashing. They remained calm and rang around all of our parents before making us all a hot drink. As it was so late, we were all allowed to stay over. None of us slept because we were all concerned about Robert. We got an update in the middle of the night to say that he'd sustained a punctured lung and he'd lost two pints of blood internally and his condition was very much touch and go. The four of us sat there with our head in our hands at the predicament we'd landed ourselves in. The next morning, we all had to go into the police station to answer further questions. Luckily Robert did pull through but that dark event really screwed Robert up and he had to miss three months of school in his final exam year. The worst thing about it was the gang who stabbed Robert were caught the following week doing the exact same thing to some other poor unsuspecting sod. This gang had borrowed one of their dad's cars on the weekend and they were driving up the Seaburn front looking for trouble. The lads received a custodial sentence and we learned a valuable lesson in life.

As I've already said I've never been one for trouble at games but I was arrested once in 1989.

Newcastle were playing at home that day and me and my mate Paul went to see Newcastle v Sheffield United which we won 2 – 0 in a big top of the table game. Before the game me and Paul were drinking in The Farmers Rest in Haymarket which was my usual pre-match haunt.

The Farmers Rest was a great place and it would have all my favourite music on the free jukebox such as The Sex Pistols, The Jam, The Clash etc... A lot of my music influences came from that bar. That day before the match we'd had a right skinful and were pissed walking up to the match. We watched the game, had a great time and enjoyed our victory.

After the match we both stopped off at McDonalds on Northumberland Street to get some scran and sober up a bit. Paul for some reason thought it would be a great idea to steal the squirty bottle which was used to clean the tables. We left the restaurant playing footy with it and Paul kicked it to me whilst we were both commentating pretending to play for Newcastle. As we continued to play football up Northumberland Street, we came up to the junction just where the Odeon used to be, where The Stack is now. Me and Paul weren't doing any harm, we were just two lads getting carried away in the moment celebrating Newcastle's victory, I kicked it for the last time onto the road, but as I did that, this unmarked white van came around the corner, opened the side door and out came the police. I was shocked. It was an ordinary van and I hadn't expected to see the police. One of them pointed towards me and said, "We'll have him". I was looking in amazement thinking, 'what have I done' but of course I'm still pissed. I suppose instinct took over next and me and Paul legged it towards The Monument with four police officers in pursuit. I turned left at the jewellers and then left up the first back alley towards the Tyneside cinema. When I'd reached the cinema, I was bloody knackered from drinking and my adrenaline was wearing off so I'd dipped. I just remember being at this bus stop which was crowded with lots of people so I tried to mingle in and look casual. I'd even took my coat off to disguise myself when all of a sudden, my hands were put behind my back and I was nicked and bundled into a waiting van.

I couldn't believe it. I was then taken to the police station at Market Street which was a short ride. It was 7.30pm in the evening. I was checked in but as I was only 17, I gave a false date of birth. I was then taken down the stairs and put in a cell to sober up. A couple of hours later I could hear a policeman shouting 'Which one of you has given me the wrong date of birth?' He opened the cell door. I was starting to sober up a little now. 'Me' I groaned. I gave him my correct birth date and he told me to follow him. I went back to the desk and was told that they were going to charge me with drunk and disorderly and would be letting me out soon.

They then pushed me some paperwork to sign. Without reading it I signed it and they took me back to my cell. I knew I was going to be in trouble at home and just wanted another few hours' sleep. After I signed it, I was put back in the cells until 3.30am then they rang my parents up for maximum effect. I was let out of the cells and I had to make my own way home. When I arrived at home my dad was foaming at the mouth like a rabid dog wanting to go through me like a hot knife through butter. My mam was crying saying I'm an embarrassment and what had she done to deserve this? Then my dad chipped in with, "All that money we spent on your education and this is how you repay us". I tried to defend myself and explained what had happened and that the van wasn't even a marked police van! After the initial shouting they began to calm down and they seemed to be taking what I was saying seriously.

I handed my Dad the paperwork I had from the station which I still hadn't read and as my Dad read it he started shaking his head. The police had charged me with drunk and disorderly as they had said they would but also charged me with kicking a bottle at a marked police van which caused it to swerve which was a lie. They'd also claimed that I had said "Fuck off you pig bastards" which was a total fabrication. All I was guilty of was re-enacting the goals from the game we'd watched earlier and I kicked the bottle into the road. I suppose we'd committed a crime by nicking the squirty bottle out of MacDonald's but that was it. Now what the police were saying was I knew it was a police van and I kicked the bottle at it on purpose which I hadn't. I was as green as grass and a complete novice in this game as I'd never been arrested before and of course as I had signed the bottom of the charge sheet they had me bang to rights now. My parents told me to get to bed and we'd sort the next steps later that day.

When I got up my Mam had spoken to my Aunty who was a solicitor and she agreed to defend me in court. It took a few weeks for the case to be heard and I was given a 12 month bind over for my first offence. I pleaded NOT GUILTY saying I didn't do what had been said but foolishly I'd already signed the statement. As we left court that day I was gutted. My Dad put his arm around me. The nightmare was over. From that day forward my opinion towards the local constabulary definitely changed. If they can lie about an average nobody like me then they can tell lies about anybody.

8

The Fanzine Explosion

The late eighties saw a fans revolution of sorts. With the beautiful game at the precipice of self-destruction with dwindling attendances, decrepit grounds and horrifying players' haircuts, namely the mullet, fans decided that the pen was mightier than the sword and started to produce their very own fan magazines. Within the pages of what were quickly to be known as 'fanzines', fans could praise, ridicule, patronise and fantasise about their club and their players. There appeared to be no boundaries and it became apparent that there was an abundance of literary talent standing on the terraces week in week out, who had plenty to say and knew exactly how to say it. One of the first 'fanzines' to hit the streets was 'The End' in Liverpool. It was written and produced by a group of scouse scallys who later made it big in the music charts as the band 'The Farm'. Their biggest hits included, 'Altogether Now,' and the 'Groovy Train'. Lead singer Peter Hooten took a great deal of pride in 'The End' and its coverage of the scouse music and football scene was second to none.

The late eighties and early nineties were quite bleak as a Newcastle fan. I suffered my first relegation season in 1988-89. I have often watched the DVD of that season when things have not been going well at St James to remind me that things could be worse. I mean how many times did Dave Beasant get lobbed that season man? I did not know what to expect from season 89-90. I knew we'd be visiting the likes of Port Vale, Wolves and of course Sunderland, but they always say getting out of the Second Division is harder than winning the First Division. Well we were about to see. Jim Smith had a job bigger than Jimmy Nail and Tim Healy on Auf Wiedersehen Pet and he set about re-building the Magpies nest with the acquisition of two strikers. Mick Quinn and Mark McGhee. He also brought in midfielders Kevin Dillon and youngster John Gallacher. Our first league game of the season was at home to Leeds United on Saturday the 19th of August. The pre-season had seen the formation of 'United Supporters for Change', a fans group that wanted the present board removed from power and the club re-vamped and run properly. I knew a few of the lads involved. I also made a few friends amongst the group, none more so than Bryan Williams who I still travel to games with to this day. 'USFC' wanted fans to boycott our first home game of the season as a vote of no confidence towards the board of directors. I just couldn't. I felt a bit disloyal to Bryan and the lads. I agreed with their principles but as a fan just could not stand outside the ground whilst the lads were playing. There is a famous saying in Newcastle that the fans would simply pay to watch the grass grow. That was certainly true in my case! As I reached the ground I felt the familiar tingle that every fan gets at the start of a new season. There is a freshness about the ground. Every team is equal, it's the beginning of a nine month quest for glory and your team is going to do it this year. The sun was beating down on a lush green surface as Newcastle Kicked off towards the Gallowgate End. The crowd roared United on.

I took my place at the front of the scoreboard end in the Gallowgate. The boycott had affected other parts of the ground but the popular end was packed. Eric the Radio Man was there as usual in his grey coat and magpie hat and with his radio tuned in, so I stood next to him as the game kicked off. It was refreshing to see the game without the fences in the way.

You felt closer to the players. My dad had often mentioned Malcolm Macdonald, his goal scoring hero, to

41

me. He could recount his many goals and said that it would be a long time before we would see the likes of him at the club again. 'Supermac' had become a legend in his time on Tyneside and crowned his St James debut with a hat trick against Liverpool. Had my dad spoken to soon? What unfolded on that hot summers day would stay with me forever. Mickey Quinn, (he's fat he's round he's worth a million pound Mickey Quinn!) hit four past our Yorkshire rivals and John Gallacher a fifth as we ran riot. It was the stuff dreams were made of, and Quinn was a terrace favourite from the start. The 24,482 that had defied the boycott had certainly got their monies worth and as the game came to an end and people filed away from the ground the talk was already of finishing as champions. I left with a warm glow, from the result and the fact that the sun had burnt my face! I also had a hero....Mickey Quinn.

Quinn seemed to be on a one man mission to take us back up as everything he seemed to hit went in and he was ably assisted by Mark McGhee who was in his second stint at the club.

They complimented each other well and spelt double trouble for defences home and away. The football we played was a pleasure to watch but it became apparent that we would have our work cut out winning the title with both Sheffield United and Leeds starting well. By October we were lying in third place behind our rivals and had just defeated Bradford City at home with a great goal by McGhee. Mick Quinn had missed a penalty and we looked to be heading for a draw, until McGhee picked up the ball from a Mark Stimson throw on the halfway line. McGhee turned and left Jackson and Abbot for dead, he dribbled past three other players before wrong footing keeper Tomlinson to grab all three points. Maradona eat your heart out!

We never seemed to do ourselves justice in the Cup competitions, the league cup is a particular bug bear of mine. So many average teams seem to do well in this competition, but not us! This year was to be no different as Chris Whyte scored the only goal of the game to dump us out once again.

My brother Rob was 10 years old now and like most younger brothers was keen to follow in his older brothers footsteps. He would often listen to the games that I attended and wanted me to take him through the goals that I had witnessed first hand. He was fascinated by the noise the crowd made on the radio and was keen to go to the game himself. I decided to ask my dad if he would be okay with me taking him along with Matty Gregory. He said that it would be fine as long as we looked after him. Port Vale were the visitors to St James Park for Rob Wraiths first game on the 28th October 1989. The crowd was a paltry 17,809. United were in the running for promotion but were not exactly setting the division alight, and some fans were still clearly not happy with the way things were going.

Rob was quite a small lad and we had difficulty finding a good vantage point for him as we wandered onto the Gallowgate Corner terracing. He was in awe of the ground, just as I had been and took in the atmosphere as the crowd started to sing their usual array of songs. The game was a tense affair but Quinn and McGhee gave Newcastle the advantage. Rob missed both goals...he was devastated. With the crowd in the corner swaying almost constantly, keeping a spot was almost impossible and as a result Rob ended up behind the biggest fan in the ground. Never mind at least we were winning I told him. I had spoken too soon.

Newcastle's rear guard committed footballing suicide and the visitors capitalised on their mistakes twice to snatch an unlikely point. Rob had managed to catch both of Vales goals! It would be a wonder if he ever asked me to go to another game again. As we made our way home Rob told me that he had enjoyed the day, and asked 'Will you take me again?' Another magpie was born!

1990 would be the year that we would return to the First Division, of that I was convinced.

Every team has a blip during the season however and we were in the middle of ours. 1 point out of 12 was not the form of a title winning team and the visit of Wolves on New Years Day gave us no reason to toast the New Year. Steve Bull Wolves Legend, ran riot scoring all four goals for his team in a 4-1 win. Kevin Brock notching the consolation for Newcastle. It was becoming apparent that Newcastle United needed to stop the rot at the back. Jim Smith pulled off a coup bringing in Celtic stalwart Roy Aitken for half a million pounds. He made his debut on 13th January 1990 and Leicester City were the visitors. Aitken didn't quite plug the gaps in his first game as United ran out 5-4 winners thanks to a late McGhee strike but he did enough to win the fans over who were sporting half Newcastle and half Celtic woolly hats and chanting 'Feed the Bear' an Aitken song. The F.A.Cup always makes the hairs stand up on the back of Newcastle United supporters necks. We have a proud tradition in the competition and there is always an air of optimism once we get passed the third round. 1990 was no exception. A fifth round tie against Manchester United was our biggest game of the season. The build up to the game was fantastic. I had just celebrated my 18th birthday and a win over Manchester would be the greatest present of all. The game was played on the 18th of February and I met up with a mate of mine from Scunthorpe Stephen Cross. I decided against a drink before the game, preferring to get high on the atmosphere. Our tickets were for the West Stand Paddock next to the tunnel. As we walked up to the ground we could see Television cameras interviewing supporters. I had decided to dress up for the occasion. I had a false moustache on, in honour of my hero Mickey Quinn. As we walked past the cameraman I heard a familiar voice. 'Excuse me….Gerald Sindstadt ….BBC …Just wondering if you would mind having a few words on camera?' I agreed and he asked me what I thought the result would be in the game and who did I think would score. I told him Newcastle would win and my brother Mickey Quinn would score much to the amusement of the fans around me and to the 13 million armchair fans watching at home! Fame at last. The 31,748 crammed into St James raised the roof and the team gave it their all, but unfortunately that was not enough as the visitors ran out 3-2 winners. We had chances to equalise and the last five minutes were tense. Stephen had been carried off by St Johns ambulance men when we had scored our second goal. With minutes remaining and the game on a knife edge the tannoy crackled into action, 'Would Steve Wraith please make his way to the First Aid Area'.

First an appearance on national television now my name being read out to the fans! Mental.

I made my way along the cinder path at pitch side as the teams were applauded off the pitch to try and find Stephen. A steward took me to the first aid area. Stephens' ankle was really swollen and we spent the next few hours at Newcastle General Hospital. An eventful end to an eventful day.

April 15th saw Liverpool take on Nottingham Forest in an FA Cup semi-final at Hillsborough, home of Sheffield Wednesday. It was a bright spring day and no one could have anticipated the horror that the afternoon would bring. A sudden surge of fans on the Leppings Lane End crushed those already on the terraces against the metal fences. 96 football supporters lost their lives. Every fan the length and breadth of the country and millions overseas sympathised with the people of Merseyside who had lost friends and loved ones. I rang a few friends in Liverpool to make sure they were ok and offered my help if they needed it. That loss of human life put everything into perspective. An immediate inquiry into the disaster took place. The report had a knock-on effect for supporters up and down the country with the high security fences ordered down at all grounds. The disaster also had an effect on me. I felt compelled to write about the Hillsborough disaster and sent my articles in to different football magazines. I was buzzing when one was printed in full in '442 magazine,' in the letters section. I had a taste and a talent for writing.

I had seen my first fanzine a few months earlier. I had been nagging at my dad for a few months now. I wanted him to start going to the games with me. He had not been back to Newcastle on a regular basis since they sold Supermac, although he still supported the team from the comfort of the family home. I managed to persuade him to go with me to the home game with Bournemouth on February 28th.It was a night time kick off so too late for Rob, although he had just celebrated his 10th birthday. We got the metro over to Monument and walked up to the ground. Outside were the familiar smells of hot dogs and burgers from 'Keegans' vans, and the sights of programme sellers and now fanzine sellers. Fanzines were magazines written by supporters independently from the club. At the time Newcastle fans had the choice of 'The Mag' or 'Jim's Bald Heed'. 'The Mag' was the first and was a good mix of humorous and serious articles and a good smattering of cartoons. This particular night there was also the rare sight of visiting fans selling their own publication. 'Not The 8502' was a fanzine covering the ups and down of Bournemouth AFC. The game itself was a pleasing one with a 3-0 win. My dad thoroughly enjoyed it and although the crowd was low at 15,119 it was a memorable night for father and son. We decided to celebrate the win with a drink or three in the Duke of Wellington Pub. As we chatted at the bar, a few Bournemouth fans came over to us and started chatting about the game. They said that it was unreal for them to visit a stadium like ours and that despite the result that they had enjoyed the occasion. Before they left they handed me a copy of the fanzine that I had seen earlier. It turned out that the lad I was speaking to, Mick, was the editor and that he'd like me to write a piece for the fanzine. I was flattered and told him I would. I posted him a match review the next day and a month later I received a copy of my masterpiece! My first published work. I was so proud and showed everybody that I knew. This experience had given me a taste for writing and I decided to write a few pieces for the Newcastle Fanzines. I wasn't going to be deterred.

The first Newcastle United fanzines had hit the street in 1988. 'The Mag' was the brainchild of Mark Jensen and this was closely followed by 'Jim's Bald Heed', (a term of endearment for Newcastle manager at the time Jim Smith), and then 'Talk of The Tyne', a second rate attempt at copying the far superior 'Mag'. I decided to try my hand at writing a few articles for each magazine but was dismayed to find my work was obviously not good enough. Mark Jensen was at least kind enough to send me a letter of explanation, stating that they couldn't publish all work received, which was fair enough. Anyone who knows me will tell you that once I feel that I've been rejected, then I will re-double my efforts and try, try and try again. I don't give in that easily. So, I decided to set up my own fanzine. I recruited my good friend Stephen Cross from Scunthorpe whom I'd befriended on the Gallowgate End, and my young brother Rob as the editorial team. For our first issue we would have to put our money where our mouth was and dig deep into our own pockets. Stephen managed to obtain some paper from his work place, whilst I started writing my own news and views on life at Newcastle United. Stephen's Dad volunteered to draw some much-needed cartoons, whilst Rob set about cutting suitable photos out of various newspapers and magazines. Watch out Rupert Murdoch. The Wraith brothers were about to take the media world by storm. The hardest part about putting our first fanzine together was the folding and stapling. Stephen managed to blow up his work places photocopier, but not before he'd managed to run off 500 copies of 'The Mighty Quinn'. We had deliberated over the name for some time. Mickey Quinn was banging in goals left right and centre for us at the time and the fact that he wore the sacred 'Number 9' shirt meant the magazine could not fail to grab the public's imagination. Stephen brought up the photocopied sheets on his next trip north and Rob and I spent two exhausting nights folding and stapling. We also had to check that the pages were in the right order and the right way around. Painstaking but well worth it when we saw the piles grow each night.

The first game of the season saw us take on Plymouth Argyle at home. I asked Rob Blaylock who worked for me as a paper lad at my Post Office if he fancied making a few extra quid by selling the magazine. He jumped at the chance. So, at 1pm Stephen, the two Robs and me stood outside the ground and started selling issue one of 'The Mighty Quinn'. Business was quite slow at first, but as the queues started to form outside the turnstiles, people started coming up to me and asking what I was selling. 'Fanzine' was still a relatively new term so I described it as a fan's magazine. The first issue was 40p, quite competitive. As kick off time grew closer business became quite brisk. On more than one occasion people asked if it was the match programme? Before I had time to answer they had paid me and were gone. Easy money. My pockets were full as I met up with the lads at the Strawberry Pub outside the ground to share out our spoils. The total cost of production for issue one was roughly eighty pounds. On our first match day we had sold just over 200 magazines between us, so we had broken even. Anything else was profits. We were in business.

Within the first couple of weeks of the fanzine hitting the streets I started to receive letters from people who had bought the magazine. Some just praising our work, others wanting to contribute. We also received letters asking for quotes on advertising space in the magazine, something that we never really gave much thought to. We were more concerned with getting our views aired rather than making a quick buck. I was beginning to build up a network of contacts the length and breadth of the country which would prove invaluable to me. We produced issue two in much the same way that we produced issue one and again it sold out.

The fans loved it and as time progressed, we invested our profits into the fanzine giving it a bit of colour, more pages, and a larger print run. I managed to get mates to sell it with me at first and then I had people asking me to sell it. The business was growing and soon we had a deal with local distributors through my contacts in the newsagents to get it into shops across the North East. What had started out as a hobby was fast becoming a full-time role. It was here that I learned how to market a product too. With other fanzines on the streets we needed to be different so we started doing 'free gifts'. For example, when Tino Asprilla signed for the club at the next home game I took a jar of sarsaparilla sweets with me and gave away sweets to anybody buying a fanzine. I was shouting 'Get your Asprilla Sarsaparilla free when you buy our fanzine only fifty pence' every five minutes and the gimmick worked as I sold out just before kick off. The cut out Steve Howey beard was an idea that we nicked from 'Viz' which made fans laugh. It was all about being creative and I had a lot of ideas going around in my head.

The climax to the season of 89-90 was a roller coaster ride for everyone black and white. Jim Smith's team had managed to keep up with the leaders and were determined to finish in a top two slot. The previous season finishing 3rd would have been enough for a quick return to the top flight. This season however was the launch of a new scheme called the Play Offs. They were brought in to give teams at the lower levels something to play for at the end of the season. It meant however that a team finishing 6th after a full season could end up leap frogging a team in 3rd place who had been the better team over the course of a season.

This made finishing second imperative. Dropped points throughout the season however had proved costly. We went into the final weekend of the season needing to win at neighbours Middlesbrough and hoping that Leeds and Sheffield both lost their games so that we could clinch an automatic slot. Dad wasn't keen on away games, but I really wanted to go to this game. After all we could clinch promotion and what better place to do it than Ayresome Park.

Well Roker Park would have been sweeter but I wasn't going to complain. Tickets were like gold dust. It looked like my bed and radio were the only option. Dad arrived home from work on Friday beaming. 'Guess what we've got!' I couldn't believe it. In his hand were two tickets for our biggest game of the season. Brilliant. There was however a down side to this happy tale. The tickets were for the home end…the notorious Holgate End!

We travelled down early and met up with the kind 'boro fans that had sorted Dad out with the tickets. We parked up in a hospital car park, I just hoped that we wouldn't be visiting there later! I had butterflies in my stomach as we walked to the ground …not because of where we would be watching the game from but because of the enormity of the game. Dad had said strictly no colours, but I couldn't resist putting on my green and yellow away shirt on under my jumper. The police and stewards were checking tickets stringently but we slipped the net and climbed the steps to the Holgate. You could cut the atmosphere with a knife. The tension was building and it exploded as the teams ran out onto the pitch. I tuned my radio in and put on my headphones. I wanted to keep a check on other results. I couldn't get a thing so would have to wait for half time like everyone else. As the game unfolded it was quite clear that what happened elsewhere would be academic. Boro ran riot with Slaven and Baird doing the damage. Newcastle looked tired and jaded and were never at the races. The 4-1 defeat was embarrassing and the news that we had finished third and Sunderland 6th meant that we would face our biggest rivals in the first ever play offs.

The national and local press were in a frenzy in the build up to the first game which was at Roker Park on Sunday 13th May. I managed to get a ticket quite easily for the game and travelled down alone on the train. I had popped into the bookies and put a fiver on Newcastle to win 2-0. Having turned 18 I had started having a flutter and had a bit of success in March taking John Anderson to get the first goal against Barnsley and he obliged. Since then I had put my money on Kevin Dillon and continued to do so until he left the club. (Ironically the bugger scored on his debut for his new club having drawn a blank for United!) I never liked travelling to Sunderland when I was at school there and this trip was no exception. This was my first visit to Roker Park.

I'd missed the 0-0 draw there in late September but had managed to see Mark McGhee grab a goal in the 1-1 return at St James in February. The saying that form goes out of the window in derby games is so true and as far as we were concerned that was a blessing in disguise. The Sunderland Fans were well up for this game and this was by far the noisiest atmosphere that I had ever experienced. We gave as good as we got though and with both teams still level at half time I had lost my voice with all the singing that I had done. The second half was another tight affair but with the majority of the 26,647 fans shouting for the team in red and white there was always the chance of a mistake by one of our lads or the referee. That moment came when Mark Stimson was adjudged to have fouled Marco Gabbiadini inside the box. Penalty. Our hopes were on journeyman goalkeeper John Burridges shoulders. He had been signed by Jim Smith in October from Southampton and had performed miracles. It seemed like an eternity....the spot kick taken....BURRIDGE SAVES!!!!!! Paul Hardyman follows in on Burridge and appears to kick him in the head.

Bedlam. Fans baying for each other's blood. Minor scuffles around the ground, pitch invasions, it's all over. The final score 0-0. The two teams just can't be separated this season and the chance to play in the playoff final at Wembley is going to go to the final game of the season.

You could see St James Park from my parents' bedroom window in Heworth. Wednesday the 16th May 1990 was a horrible bleak day. The rain was fine but constant. The sort that wet you through within minutes of being out in it. Dad and I set off a little bit earlier than we had for the Bournemouth game as we expected large crowds at the turnstiles, and we were right. We chose to stand in the West Stand Paddocks right on the half way line. The accordion clap clap song was playing over the crackling tannoy. The Sunderland fans had taken over the old popular side the Leazes End and were making themselves heard. It did not take long for the Newcastle fans to find their voices and make themselves heard, 'We hate Sunderland and we hate Sunderland'. As the teams came onto the pitch the noise was deafening. Sunderland had opted for their change strip of blue. Newcastle were in their traditional black and white stripes. After three draws in the last three encounters it was a tentative start by both teams, but Newcastle drew first blood with a thundering McGhee shot which thudded off the post. As the minutes ticked by the crowd became more nervous. Every mistake drew a collective sigh, each attack a short intake of breath. The game, the tie was anybody's. Then a Sunderland attack down the right saw the ball fall to Eric Gates who tucked the ball past Burridge.. 1-0.

Newcastle tried in vain to claw back the deficit, but by pushing forward gaps started to open up at the back and the second half of the G-Force Marco Gabbiadini slotted in the Makems second to send their fans into rapture and their team to Wembley. Some fans invaded the pitch in an attempt to get the game abandoned, but the police were equal to them with the help of their Alsatians. At the final whistle some young fans invaded the pitch in an attempt to get to the celebrating Sunderland fans but once again the police and their dogs stemmed the juvenile tide of would be trouble makers. Dad and I were in shock. I had tears streaming down my face and as I looked around I saw that I wasn't the only one. Men of all ages wept as the team trudged down the tunnel and the Sunderland Fans sang their hearts out revelling in our demise. A season that had started full of so much promise had ended with heartache. Typical Newcastle United!

9

The Public Spotlight

What caused a dramatic change I suppose from a media point of view was the introduction of Sky TV. That's when the real money came into football in the Nineties. Kevin Keegan had come back in 1992 after Ossie Ardiles was sacked and Kevin took us up in his first full season. Kevin brought players in such as Rob Lee, John Beresford, Kevin Sheedy, Scott Sellars, Brian Kilcline, Paul Bracewell and of course my good friend Pavel Srnicek. With that lot of players Kevin won the old Division 1 and took us to the elite in English football. That was the birth of Keegan's team who were known as "The Entertainers."

With Newcastle now in the Premiership I was invited onto Sky Sports in my capacity as a Fanzine editor. There was a programme called The Footballers Football Show which used to be on Sky Sports after a live match. The show had celebrity guests on a panel with various supporters from different clubs. When Newcastle played Sheffield Wednesday and won 4-2, I was invited along to be in the audience. I took along my brother Rob and one of our mates Rob Blaylock. The participants on the panel that day were Sir John Hall, George Best and a couple of others.

During the show the host asked if any of the audience had any questions? I put up my hand and the boom mic operator headed over to me. Richard Keys pointed to me and told me to ask my question. I said that I was at Old Trafford on the first game of the season to watch Newcastle and I wanted to ask Sir John Hall why there was tickets being sold outside the away end by touts when some of my mates couldn't get tickets? Keys told me it was a great question. From that moment on it was the start of me appearing on TV on a regular basis to talk about the club. I had clearly made a good impression. I think the media saw me as a guy who was passionate about Newcastle but more importantly, I was someone who could hold a good conversation on TV without swearing. If you have a broad Geordie accent it's very difficult for people from outside the area to understand, whereas I had a mild Geordie accent.

The elocution lessons I had as a child were starting to pay off. I was lucky that my first TV appearance had been seen by local television people too as I got a call from the North East sports present Roger Tames and I was asked to do the odd bits and pieces with him. Roger told me that he'd really enjoyed watching me on Sky and had asked for my number. Roger said that he'd be doing a few local programmes about Newcastle, Sunderland and Middlesbrough and would I come onto the programme and do more of the same? I jumped at the chance. The programme with Roger was shown on Tyne Tees and as result of being the guy in the audience who asked the most controversial questions it really opened the floodgates for me regarding media work. It was then I noticed that I'd obviously got some of the other fanzine editors backs up. I think a few of them had thought I'd overstepped the mark and that I was just some upstart who didn't know his place. I was seen as the new kid on the block and it didn't sit well with them.

A lot of people won't watch themselves on the TV but I did and I was my biggest critic. I wanted to know what my mistakes were so that I could make a mental note not to repeat them. I didn't like the way I said "Er" often so I learnt to put my mind in gear, to pause and take my time. Another programme I featured on was called 'The Seat in the Stands' and there was a very famous guy who launched his career off the back of it called Eamon Holmes. I received an invite from Eamon to go on the show and talk about women's football which at the time was in its infancy. On that show in particular they were dead against it. If that show was broadcast now it would cause uproar with some of the blatantly sexist comments, but that was the mentality back then. On shows like that it became a bit of a habit of mine to support the polar opposite of what everybody else was saying. I started defending female football on Eamon's show saying it was a great idea. I also said in 20 years it will have a huge following which it has. I didn't set out to be a spokesman for the minority view it just turned out like that. I worked with Eamon Holmes five times as he liked me and we got on really well. Not only was I on the telly a great deal in those days but the local radio stations started inviting me on too. These media appearances meant that I was starting to get well known in the local area. Many times, when I was doing my drinking in Felling, I would be stopped by people I didn't know to tell me about all these good points I'd made.

Then there's the downside and I'd go to places and people would be like, "You're a fucking idiot you" and "Who are you to speak for me?" etc... That was my first taste of trolls, I didn't know at the time but the 'trolling' would go on to become a lot worse in the future. I didn't expect it. I never had any violence against me but it was incredible the amount of people who knew me. All my mates thought it was great when I'd get abuse, they thought it was hilarious and to be honest that kept me grounded. Many of them would join in with the abuse which I loved because that's what mates are supposed to do.

A lot of people were under the impression that I was making a fortune from all these interviews. I didn't receive any payments; I was just happy to build my reputation as Steve Wraith the editor of The Mighty Quinn. When Micky Quinn left, I did a poll in the fanzine on what we should call it now and people voted The NO.9. All those appearances on telly made the sales of my fanzine go up so it was worth doing.

For any football man from Tyneside like myself in their mid-to late 40s, you look at that era as a golden generation. Kevin Keegan had built 'The Entertainers' from scratch and now it was paying off. Keegan brought back in Peter Beardsley who was my hero and the best player I've ever seen in a black & white shirt. It was Beardsley who made Andy Cole at Newcastle in his brief spell at the club. Those early days taught me about PR but I wasn't quite the self-publicist I would go on to become.

10

'Nipper and Super Sundays'

I had always wanted a Staffordshire bull terrier. They are loyal dogs, full of energy and I had the time and the inclination to look after one. A mate of mine Keith who is sadly no longer with us, had puppies for sale, so I popped up to see him and his litter. I picked out a red coated pup with a white chest. He fitted in the palm of my hand and could barely see. I had given the name a lot of thought before I handed over a couple of hundred quid to Keith to buy 'Nipper' named after the policeman who tracked down and arrested the notorious Kray brothers. For the first few weeks Nipper whined and cried as puppies do. They miss their family. As the weeks and months passed by Nipper made himself at home and he started developing his shape and character. By his first birthday he was well over the average size for his particular breed.

Nipper loved Sundays. It was the one day in the week where he could spend all day with me. In my early 20s I also discovered my love of Sunday league football. Not many will know this but I ran Felling football club for 20 years. I was a Sunday league player also. Although I had two left feet, I'd always enjoyed playing football. If you want me to describe what kind of player I was I would have to say I was a big ugly centre-half. I was all elbows and would tackle a brick wall. When I played, I was given the nickname 'Vinny' because Vinny Jones was about at the time. I'd also just shaved my hair off so it fitted. As a kid my dad made me play rugby at Gateshead Fell rugby team but I would just mess around when I went. I had three years at the rugby club but I didn't enjoy it. They nicknamed me 'trouble' because I was always messing around. The only reason my dad got me into rugby I'm sure, is because he liked to go drinking there on a Sunday. I think that's why I joined the Sunday football teams because I was rebelling from all the years my dad told me I'd never make a footballer.

On a Sunday I would be up early to pick the team and then I'd take Nipper out for a walk. I'd then have breakfast and take him to watch a game at the local park. Like most dogs he would watch the ball with intent. To him it was a moving target that he must have at all costs. I'd let him loose at half-time then put him on his leash again as the second half kicked off. After lunch I'd meet up with my squad of players and give them the good or bad news and then we'd prepare for the game. Wherever we played we always had a good following. Regular supporters included Anthony Halpin, Mickey D, Steven Spence, Stuart Collings Chris Liddle, Ian Brown, Andy Wilcox, and Arron Parker. This particular day we were short of players, so I asked Arron to look after Nipper as I would have to pull on my boots and play. It was a meaningless game against Washington Coach and Horses so I couldn't do much damage.

As I was pulling on my top Arron was dragged into the changing room by a panting Nipper. I gave him a drink of water and Arron asked me if it was okay to let him off the lead. I said yes, on the understanding that he must be back on his leash by kick-off. No problem Arron assured me. Sure enough as the game kicked off Arron and Nipper stood side by side, almost regimental. The game itself was a high scoring affair, and mid-way through the second-half the teams were locked at 4-4. With five minutes remaining enter Nipper stage left. With skipper Chris Liddle on the ball, Nipper slipped his leash and set off for his target. Reaching the 18-yard box Chris faced two defenders and the keeper. Just as he was composing himself for a shot at goal the two defenders ran off in opposite directions, whilst the goalkeeper was rooted to the spot. It was as if they were scared of Chris and his lethal left foot. Then Nipper made his move tackling Chris unceremoniously from behind using his nose and teeth, which incidentally is within the rules of the beautiful game and he nudged it past the keeper for the winning goal. The referee stunned by the turn of events awards the 'goal' and Nipper is crowned a hero. We won the game 5-4 and all had a laugh about 'that goal' back at our base 'The Portland Arms Pub' in Felling. I thought nothing of the incident until the following week when local journalist and good friend Ian Willis rang me up from 'The Gateshead Post' to say that a match report had been filed by league secretary Tommy Richardson and that the newspaper wanted a photograph of me and my four-legged hero. I agreed as it would be great publicity for our sponsors. Little did I know how quickly this story would escalate. After posing with my star pooch and the paper going to print with the headline proclaiming a new 'Kenny Dogleash' I was being inundated with newspaper hacks wanting an exclusive with Nipper.

Channel 4's highly successful breakfast show 'The Big Breakfast' wanted him to appear on the show and take a 'Dog Soccer School', Radio Newcastle actually got him to bark and he conducted his first and last interview!

Those days with my football team were some of the happiest days of my life. I lived and breathed football and the 'Super Sundays' and we all lived for the all-day sessions afterwards. I was crap at tactics but any of the lads who played for me will tell you I was a good man manager. I also honed my PR skills with the team. Over the years we had various ex professional players turn out for us such as John Beresford and Frank McAvennie. They only played a half each but it got us column inches. We always had an ex-player attend our presentation nights and over the years the likes of Supermac, Lee Clark, Obafemi Martins and Nicky

Butt did the honours. We even had top rave band QFX play at one night in Felling for us. One season our squad competed in a Sunday Morning and Afternoon League and won both. As a reward for the lads' hard work, I held the presentation at St James' Park and we had our photo pitch side. Spencer couldn't resist running onto the pitch and was hollered at by the groundsman who was doing me a favour. You can take the lad out of the Felling!

One season after winning the league I booked an open top bus to drive around Felling. The lads weren't keen but all got on. I hadn't quite thought the route through and we spent an hour dodging branches, but it got the team and our sponsors some good PR. End of season trips were always special too with trips to Blackpool, Wakefield and Liverpool the norm, but don't expect any stories from those trips because as you all know what happens on tour stays on tour

I look back at my dust collectors (trophies) from those days. Over 20 of them. As a team we were never relegated. I had a great squad of lads who stuck together through thick and thin, and we are like that in life too. We all have a WhatsApp group which helps us keep in touch because life gets in the way these days. Love you all lads. Felling till I die....

11

I Found Eden in Ibiza

All work and no play make Steve a dull boy so they say. Lads holidays are a must if you are footloose and fancy free, and any young man or woman for that matter who has never ventured abroad on a club 18-30 before settling down is making, in my opinion, a serious mistake. I count myself lucky that I had travelled abroad with the theatre group to America and Russia respectively and they were good rehearsals for my first fully fledged trips away with 'the lads.' The Lads in my mind are whoever you are knocking about with at the time.

My first trip away was to Faliraki in Greece at the age of 21, a late starter by today's standards, I travelled with Steve Graham, Steve Thomas, Graham and about 20 others who worked with the lads, and I followed that the next year with a trip to Ibiza a Spanish island with Martin, Ballsy, Bobby and John Dafter, Steve McTaggart and John Nicholson. It was a wicked holiday and I loved it that much that I said I would return to San Antonio. Sometimes going back can be a mistake but 2 years later I was stepping off the plane again this time with Peter and John Clark, Melvyn Gates, Titch and Brewis. I loved the place, and my return was welcomed by the bar staff at the Pink Panther who remembered me from my previous visit. I had performed quite well in their karaoke competition and pool competition on my last holiday and they were keen to enrol me in their activities again. I sing a wicked Elvis! Well I think I do. Again, a holiday fuelled with alcohol resulting in a lot of high jinx and sexual activity resulting in sand getting into places it should not! I really liked Ibiza the sand and sea, the weather, and the music. The place was only just really taking off when I first visited its idyllic shores. A lot of the super clubs and big names from the UK had not discovered this paradise, but it was only a matter of time.

The Summer of 1999 was to be my next venture to the Spanish resort. By now the place had been taken over by big name DJs and Promoters. The lads could not decide where to go this particular year and as a result myself, Carl Douglas and Paul Donnelly decided that we would go to Ibiza regardless. It was hotter than previous years and the numbers of visitors to the Spanish island seemed to have trebled since the early nineties. The clubs had trebled also, and with the big-name promoters came the big-name DJs and with them came plush new interiors for the venues. A lot of money was pouring into the Spanish coffers and they were lovin' it, lovin' it, lovin' it!!! The first couple of days were a laugh as I reacquainted myself with old friends who had decided to work out there for another season. I also made some new friends at the old 'Star Club' now called 'Eden'. It was just as well as there was a lot of friction at the end of the first week between me and the lads. Nothing serious but enough to make me take on a job at 'Eden' as a doorman.

Working the door abroad is so different to back home in England. It is far more relaxed. The lads were bemused at my decision to work but I was sticking to my guns. I teamed up with James the only other English lad from Nottingham and a Swedish steroid freak by the name of Magnus. The manager of the club Mario explained to me that I was expected to work 11.30pm till 6.30am and that I would receive the equivalent of sixty pounds cash in hand. Result!

My first night was the start of the second week of my holiday and resident DJ Dave Pearce was spinning the discs. By 1am the club was ram packed with 3000 twenty somethings all up for it. The club itself was a credit to the owners. It had originally been a worker's club, a very run-down establishment but a million-pound makeover had transformed it into Ibiza's very own garden of Eden. The dance floor was the club's main attraction surrounded by four 6-foot podiums with a rotation of dancers performing till the early hours. Any punter trying to climb onto the podiums I was told must be thrown out. The front of house doormen were all Spanish and obviously didn't take kindly to having to work with English door staff. I never received any welcome or recognition from them, so I decided to return the compliment. It was creeping towards 3am as Dave Pearce took the stage and started his set and it was at this moment that one punter made a very big mistake. With a bottle of cheap champagne in one hand he tried to climb up one of the podiums and grab a female dancer. I caught him out of the corner of my eye and lunged towards him grabbing his leg. He hit the floor sharply smashing his cheap plonk. As he staggered to his feet, he started shouting abuse at me in Spanish and took a mis-timed swing for me. Big mistake. I ducked his punch and then grabbed him in a headlock and rammed him headfirst out of the fire exit. He tried to punch me again, so I side stepped him and gave him everything I had with a sweet right hander. Bullseye. England 1 Spain 0. With that I shut the doors on my amigo and went back inside to enjoy the rest of the night. The dancer thanked me in her broken English, but there was no praise from my English compatriot James. "Do you know who you just hit then?" I shook my head, just happy that I had dealt with a very tricky situation very well on my first night. "The Governor of Ibiza's son!" I thought he was having a laugh but sure enough within fifteen minutes, it must have taken him ten minutes to come round, he was back in the club and heading straight for the manager's office. Paul and Duggy were in hysterics as I told them what had happened and as they went to the bar for another drink, I was asked by James to pop in and see Mario. The meeting was short and sweet. He knew the lad was a pain in the arse and he was pleased that I had taught him a lesson but he had told him that I would get a ticking off and that he would not pay me for that night's work. He did pay me, but he told the lad that so that it would not get back to his father about the incident. It turned out that his dad granted the club's license. What a headline that would have made 'Geordie Doorman and Former Kray Man Closes Ibiza Super Club!'

The next night was foam party night with Boy George as the special guest. Foam Parties are messy but fun and on holiday you do not really care about getting covered in bubble bath!

Word had obviously got around about my exploits the previous night as the Spanish Doormen were a little more receptive and respectful as I entered the club. They put their hands out to greet me, so I shunned them and decided that it was me and James against the world. About an hour into the night a cockney bloke tapped me on the shoulder and asked me to do him a favour. He was in his mid-forties, tight curly hair and very tanned. He introduced himself as Tony a partner in the club. He had arranged for a film crew to visit the club and record an advert for the Ministry of Sound. He wanted me to look after them and the girl who they would be filming for a TV commercial. Great I thought, a night skiving with a star and I would be getting paid! Little did I know.

After the formal introductions I was a little disappointed. The girl who I was looking after was an unknown but would be world famous apparently after this advert. The story then unfolded. I was to carry Lisa on my shoulders onto the dance floor and she would be performing dance moves above me to the camera. Sounds simple enough, until you recall that it is foam party night! As the foam started to pump out of a tube above the dance floor the director shouted action and we were off. The dance floor was packed, and I was struggling to keep a hold of my star as the foam was making her legs around my neck very slippy. Within five minutes I was completely covered and choking on the bloody stuff as the director asked me if I could try and look as if I was enjoying it! Like a trooper I managed to battle on 'til the end with her safely on my shoulders, and when the director shouted cut, I let Lisa down and walked off the dance floor looking like the Snowman on holiday! The director was happy, I was soaking wet and my shoulders were aching, and Lisa was looking forward to a blossoming career. The director promised to supply me with a final copy, which he duly did a few months later. Unless you are looking for me you can't even see me on the advert but at least I know I was there!

I was making good money on the door and was offered some work at a worker's bar after 6:30am. I can't remember the name of the place, but it was walking distance from Eden and was an outside bar surrounded by hammocks a perfect chilling out place and an ideal place to watch the sun come up over the island. I was not getting paid in cash for looking after the bar, I was being paid with free drinks and a breakfast, which saved me money. I also made a couple of quid shaving lads heads down to the bone with a Bic razor. The doormen started to resemble the cast of Romper Stomper on the island courtesy of Stevey Todd!

I was beginning to toy with the idea of staying in Ibiza and giving up on my life back home for a while, but I had enjoyed my time there and decided that if things did not work out for me in blighty then I would return the following year and pick up where I left off. I said my goodbyes to James and the lads and my friends from the bars and clubs on both sides of San Antonio Bay and stepped on a flight bound for Newcastle upon Tyne. I was coming home and hoped that if I did return to Ibiza that it would be for another holiday and not to work because it would mean that I had failed in my home country. I was going to give it a go back home on the doors again and attempt to write a book about my life and times with the brothers Kray.

12

Scoring past Steve Harper

A few of my mates had been invited by former Blyth Spartans goalkeeper Dave Clarke to train with the Gateshead team from the Unibond League. Colin Richardson was the manager at the time and their latest star player, a certain Ali Dia. Ali arrived in England in a hail of publicity. He was signed by Graeme Souness at Southampton on the alleged recommendation of George Weah a former 'FIFA World Player of the Year' who Dia claimed was his cousin. As the ink dried on Dias' contract Weah denied all knowledge of this 'relative'. It was one of the biggest cons the premier league had ever seen. Ali actually came on as a substitute for the Saints but failed to impress, and after a drop down the various leagues he found himself on the Southern Banks of the Tyne.

Steve Harper, a reserve goalkeeper at Newcastle United was also at the club at the time on a short term loan. He was there to gain some much needed regular match experience at a competitive level. It was a sunny Wednesday night when I got a call from Dave Butterfield asking if I wanted to train with Gateshead at Wardleys Welfare pitch. I had nothing else arranged so I agreed. We joined up with the team in the changing rooms and after various introductions we got changed and straight into a warm up. I have to admit that I found the relays and the running quite hard. I've never been what you would call a top athlete, but when it came down to the ball work I was getting by quite well. Ali Dia was slow and lethargic and treating the management regime with very little respect. By the latter stages I found myself growing stronger and more confident, and although I was yards off the pace I was still finishing ahead of Ali!

Steve Harper was being warmed up by Dave Clarke as we all took a breather. We were then told to line up on the edge of the 18 yard box. Dave Clarke was to throw the ball at us. We had to chest it down and then hit it first time at Steve Harpers' goal. I was to go last, number 13 behind former professionals, top amateurs, and of course Ali Dia. It didn't take long for those in front of me to take their respective turns. Harper pulled off save after save, some high some low, some fast some slow. My time had come. The impregnable Steve 'Golden Gloves' Harper versus Steve 'Vinny' Wraith. You could hear a pin drop as Dave Clarke threw the ball to me. I chested it down perfectly and launched my right leg forward. The connection was abysmal. I toe ended it and the ball skidded away to Harpers' right. He had it covered but it clipped a divot in the pitch and this carried it over his outstretched hand, onto the post and into the back of the net. The lads cheered and laughed out loud as I pulled my top over my head Fabrizio Ravanelli style and ran blind with my arms aloft. It was my greatest moment. Steve saw the funny side too and I told him that I hoped one day that he would play for England so that I could say that I'd scored past England's number one. As squad numbers were introduced into football it gives my story an interesting footnote. Harper opted for number thirteen. Did he choose that to remind him of the lowest point of his career. The night number thirteen put the ball past him on Wardley Welfare. I wonder?

Ali Dia did not last long at Gateshead, but he did sign for my Felling team later that season and played one game, coming on as a sub for twenty minutes scoring two headed goals. We never saw him again…

13

Dalglish

Kenny Dalglish might not be a manager that fans remember fondly but he was great for me at the club. When he arrived at the club, he contacted me straight away. To this day I have no idea who gave him the heads up or who pointed him in my direction but I'll always be grateful. Can you imagine how strange it was to get a phone call saying, "Steve this is Kenny Dalglish I'm taking the Newcastle job would you like to come to the press conference when it gets announced?" Mental.

I turned up at the press conference in true Wraith fashion, Samba's, jeans and a shirt. When I walked into the conference, I could see all the other press guys like Alan Oliver and John Gibson staring over to me thinking, 'what the hell's he doing here?' Then Kenny Dalglish came in and out of everyone in the room he walked up to me standing at the back, put out his hand and said, "Hello Steve nice to see you". Somebody must have pointed me out because we hadn't met. The press conference went well and it was great as a fan just to be there and watch how it was run. After he had fulfilled his media duties, he invited me to go to Maiden Castle for training the next day and he said he would give me the exclusive first interview with him.

I headed up to Durham early the next day. I watched the lads train and then headed to Kenny's office afterwards with my mate Mark Collingwood and I got my exclusive. I found Kenny to be very honest. He opened up to me about the papers that would be attacking him from day one and that he wouldn't get the chance to succeed unless he had the fans support.

That's all he said to me. We got a couple of photos and headed off and ran the interview in our fanzine that weekend. It went down well and a few of the tabloids ran the exclusive too giving us some great PR.

I found Kenny to be very honest and open. He told me that certain newspapers would have it in for him from day one. He was right about that. As every Newcastle fan knows, the sale of Ferdinand was followed swiftly by an injury to Alan Shearer in a pre-season friendly against Everton leaving the inexperienced Jon Dahl Tomasson as a lone striker that season. With no money to spend Kenny started calling in favours and brought in ageing stars such as Ian Rush, John Barnes and Stuart Pearce. It didn't go down well with the fans or the press. Despite this, Kenny managed to get us second place in the premiership in his first season and in his second season he got us to the F.A. Cup Final at Wembley. We celebrated getting past the third-round days.

The highlight for me was the night, at St James' Park, when we took on Barcelona in the Champions League. I was pitch side before kick-off. Kenny had sorted me out a press pass. I watched as some of the greatest names in Spanish football were put through their paces in the warm up. The atmosphere that night was spine tingling. The 3-2 win has gone down as one of the greatest nights in our history and rightly so. Tino Asprilla and Keith Gillespie were unplayable that night and rarely have to buy a drink when they visit the city these days.

By the start of the following season the knives were well and truly out for him and after a 0-0 at home to Charlton the boos rang out around the ground. I was doing a shift on the doors that night after the match at Scruffy Murphy's on Percy Street and well-respected journalist Doug Wetherall who I knew well came up to me. He was making small talk about the game and I told him it was a shocker and that the players needed to gel more. So, you can imagine my surprise the next morning when I picked up the paper to see the headline, 'Bore Draw' and underneath 'Kenny's Final Ally Says Enough Is Enough'. The reality is I never said anything of the sort and I'd been stitched up. That was the first time I've been stitched up by the press and I wasn't impressed. I managed to get a message to Kenny to make sure he knew what had happened. That was a real harsh lesson to learn. When I questioned Doug on it he just said, "Just doing my job Steve". Of course he was but I would make sure he never got anything from me again.

14

The Fake Sheikh

As a boy I had always dreamed of signing a contract for my team…Newcastle United. I would envisage large crowds milling around Gallowgate waiting in anticipation for the return of their prodigal son to lead the team to domestic and European glory and make St James Park, to quote Bill Shankly, "A bastion of invincibility". Sadly, that particular scenario is still but a dream, however I can at least say that I did achieve part of my dream in a roundabout way in quite unusual circumstances.

My constant appearances in the media arena in my eight-year stint as fanzine editor had brought my name and face to the attention of some very prominent board members and directors at the club. In the early years the club would not recognise the likes of myself and the Mags Mark Jensen or True Faiths Michael Martin as anything other than troublemakers. But, as the meeting with Sir John Hall had shown, the club was beginning to see us as allies and possibly thinking about taking us on board in some capacity.

The first indication of their change in attitude came during the 'Save Our Seats Campaign'. During the ground restructuring a group of fans led by Jane Duffy objected to being re-seated in the oxygen starved level seven in the 'Milburn Stand'. They felt that the club were giving their seats to the corporate fans and sticking them up in the gods and out of the way. They weren't happy and mounted a legal battle against the club in the high court. The press and local media had a field day and the only loser was the club's reputation once again.

I was interviewed on local television and radio about the situation and I gave my honest opinion as always. I felt that the fans were wrong to object and did not see why I should support them. After all I had been in a similar situation in the early nineties when the ground was made into an all seater stadium. I had to give up my place in the Milburn paddocks for a seat way up high in the newly built Gallowgate End. Where was Jane Duffy and her merry band of discerning voices then? Some supporters slated me for my view, saying that I was 'in the club's pocket' but I was not. I genuinely felt that had their seats been safe then they would not have kicked up a fuss and there would not have been any campaign.

In all good battles there has to be a patsy, a fall guy if you like. As well as Shepherd and Hall having their dirty linen washed in public again, they managed to get off lightly in the 'Save Our Seats' fiasco and in my opinion, it was Chief Executive Freddie Fletcher who was the scapegoat.

He was painted as public enemy number one and departed the club under a very black cloud indeed. A week before his departure he invited me to meet him at Newcastle Breweries in my capacity as a supporter for the launch of a new photographic book depicting various sections of supporters in St James Park. I decided to go along and took Mickey Davidson and Chris Liddle. We had a tour of the breweries and a chance to look in on the Newcastle United museum housed in there at the time. We then posed for a few photos for the local paper for an article about the release of the book. After all of the formalities Freddie pulled me aside and said that the club were thinking about appointing a fans' spokesman...would I be interested? I told him that I would be, so he told me that he would be in touch.

I never gave the 'job offer' another thought, and Freddie's subsequent exit from the club put the idea of working at the real theatre of dreams to the back of my mind. My invites to the club press conferences continued thanks to Kenny Dalglish who I had struck up a good relationship with and I was still contributing on a regular basis to a lot of Sport shows. I was getting to know a lot of the staff at St James and was becoming a regular face in and around the ground. I had met Douglas Hall and Freddie Shepherd on a couple of occasions. Both were definitely black and white daft!

Their subsequent exposé by 'The News of The World' newspaper and its 'fake Sheikh' brought me unwittingly even closer to the club. Kevin Miles was the chairman of the Independent Newcastle United Supporters Association (INUSA) and was portrayed by the media as the fans' spokesman in this soap opera. He seemingly wanted their heads dangling from a noose at Gallowgate. I on the other hand was calling for calm and for supporter's minds to be focussed to matters on the pitch and not off it. It was also apparent to me that there was no chance of Hall and Shepherd leaving the club in the near future as they were major shareholders. They owned the club. They were not going anywhere.

I decided to carry out my own investigation. A good friend of mine in the media loaned me a full transcript of the interview and an un-edited version of the tape with our directors on. It soon became apparent that all was not as it seemed and that they had been set up. Reading between the lines the directors in some areas had said things regarding north east women being dogs and comparing Alan Shearer to Mary Poppins, but they had been taken out of context and sensationalised. It was made to look a lot worse. In the course of that week I must have taken part in over one hundred interviews on radio and television, many of them with Kevin Miles. Although we had very different opinions, we remained friends throughout a very busy period. The highlight for me was an all-expenses paid trip to London, (a good excuse for a night out with the chaps) to face the daunting Jeremy Vine on Newsnight. I had been asked to make myself look presentable and wear a suit. So, not one to disappoint I shaved my head, put on my Newcastle tracksuit top jeans and sambas. Jeremy Vines jaw dropped as I arrived on set. The interview consisted of myself and Jeremy in the studio, and former Newcastle United legend Malcom Macdonald and INUSA member Nicola Hawkins live via a link from Newcastle. Nicola had been brought in to give her views on whether all Geordie women were dogs. I knew that I was going to be in for a rough ride. Malcom and Nicola both went for my jugular saying that I had changed my stance over Shepherd and Hall. I weathered the storm and was giving a good account of myself but was stunned when Vine asked me, "Yes but isn't it true that you would play the Kray Twins for Newcastle United if you could?" Vine had certainly done his homework. Someone had told him of my association with the twins. I was on the ball though and retorted, "Yes that's true, but sadly one of them has passed away." Both Malcom and Nicola were smirking on the giant video screens. I was just pleased that I'd managed to parry Vine's verbal blow and left him looking rather stupid for mentioning it. I didn't take it personally, and Vine congratulated me after the show for the way that I'd handled the question. Like every good journalist however he wouldn't reveal his source.

Over the next few weeks Shepherd and Hall distanced themselves from the day to day running of the club, preferring to keep a low profile. When the dust had settled, they returned to the club with this statement:

A Personal Message from Douglas Hall And Freddy Shepherd

Dear Sir/Madam,

Following the controversial News of The World article which appeared over four months ago we issued a statement through the media on the 18th March 1998 which said: -

"...Both Douglas Hall and Freddy Shepherd sincerely apologise for any offence that has been caused to members of their families, the fans of Newcastle United, and the people of the North East...".

We are now writing directly to you as a Newcastle United fan to reaffirm our apology and to tell you of our hopes and aspirations for Newcastle United Football Club in the next stage of the Club's development as one of the greatest clubs.

We are pleased to accept the invitation of the Newcastle United PLC board to re-join the club board and look forward to working with our colleagues at all levels of the club again. The events of last March inevitably diverted everyone's attention, but we now once again wish to devote our energies towards giving the people of Tyneside the sort of football club they deserve. It took creativity and hard work to transform Newcastle United from a club which was teetering on the brink of descent to the old Third Division to one which, only two years ago, came second in the Premier League and qualified for Europe.

Last season's league performance was not as good as previous seasons, but we did nevertheless qualify for the Champions League, reach the F. A. Cup Final, and qualify again for Europe.

The Club have, during the close season, already signed a number of players to strengthen the squad. We will continue to ensure that Kenny Dalglish and the team receive our full support.

The stadium extension, which you will have read about in the local press, will be completed for the start of the season beginning in August 2000/2001 and will result in an increase in seating capacity to 51,000.

Our intention has always been to make Newcastle United one of the greatest football clubs in the World. We have started something exciting, and with your help we intend to finish this task. We have, unfortunately, lost ground since March, for which we are truly sorry, but we now intend to concentrate our energies in recovering that lost ground and repaying you the supporters with the footballing success your loyalty warrants.

Yours Sincerely - Douglas Hall Freddy Shepherd

I decided to strike whilst the iron was hot and contacted the clubs press officer Graham Courtney to see if I could interview the two men in question. It was an audacious bid to get them to set the record straight. To my surprise they agreed. Hall had never granted an interview to anybody, so already I was breaking new ground. The interview was set for the following week. On the day I arrived at St James' early and reported to the South West reception. From there I was escorted to Level 5, home of the club's directors. I was met by Douglas Hall with a firm handshake and offered a drink. I asked for a coffee. He then walked me to the boardroom. The boardroom was very long with the kind of furniture you see in Barker and Stonehouse. You're scared to sit on it. You could see your face in the table it was so polished. As we sat waiting for Freddie, Douglas made small talk about the team and about my job and family. I told him that I was a doorman. He told me that 'I didn't have the build'. The door swung open and Freddie came straight to me and shook my hand then took his place at the head of the table. He seemed quite nervous compared to Hall.

With the pleasantries over and done with I ran through the questions to make sure that they were happy before I started to record them. Hall laughed and said that he did not want everything recording and that 'I'd better not have another machine on me to obtain any private conversations that we may have.' Paranoid or what!

I had typed up a set of questions and started interviewing the most powerful people at Newcastle United Football Club. The question on most fans lips was how they felt about what had happened. People had heard their apologies and wanted to know what they were going to do to appease the fans. I was keen on finding out whether these two men were football people or just businessmen trying to milk the club dry.

Steve Wraith: "How hard have the last 12 months been?"

Freddy Shepherd: "Very hard. I can only speak for myself.

It's probably been a season horribilis, or annus horribilis as the Queen said. It has been a dramatic time for Douglas and I. Our lives have been hard to say the least. But like all good Geordies we've come through it. We've put it all behind us now and are just looking forward."

Douglas Hall: "I look at it slightly differently. Problems started in March; I think. Up to March it was a great year. Barcelona were here in the Champions League. Stuffed them. The League would have been a different story if we hadn't lost Shearer early. After March it all changed. It was a nightmare. Me and Freddy couldn't comment on the situation. If we did, it could have had an effect on an important match, the six pointer against Barnsley, the semi-final, even the final. Anything we said would have been used. We had to keep our gobs shut, if you like, not able to tell our side of the story and we still can't for legal reasons. The worst part was reaching Wembley and not being able to go. We had our tickets booked and up until the Friday night I was going to go. Freddy wasn't certain but I wanted to stick it up the press.

They weren't going to keep me away. But Freddy kept saying we can't affect the team's performance on the day. If we had gone, there would have been a media throng all around us and it would, with hindsight, have ruined the day for the fans and the team. It broke my heart not to go. I didn't think we deserved that because I think whatever we're accused of, if someday the fans hear the real truth about it, it'll put us in a different light. So, it was a bad year, a nightmare. Especially with all the bits and pieces that have gone on recently."

Steve Wraith: "The public relations left a lot to be desired last season. How do you intend to improve this at the club?"

Douglas Hall: "We're doing it now by talking to you. It's something we will build on. My father was a great communicator, but myself and Freddy have always preferred to sit in the background. We realise we have to talk to the fans more."

I was happy with their answers to my questions. After checking that my tape had recorded this historic conversation, I asked them if they would have a problem with me publicising the interview or selling it on. They said that they didn't. At this point we were interrupted by club stalwart Russell Cushing. He didn't seem to have a reason to enter the room. I got the impression that he had been asked to appear after a certain amount of time in case the interview was not going according to plan. It didn't bother me. I had what I had come for. My first real exclusive.

Freddie Fletcher's departure from the club as chief executive paved the way for David Stonehouse's appointment. Stonehouse, a self-confessed Newcastle United fan, had been employed by rivals Sunderland and was the major reason that the black cats flourished off the pitch. David was appointed as chief executive and given the job of building bridges between the club and the fans in the wake of the 'Save Our Seats' campaign. The first man approached was Dr. Rogan Taylor a 'scouser' from the red half of the city who came to prominence throughout the dark days after the Hillsborough disaster. He was given the position 'Fans' Liaison Officer'. His job was to go out onto the streets and talk to Newcastle United fans to find out how their relationship with the club could be improved.

Taylor organised meetings with carefully selected groups of season ticket holders. The club oversaw this particular process, saying that they wanted to make sure that there was a wide spectrum of its supporters included in these ground-breaking discussions. The meetings were to be held in the Swallow Hotel in Newcastle City centre over the course of two weeks. I received a call from Rogan out of the blue asking me if I'd be interested in attending the meetings with him. He wanted me there to help him with his research and to give him an honest opinion of how things could be improved. I took up his invite but warned him that there was a lot of bad feeling towards the club and that this process would be anything but plain sailing. I was looking forward to meeting up with Rogan again. I had helped him way back in 1989 when he was involved in the Hillsborough campaign.

We arranged to meet up for lunch prior to his first fans forum and I told him in no uncertain terms that he would be in for a rough ride. I explained that the relationship between the Club and its supporters was at its lowest ebb and that there was a lot of animosity and hatred towards the men at the top. Rogan appreciated my honesty and spelled out his blueprint for the future to me over a chicken madras. It all sounded too good to be true. He wanted the Club to sanction a 'Fans' Liaison Committee'. They would meet on a regular basis to discuss important matters that affected the fans. They would express the fans views to the club via the Fans' Liaison Officer. The committee would be elected democratically by the fans whilst the Fans' Liaison Officer would be appointed by the Club and salaried. In theory to me it sounded like a really good idea. But what would the fans think?

I managed to attend three meetings hosted by Rogan. As I predicted there was a lot of hostility. Rogan was genuinely taken aback. There was even some directed towards me which I had expected. The one positive thing was that the fans attended these meetings rather than ignoring them. Newcastle United fans live and breathe football. Our passion is second to none. If they thought that the FLC would help then they would give it a go. That was the general consensus of opinion. A lot of the same fans felt that it was the club trying to pull the wool over the fans' eyes. How right they would prove to be.

With Rogan's work complete he set about writing up a report for the board of directors and asked me how I would feel if he nominated me as his choice for the position of Fans' Liaison Officer. I was rather taken aback at first and thought about the implications. I decided that there would be no harm in being put forward. I could make a decision at a later date if I was offered the position.

A couple of months had passed when I was contacted by new Chief Executive David Stonehouse. He had received and read Rogan's report and wondered if I'd like to pop into the club to see him for an informal chat. I agreed and we arranged to meet in his office at St James' on the infamous Level 5 a week later. When the meeting came around, I'd had time to think about how I was going to handle this. I knew that David wanted to pick my brains, but in the back of my mind I knew I may be offered the position of Fans' Liaison Officer. I was unsure about how I was going to handle any offer but I was quite excited. David met me outside the lift on Level 5 and we met like old friends. There was a calming influence with David. He took me to his office and made me feel very welcome. We chatted for almost an hour about the team, new signings and memories from yesteryear. We were two football fans in our own theatre of dreams ensconced in our favourite passion. Newcastle United.

David then became quite conscious of time and turned our conversation to the matters in hand. Rogan Taylors report. David wanted my honest opinion on how the meetings had gone and how I felt about the proposed Fans' Liaison Committee. I told him that I felt Rogan had done a good job and in theory the FLC looked a sure-fire winner but that the only way we would know is by giving it a go. As the meeting went on, I felt as if I was talking myself into a job. Creating a position for myself at the club. It was a really weird situation if I'm being honest. David thanked me for my time and told me that he would ring me when he'd had time to digest all the information given to him.

'United Make Big Signing!' This is what you are brought up with when you live in Tyneside.

The Evening Chronicle Billboard always screams out all the latest news on Newcastle United and we always hurry to the newsagent to find out who has signed for the toon. Inevitably we are always disappointed. I remember one-year

Alan Oliver and John Gibson the chief United reporters broke the news that Brazilian ace Socrates was all set to sign. Of course, he didn't.

Years later I asked them where the story had originated from. They had to admit that it was a conversation that had been overheard and they went with that as copy. A few days later they realised that their 'source' had been talking about a band playing at the Student Union called 'Socrates'…priceless.

I'd been waiting a couple of months for David Stonehouse to call but had put all thoughts of a job at the club to the back of my mind when eventually he got in touch. He invited me up to St James again for a formal meeting this time. I have to admit I was a little nervous but excited as I entered the lift going up to Level 5 once more. David's secretary showed me into his office and provided me with a much-needed coffee. David got straight down to business.

"We want to offer you the position of Fans' Liaison Officer at the club Steve." I was blown away. I'd had time to prepare. I suppose I knew it was coming but it was a dream come true for me to actually be working at the club that I had supported as a boy. 'That's great' I replied as I shook David's hand. 'Now we need to work out a rate of pay. Any thoughts?' I'd spoken to my dad about this but didn't really know what to say. I mean what do you ask for? £100, £200 a day? A week? It was a really surreal situation. I'd in effect created a job for myself, now I was being asked to name my price! Crazy! I asked David for time to think about it and he obliged. With the formalities out of the way we chatted again about the team, imminent signings and possible ground alterations. He suggested that there may be a deal in the offing with the University to buy their listed buildings and incorporate the fronts of the buildings into a 'new East Stand'. He also mentioned development at the Gallowgate End with view to building a hotel linked to St James. It was great to hear all of this kind of information before anyone else.

I mulled over the money situation and agreed that I would take £100 for each day that I worked. I didn't want to be too greedy but at the same time I didn't want to cheat myself out of a good pay day. As it was to be a part time job and we didn't know what it would entail I may be required to be in 5 days a week so £500 a week didn't sound too bad did it?

15

Not So Sexy Football

I was half tempted to leave this page blank as a tribute to what Ruud knows about football management, but he warrants a page. I'll put as much effort into this chapter as he did managing our club.

After Kenny we had Ruud Gullit and sexy football. Another huge name in football and a magical player. Sadly, the sexy football he promised did not materialise and he upset players and fans alike with his arrogance. Not giving Rob Lee, who pound for pound is our greatest signing, a squad number beggared belief. Then there was dropping Shearer and Ferguson for a derby match against Sunderland and playing the game down as a non-event which eventually cost him his job. For me his reign was more damaging than Kenny's, but it's all about opinions.

With Kenny's departure my exclusive access with the club was over as quickly as it had begun so I concentrated on writing about the club in the 'Number Nine Fanzine.' We had reached 30 issues by the start of the season which for a home-grown publication was something to be proud of. We had some great regular columnists over the years including Michael Martin who went on to set up 'True Faith' which still runs to this day. I'm not sure whether it was Ruud's negativity and the apathy surrounding the club or whether the fanzine had run its course but we were all starting to find the whole thing a chore. It was getting harder to find match day sellers too which meant that as well as writing and producing it I was having sell it to. After a chat with my Dad and Rob we decided that we would call it a day at the end of the season. Unbelievably the side reached a cup final under the much-maligned manager but for the second year running we came up against a team chasing a domestic double. We were beaten again and me and Rob sold the 'Number Nine' under the old Wembley Towers for the last time. It was sad that we didn't go out on a high.

Ruud's departure came the following season with a defeat against the Makems. In the build up to the game I was interviewed by the local news about Ruud potentially dropping Shearer for the game. I couldn't believe he would be so stupid. When the team was announced and he had left our 'Number 9' on the bench nobody could believe it. We lost the game and Ruud lost his seat in the dugout. His departure after the defeat in the Tyne And Wear Derby meant that United were looking for another manager. Little did we know that the good times were just around the corner with the return of a local hero.

16

Top of the Pops

As I have already said Football has always been a great passion of mine and Newcastle United have always been my team. Now, although a great cup team in the 1950s, Newcastle haven't much to show in way of honours over the last five decades. The late nineties promised so much but delivered nothing but very entertaining and colourful players and with them attractive and attacking football. It was United's defensive frailties which would deprive the fans of the silverware they so desperately craved. 1998 saw my beloved magpies reach the twin towers of Wembley in the showcase of the footballing season the F.A. Cup final and what better way for me to mark the occasion than by releasing an F.A. Cup final record!

Football records of any type are par-se usually bloody awful. Take Kevin Keegan's 'Head Over Heels' or Chris Waddle and Glenn Hoddles' 'Diamond Lights', sorry lads! I decided to ask my mates from all boy band 'Cryin Out Loud' to help me out. Paul Martin was the lead singer in the band, I had gone to college with him after I had left school and we had kept in touch from time to time. I told him what I wanted and he set to work with another of my mates Kris on writing some lyrics. A week later the lads came back to me with a witty little number called 'Friday Neet And We're Gannin To the Toon', about a night in the Bigg Market. They had also composed a version of Ronnie Lamberts' classic, 'Home Newcastle', about coming back to the Geordie nation!

Another week passed and the lads had a copy of their tunes on a cd and I have to admit I was blown away. I agreed to finance the recording studio and the production of 2000 CDs. Top of the Pops here we come! First though we needed a gimmick, so I turned to Gazza's best mate Jimmy Gardner aka 'Five Bellies'. I had known Jimmy for a few years and when I told him what I wanted him to do he was up for it. So, I set the publicity ball rolling and within a few days the locals and nationals were plugging our cd before the first disc had been printed.

Jimmy was due to meet up with the lads at the recording studio that Friday and I had arranged for a photo-shoot with the lads too. I was away for the weekend so was looking forward to seeing the results on my return. It wasn't until I was on the train to Kings Cross that I realised that I had left my mobile phone at home. I felt like I'd lost a limb. Still at least it meant I couldn't be hassled on a rare weekend off.

After a relaxing weekend in London with my mates Christian Simpson and Dave Courtney I arrived to find countless answer machine messages at home and on my mobile.

Jimmy had got tied up and couldn't make it to the recording studio, so as a result we had no star, no star vocals and no star photo! Great. As the lads couldn't contact me, they took the initiative and recorded the song anyway. I met Paul that Monday and we listened to the songs and I had to admit it was brilliant! This could still work but I needed another angle. Paul, although a great songwriter, didn't have the nouse to promote the CD and the cover the lads had made for the cd was horrendous. I wasn't happy. It was a photo of the band posing and pouting and trying to look all serious! This was supposed to be a cup final cd and I had a great cartoonist Joe McKeough all set to do a cover of Alan Shearer but the lads had dotted the I's and crossed the t's because they couldn't contact me. I only had my absent mindedness to blame!

I tried to look on the bright side and was determined to get my outlay of cash back. We had competition though two other groups had decided to bring out cup final records due mainly to the fact that it was the first time we had been to Wembley in a major domestic cup final since 1976. This had the media in a frenzy and local tv station Tyne Tees decided to run a poll on their nightly news program. They gave each band a chance to perform their songs on separate nights of the week and then let the viewers vote on which song should represent the club on their trip to Wembley. The lads did me proud and won the publics votes by a massive majority! I felt like Pete Waterman as I watched the lads give it their all that night! The team performed poorly at Wembley losing 2-0 to double winners Arsenal, and the cd didn't fare much better, but I did get my money back and at least a chance to say that I can join the likes of Keegan and Waddle in the football records hall of fame.

17

'United Make New Signing!'

I was given a start date of 25th September 2000. I was counting the days! The big day arrived.

I was a little unsure what to wear on my first day. Suit, Shirt, Tie? Naaa I decided to settle for Jeans, sambas and a Ben Sherman shirt!

I was told to report to Pam Nichol at 9.00am on Level 4 for my induction. Pam was a lovely middle-aged woman with an air of authority. She had that knack of speaking to you like a head mistress but making you feel like you had been school mates for years. I liked her. She gave me my handbook with all the club phone numbers in. As I looked through, I recognised some very famous names, Freddy Shepherd, Douglas Hall, Sir Bobby Robson and Peter Beardsley. Pam then took me through the rules and regulations of the club. I decided to bring up my association with a few notorious criminals at that point and my intention of doing a book or books on them at some point. I thought it would be best if the club were aware of my association with these types of people in case any criticism was levelled at me. She thanked me for being so honest and made a note on my records and then the moment that I had been waiting for. Something that no one could ever take away from me. I signed my official contract at St James Park. It wasn't quite how I'd imagined…me sitting in between the manager and the chairman with the world's media quizzing the local boy returning to his roots…but it would do! Pam then gave me my copy and looked at her watch. "I've just got time to show you around the ground and introduce you to a few more people." I clutched my copy of the contract tightly ....

I could have probably shown Pam a few places that day that she didn't know about. I'd had access to most parts of the ground over the last few years but I followed Pam quietly and took in what she had to say. As we reached the new atrium at the Milburn Stand it suddenly hit me that I was now part of the greatest club in the World. My club...Newcastle United.

This new entrance led to the St James Café, the new magpie lounge and platinum club and the early learning centre. Greeting you at the door was a life size Alan Shearer waxwork model in typical scoring pose. The club had bought this and removed the England shirt that adorned it and replaced it with the obligatory number nine toon shirt. We entered the learning centre and I was really impressed. There were at least one hundred kids all working hard on their latest project on a top of the range computer. The room was state of the art and was very impressive. I was introduced to Phil the man behind the scheme who welcomed me in and let me try out one of the computers. If I'd been allowed to study at St James maybe I'd have put in a bit more effort!

Pam then showed me the corporate areas. I'd had offers to attend games here but never accepted them. Maybe I was stuck in my ways but watching the match in there wasn't my cup of tea. It was however just what I'd expected. Full of Ikea like furniture and photos of yesteryear. Pam received a call saying that she was needed back in the office so she took me down to the dungeons to meet up with the security staff. They were to issue me with a security pass for the ground and I would need to have my photo taken by them. Pam introduced me to Dave Pattison the head of security. I'd met him a few times and he had done me a few favours in the past by letting me into press conferences etc... My next scheduled meeting was in an hour's time with the head of the public relations department Hazel Greener. I was advised by certain people to be wary of Hazel. I like to make my own opinions about people so I would certainly reserve judgement. Dave hunted high and low for the camera to take my photo but to no avail. He said he would come and see me later and get it sorted. In the meantime, I was to be shown all of the fire exits and fire meeting points and the pitch side. The final part of my tour was given to me by an old tour guide who I would guess was ready for retirement. His recollections were a little hazy and his facts often muddled with fiction. He showed me the stadium and the pitch. I took a deep breath as I walked down the tunnel like so many of my heroes before me and walked out onto the pitch.

Trying to imagine what it must be like to play for the team in front of 52,000 fanatical fans week in week out. My moment was spoilt slightly by the old gent recollecting the day Jackie Milburn scored after a great through ball by Keegan. Poor bugger!

My date with Hazel Greener had arrived. It was held in one of the many meeting rooms at the club. As I approached meeting room number one, I caught a glimpse of a woman with short white hair wearing a trouser suit. It was Hazel. She was older than me and wore glasses which she peered over the top of. She gave me the impression that she obviously had more important things to do than to meet me. She asked me what I had been shown and whether I had received an induction. I told her I had. She seemed at a loss at what our meeting was actually about. She explained that she was head of the media department and that if I needed any help or advice then I was to report to her. When asked if I had any questions I said, "Where will my desk be?" Hazel peered over her glasses. "Your desk?" This seemed to throw her into complete disarray. I thought, I'd hate to see her if a big story broke at the club if this was the way she reacted when she realised I did not have a desk. She explained that the problem would be rectified by the end of the week. She would take me through to see the media department however and introduce me to a few of my new work colleagues. I must admit I couldn't get out of that room quick enough. Hazel was my line manager in effect. I could see that we were going to clash if not sooner than definitely later.

My new 'office' was on Level 4 and was a huge expanse of phones, computers, desks, and chairs. At one end was Pam's office which was next to the overworked telephone receptionists. The office then panned out and the marketing department, junior magpies, charity requests, IT department and the newly formed customer service department surrounded the media section which I was to be incorporated into. I was introduced to Judy Waitt. She had been given the task of running the customer services department. A thankless task at our club I imagined. Hazel left me to chase up my desk. I chatted to Judy about her new role. She was quite optimistic about it and said that our two roles and the eventual recruitment of a Fans' Liaison Committee would be beneficial to both the club and the fans. I nodded and smiled. Spoken like a true club official, I thought to myself.

Hazel returned. There was still no sign of my desk. I couldn't believe it to be honest. Here I was. Day one of my new job at one of the biggest clubs in the Premiership and they couldn't even find me a desk and chair! Judy offered to clear a bit of space next to her and she had a spare chair anyway. Hazel agreed that this would do as a temporary measure. I mentioned that my job would entail dealing with the public so access to a computer and telephone would also be beneficial. Hazel gave a rather dry smile and said that she would 'do her best'. My first day at Newcastle United was certainly a day to remember. I wondered what the future would hold as I entered the lift and began my journey home.

I had to share a desk for the first week with Judy and with Nicky Child the club receptionist due to a major re-shuffle of staff on the floor that we were situated on. By week two I had my own desk and computer and was in action. I started off by going through the various complaints that supporters had sent in over the last twelve months to try and pinpoint key areas that needed addressing by the FLC. I also began to contact the various supporters' groups up and down the country, as well as those locally to let them know that if needed I was available to them to help if anyone had any problems. Judy handed me two large files to start with. This was just the 'tip of the iceberg' but was 'something for me to be getting on with for the time being.

I took my time studying many complaints from fans like myself about the infamous ticket office, catering, stewarding and seating to name just a few. It was good to see that the club was logging and filing these complaints. Whether there was any action ever taken prior to my appointment I'm not sure, but I felt it was my domain to try and help these people by speaking to them personally either by phone or in person. There was a feature about my position at the club covered in the Match Program and from that moment on I was inundated with calls, letters and e-mails. I was in business!

My desk was situated within a group of four with Paul Tully programme/magazine editor, Mark Hannen newly appointed assistant press officer and Vicky Walmsley press officer. More importantly, I was directly outside Hazel Greener's office and within her line of vision. I was obviously a thorn in her side and she wanted to keep an eye on me. I felt like a naughty schoolboy again sitting outside the head mistress's office!

The constant hum and shrill of the phones would often distract me as I worked on reports and answered queries. It was great though to be working at the club I loved, all be it on a part-time basis, and I was relishing the chance of being part of the club's history and helping establish a better relationship between the fans and the club.

The election of the FLC committee was run by the Electoral Reform Society. Season ticket holders were given the chance to put themselves forward as candidates by collecting thirty signatures from other season ticket holders. They were then asked to nominate themselves into categories which ranged from the general category to the disabled category. Season ticket holders could then vote for the candidates in the various categories. As far as elections go this was quite successful. The thirteen successful candidates were Geoff O'Brien, Simon Lindsay, Marion Williams, Ian Ferguson, Jim Beresford, Mark Havery, Peter Carpenter, Ian Gilmour, David Toor, Steve Wilkinson, Glenn Jackson, Bryan Williams and Michael Murray. Our first meeting took place in June 2000 at the club, which really had a feeling of occasion and history in the making. It was a strange feeling for all of us to be suddenly thrown together, but I was pleased to see a few familiar and friendly faces in Bryan Williams, Glenn Jackson, and Ian Gilmour, all of whom I'd met in the past as editor of the magazine.

Over the first few months the FLC agreed its constitution and elected its officers and generally got to know each other. I suggested a flag and scarf day at the club to help raise the FLC profile and to help improve the atmosphere within the ground. Both the FLC and the Club endorsed the idea and with Metro Radios help we handed out 400 free flags to supporters prior to the game. It wasn't a great success but at least the club allowed the project to go ahead. It was a start.

The FLC set up their own website and began to receive input good and bad from fans up and down the country and together with the calls letters and e-mails I was receiving and the clubs own customer services department headed by Judy Waitt, at last the fans at Newcastle United had someone to vent their spleen to and most importantly someone to talk to. There was still a lot of hard work to do, but at least we were on the right track.

Sadly, not everyone agreed. True Faith fanzine and their writers really had it in for me, my position and the fact that I was employed by the club. In each issue there would be a snide comment about me. My relationship with the Kray twins was often mentioned and used against me. It was disappointing to see fans who had called for communication with the club constantly attack me and the FLC. What did they hope to achieve? Were they jealous that they hadn't been asked to do my job? Did they not get enough votes to be on the committee? Only they know but it was very petty and uncalled for.

For the first few months I was going in 4-5 days a week as well as working weekends on the doors. I felt like I was making good progress. I was just enjoying being at St James' and I would often have my lunch sitting in the stand looking out onto the pitch as the groundsmen went about their work. By now I had put together a comprehensive database of worldwide supporters' clubs. I touched base with a lot of them and was hoping to set up meetings between them and the club. Carole Beverley was leading things on the commercial front and she was great, friendly, approachable, good at her job, happy to listen to my ideas and gave me a bit of freedom to run with things.

My new job gave me the chance to invite people to the club who might otherwise not get the chance. I had invited a few fans who had written in who said they were visiting the area. It made their trip! One guy said he was dying of cancer and had weeks to live so I made his dream come true. He is still alive now however and claims to have made a miraculous recovery. I also brought up a few 'faces' such as Great Train Robbery mastermind Bruce Reynolds, London Godfather Freddie Foreman, and Kray henchman Tony Lambrianou. I took photos of them in the dugouts and gave them all the full tour.

17th June was the beginning of the end for me. David Stonehouse's shock resignation for personal reasons saw one of the 'old guard', Russell Cushing, take his place. A few days later after he was appointed, I was summoned to his office. There was a cold atmosphere and no offer of coffee. "As you know Steven, I have taken over David's old role. You watch your back and I'll watch mine. Any questions?" I said no and walked out. We wouldn't speak again.

I had booked a holiday in late August. I was on holiday with my fiancée Dawn. When I returned home there was a rather official looking letter on my doormat. I opened it and saw the club crest and the words suspended and hearing. I went white. What the hell was this? I cannot go into the case for legal reasons but let's just say that what I mentioned at my induction proved to be vitally important. I had to take the club I love to an employment hearing. This time it was Steve Wraith with two left feet vs Newcastle United and there was only going to be one winner. Soon after we married and enjoyed a lovely honeymoon. My career at NUFC was short but nobody could ever take it away from me.

18

Sir Bobby

Had Sir Bobby Robson become Newcastle manager when Kevin Keegan left, I have no doubt we'd have won the league and a cup or two. Sadly, he was unavailable and his arrival in 1999 saw Newcastle struggling again and Alan Shearer on the verge of walking away. We all know what happened. Sir Bobby gave us hope, some fast-flowing football and he gave Shearer the chance to go on to smash Jackie Milburn's goal scoring record.

I first met Sir Bobby Robson briefly at the club whilst I was working there. He had time for everybody and we chatted about the match at the weekend and what I was up to. I told him that I was working hard to improve relations between the club and fans. I also mentioned that I was writing a book about my time visiting the Krays in prison. He wished me luck with both projects and said he would want a copy of my book if possible. It wasn't till I headed back to the office that I realised Sir Bobby had been asking me my opinion on the match and the team and had put an order in for my first book. I was blown away.

What most of you won't know is that Sir Bobby was intrigued with the story of the Kray Twins. He had 'followed my story with interest' since our first meeting he said when we met again at a Sportsman's dinner at the Hilton in Gateshead in 2003. As we were chatting, I pulled out a copy of my book signed to him. He was amazed and thanked me. As we were talking a press photographer took some snaps. He sent them to me a few weeks later. Sir Bobby was at Fulham as a player and then as a manager during the rise and fall of the twins and had heard a lot about them. He had also read a few books on the terrible twosome.

About six months later I bumped into Sir Bobby again and he came dashing over to me and he said, "Aah Steve my boy I read that book, what a remarkable story". He told me how much he'd enjoyed it and congratulated me.

On the pitch he led the team to an FA Cup semi-final. We lost again, this time to Chelsea, but at least we had the joy of seeing Shearer cross and Rob Lee stick the ball into the back of the net. His departure, which I don't want to dwell on, sickened me. Fans were calling for him to go after a fifth place finish. If only they knew what was coming up in the next 15 years, they would have kept their mouths shut. Sir Bobby left the club with his head held high but was struck by cancer again and this time it was terminal. Typical of the man he set up a Foundation to help others and with the support of his many friends in football he launched it in Newcastle. Where else.

His final public appearance was on Sunday 26th July 2009 at St James' Park when an England Italia 1990 team took on a Germany select team in an exhibition game for charity. I had received an invite from the Foundation and was sitting in the Directors Box with other prestigious guests. It was an emotional night with many people including myself close to tears. Sir Bobby by now was confined to a wheelchair and after meeting the teams he was brought up to the director's box to join his guests by his favourite member of the St James' Park security team 'Bob'. As he was coming past me, he asked Bob to stop and then said, "Aah Steve thanks very much for coming and I hope you enjoyed it." I told him he still knew how to pick a team and he gave me a wink and off he went. That was the last time I saw him.

19

Big Brother's Loss Not Mine

After watching the first series of a new reality TV show on channel 4 I really fancied entering it. I applied to go on series three in 2002 and like thousands of others I started the audition process with a 'diary room' type interview at a secret location in Newcastle. I heard nothing for a few weeks and to be honest I had forgotten that I had entered when I got a call asking me to go to another interview. This time it was a 'diary room' audition and I had to fill in a 24-page questionnaire that they used to assess your mental wellbeing. I was then taken into a room with other potential contestants and we were given scenarios to deal with as the cameras recorded us. I was just myself. No airs no graces. I had applied for the show in 2002 to promote my book 'The Krays The Geordie Connection'. My idea was to go on there and get as far as I could and that with the new found 'fame' my book sales would reach a wider audience. There was no contact after that for a few months then out of the blue a withheld number called me to congratulate me on getting to the last 24 and that I had to travel to London the following week for a final interview. The following week I travelled down all expenses paid by 'Endemol'. I had to call a number from a call box on arrival and I would be given further instructions. I arrived in London on time and had to head to a North London hotel. On arrival I was told not to mention what I was there for to the staff. A producer met me and took me up to a chair outside a room and I waited. I didn't see anyone else that day. I was then taken into a room with a man and a woman who were the series producers. We chatted for thirty minutes and then they thanked me and I was allowed to leave. Two months later a letter dropped on my mat. It was a thanks but no thanks letter. The male producer really liked me but the female one preferred fellow Geordie fireman Johnny Regan and he got the nod. I was gutted. I watched the series in the summer as Jade Goody, Spencer Smith, and Johnny took the show to new heights. I looked on in envy. The following year I decided to give it another go but I fell at the first hurdle. I wasn't going again.

Inadvertently I did have a success of sorts with the reality show. When I was working on the door at Sea Nightclub on The Quayside a young lad called Antony was working there and would come in as a 1970's dancer. He used to dance in there on a Monday night dressed up in wigs, flairs and horrendous jazzy shirts as part of the 'Stretch Limo' night. He knew I had just missed out on Big Brother and he was asking me how I had made it so far. He wanted to know how I'd acted, what I'd said and what I'd put on my forms. First and foremost, as I've mentioned you must fill in a twenty-four-page psychological review form which can help them to figure out whether or not you're likely to have a mental breakdown on national television. With all these questions I got the impression he was around that stage. I told Anthony that I was just myself but that perhaps someone might get further if they pretended to be something they were not. He took my advice. The night that series started I was sat like everyone else waiting to see the contestants enter the house so you can imagine my surprise when Anthony Hutton got out of the limo, I almost spat my drink out because it all made sense, that is why he had been asking me all those questions, I was really pleased for him.

He came across really well on the show and it's no surprise to me that he went on to win it. I felt like I'd helped him and that was good enough for me.

The following year I was working on the doors with a guy called Jonathan Leonard from Carlisle. Me and Jonathan got into a conversation about Anthony winning and unbelievably he told me he'd just applied to go onto the show. Jonathan almost got into the house but just fell short like me. If I remember rightly Jonathan got on the opening night programme but as Big Brother does it twisted it and they made a cull so Jonathan got pulled. Looking back at it today I'm glad I never got in, it was a close escape. The reason being is that I'm an actor first, so for me to be taken seriously in the industry it would have been a bad career move.

20

Closing the Doors on Another Chapter

On the doors in the mid noughties I was doing 34 hours a week and I was on anything from between £15 - £25ph so it was a full-time job to me. What I will say is once you get hooked into that industry it's very hard to leave it which is probably the reason I was in it for so long.

When I was doing that job, I had my days to myself so I was in the gym every day or spending time with my girls. When I did a 9 to 5 at the Post Office I could only do things like that on the weekend. I would have to say the last six years of my door career was when I started to get sick of it all and the reason was, they'd changed the laws drastically. The 24-hour licensing came in which essentially meant bars could stay open morning, noon and night and that killed the nightclub industry. In the old days you could go out 7pm to 11pm and after that you had a choice to make of going home or paying into a nightclub which would be busy. When the 24-hour licensing came in it meant people didn't have to go to clubs, they could stay in the bars in shorts and trainers until stupid o'clock if they wanted. I have to say the worst thing for me was the smoking ban in 2007 because with that coming in and with me being the Head Doorman, I suddenly had to round up hundreds of smokers like a Shepherd bringing in his flock of sheep. Not to mention all of them blowing smoke across my doorway and into my lungs. That used to really get me in a bad mood and I would have to be constantly telling people off for standing in the doorway.

When I was working at a certain club and people wanted to go out for a cigarette, they'd need their hand stamping to prove that they'd been in, with that it suddenly brought a big security issue to the forefront for us. On Friday and Saturday they'd be two thousand people in the club and many of them would be in and out smoking which ordinarily wouldn't have been a problem but there were the trouble makers who we had put out of the club who were getting back in because they had a smokers stamp! All of that would change me from the nice, mild-mannered and pleasant Steve Wraith to somebody who would be constantly pissed off going to work which had never been me. Another big factor was the licencing law required there to be one doorman per eighty people in your venue but that was never going to be met because of the financial implications. In there we ended up with six doormen full stop when in reality we'd have needed six Superman's to hold the fort. Sometimes they'd be 2,200 in on a Saturday which was against fire regulations anyway but I was getting told to like it or lump it because they wanted more people in the club. I think the most I ever had was eight doormen to do the job of sixteen men which was totally ludicrous, because of it all I was getting really agitated about it because my own professional reputation was at risk.

Another biggie for doormen was the invention of phones that could video you, we had a lot of people that didn't like being thrown out of the club who would then be waving their phone around in front of your face recording. Another problem was that clubs were now asking us to escort troublemakers we had ejected from the club away from the premises because they were getting black marks from the council. I was expected to literally frogmarch the rowdy individuals away from the club onto the street. This was ludicrous because If I was shot, punched, stabbed or fell and banged my head I wouldn't have been on the club's premises that I was working on then I'd have no cover if anything happened to me. I would have been seen as a member of the public and the badge of authority was worthless. Also, if I needed to push someone away and they fell and broke their ankle then I was liable to be personally sued. Although I had a badge of authority it doesn't work on the streets like the police.

Newcastle is a tough city to work in because it's a party city. Every weekend there's dozens of groups heading to our city for hen nights and stag-dos thanks to MTV show Geordie Shore. Lads and lasses would watch the show and presume that all the Geordies were like that which just wasn't the case. Big groups were even heading over from as far as Dublin because it's cheaper in Newcastle than it is for them on their own doorstep.

With me being so well known in football circles, a lot of my night would be taken up with people wanting to talk to me about what was going on at St James' Park. Sometimes I'd be having to put people out for fighting and I'd be marching them out in a headlock when a drunken lad would come up at that very moment asking, "What's going on at Newcastle Steve"? I never like being rude to people so it always made me feel bad when I had to say, "Look mate I'm at work and I haven't really got the time to be talking about Alan Shearer's hat-trick or the latest fans protest". I could tell some of them were thinking I was an arsehole because I couldn't give them the time of day which really isn't me.

A lot of my door stories can be found in my book, 'The Krays The Geordie Connection' but I do have one I can share with you. One night we threw out a local lad who was effing and blinding and telling me he was going to have me shot. I ignored him but he kept coming back. Then he went on the phone and was pointing at me. He came back laughing like a bond villain. 'That's sorted,' he said 'you're in bother.' I asked him why that was. He told me his brother was coming down to sort me out. Intrigued I asked him who his brother was, expecting one of the numerous local names

I would hear every night of the week. 'Steve Wraith' he said. Well the other lads on the front door couldn't help it they burst out laughing.

I held my laugh in and for the next half hour quizzed him about his 'brother' Steve. I eventually let him in on why my lads had been laughing at him. He saw the funny side and apologised and walked off. I let him in the following week and he wasn't a pick of bother.

In 2010 I had decided enough was enough. I just wasn't enjoying it any more. The rules and regulations were doing my head in. The cold weather was starting to get to me and with a family now the threats I would receive night in night out would not just affect me if anyone had bad intentions. I walked away just before Xmas 2010. I had no job, but had started my Performing Arts Degree at Gateshead College after regaining the acting bug and had my mind set on going into the events business using my contacts in the world of football and boxing. Do I miss the doors? I miss the crack with the lads and I know I could go back to doing the doors at any time because I still have a good reputation in the industry. It is nice to head into Newcastle and see some of the lads on a night out. The respect is still there and the camaraderie. I still don't know how I did the job for 18 years. My mates say it's the best acting I have ever done. I don't disagree...

21

Drama: Take Two

I never thought I would get back into acting. It was a chance meeting with my old mate John Altman who played 'Nasty Nick Cotton' in EastEnders that persuaded me to give it another go. John was appearing in a play called 'Bouncers' at the Sunderland Empire and had asked me if he could pop to Newcastle whilst he was looking for accommodation to stay in and do a stint on the door with me so he could get a feel for the job. I ran it past Mark Whitaker my manager and he was delighted to be getting a 'star' in his club for free. John came up and spent an enjoyable night in 'Sea' Nightclub and watched me in action. Six months later he appeared in the play and sorted me three free tickets out, so I took my Mam and my wife.

After the show I took John and his co-stars Nigel Pivaro (Terry Duckworth in Coronation Street) and local actor Chris Connel to Newcastle for a night out. As the drinks flowed Chris brought up the fact that I used to be an actor and should give it a go again or I'd regret it. I laughed it off but the next day I called him and we chatted about my options. He suggested I call his agent and ask about registering as an extra on her books. I called her, went for an interview and I was back in the game within 2 weeks.

My first casting was at the 'Mitre' where they used to film 'Byker Grove.' I had a hangover from hell and my voice was croaky as I had been to a Newcastle match the night before. Not the best preparation. My agent had put me in for a speaking role in a new BBC 1 Detective series called '55 Degrees North' which was unexpected. I was taken into a room with a Director and the producer. The Director looked as bad as I was feeling and when he heard my voice he smiled. "At the match last night?" I nodded. "Yes." For the next 10 minutes we talked about the game, the incidents, and how we saw the season panning out. He then said, "I suppose I better get you to read the script." After one read through, he thanked me and I was on my way. I hadn't reached home when my mobile rang. It was my agent congratulating me on getting the part. I was over the moon. I did two days filming on that playing a wheel clamper. I was picked up from home in a car and had my own trailer on set. I was feeling every bit the actor. Hollywood here I come! I came back down to earth with a bump on my next job though. I played a security guard in 'Byker Grove' and was a background artist. I started at 7am and had to find my own way to set. I had completed my scene by 9:30am. I tried to get an early finish but they kept me there till 7pm. I was sick as a chip. I stuck at the extra game for six years though and I networked. I appeared in Byker Grove three more times including the final episode, and also featured in 'Wire in The Blood' with Robson Green. I also spent a week on the second series of '55 Degrees North' playing a henchman. I worked with well-known North East actor and comedian Mike Elliot on that and I learnt so much from him. I was also into doing student films for free so I had those strings to my bow. What I would do was check Newcastle and Sunderland Universities for parts and I played detectives and gangsters parts, it was a good opportunity to get myself back in front of a camera again after almost twenty years away from drama and to get up to speed with how it worked now. It was around then that I knew if I was serious about becoming an actor I'd have to go back and do my B-tech diploma that I walked away from at College.

After looking at Gateshead Colleges website I enrolled for a GCSE in Performing Arts course which would take a year. I wanted to learn the craft you see. I didn't want to feel as if I had cheated my way into the career. The beauty of going to Gateshead college was Steve Melville was there and Steve and I had been at The People's Theatre together as kids. Steve was slightly older than me but he was now the head of drama at Gateshead college. I would have to go to college one night a week to do my bits of theory then I was mainly working towards a performance at the end of the year. The play I did was called 'Your Home in the West' by Rod Wooden. I got cast for the part of Micky which was the lead role. Micky was a nasty piece of work who was an alcoholic woman-beater and it was fun to play him. It was the first time I'd been on stage in seventeen years. Acting is like riding a bike though, if you're any good at it then it comes back naturally to you. I can't even remember anything about the first half of that play so that tells you how good it was.

After passing that course I asked Steve Melville what I should do next. Should I finish my diploma that I had walked away from? He told me I'd be wasting my time at my age doing that. What Steve advised me to do was forget about doing the diploma and focus on doing a full-time degree at college in association with Newcastle University which would cost £3,000 a year and it would take three years to complete. Steve told me it would be two and a half days a week so that would let me continue to work. Steve said in the third year I'd only have to be in one day a week. Steve told me that if I did that then I'd be fully trained for anything in the acting world so that was what I decided to do. I still worked the doors whilst doing it so it was tiring a lot of the time but I knew it would be worth it in the end. Dawn could see it was a passion I had and whatever happened we'd get through it and make it work. I had a great time doing my degree although it was very hard work. The degree covered acting, singing, dancing and even teaching. In the final year I had to go out and teach others and I would be marked on my performance.

I graduated at the age of 39. Steve Wraith the kid who hated school, the class clown, went back for more which I never thought would happen, although both my parents did degrees in their later years so I guess I followed suit. After graduating I went back to my agent to tell her what my position was now. Bearing in mind I'd worked a long time with her and never let her down I just for the life of me couldn't get a reply from her, no matter how many texts, calls or emails I sent her. I then was asked to go into her office to discuss something to do with me being cast on a project. When I got there, I saw my agent, she was sat with her back to me, typing away at her computer. I just shouted over, "Hiya are you ok"? She told me she was very busy and didn't even bother to turn around to look at me. I told her no problem but just wondered if she got my email, to which she replied, "I'm very busy Steve I haven't got time". I just thought, 'WOW' she clearly had got the several emails and she wouldn't even turn around to acknowledge me. I still don't have a reason to this day why she behaved like that so I just left it.

I wasn't going to be put off by her, I'd spent three years of my life at college and paid £9,000 for the pleasure so I wanted to be an actor, I'd trained to be an actor and I was bloody going to become a professional actor if it killed me. The first thing I needed to do was find myself a new agent or I would have to represent myself. I started joining various casting websites to build up my profile. North East man, 35 to 40, baldhead, dazzling good looks (joke!), height 6ft 2 and all of my other details. I would tick boxes on other various accents I could do as the more you could do the wider you could cast your net. You have to put down whether you can choreograph fight scenes, sing, dance etc...The House of the Rising Sun is my karaoke song but there was no column for that. I started to get emails informing me of auditions in Newcastle. Many of them I got booked for were student films. I was still happy to do them for free but I was ideally looking for some paid work. I had £9k to recoup! The first break was a small budget feature film set in Newcastle called 'In Our Name' which had some big-name actors in it. They were looking for a Sergeant Major, aged 35-40, stocky build, bald head, stubble and I thought perfect that's me. I submitted my application and I got an email almost immediately telling me I had to be in Elswick on Monday the following week. On the Monday I arrived in Elswick to find the casting taking place in someone's house with a couple of girls. I was given a script and had to read a few things off it and then away I went.

A couple of days later I received an email saying, 'Dear Steve we'd like to offer you the part in the film which comes out in 2010' and I was buzzing.

I was now officially a working actor and getting paid! Although the financial side of it wasn't great, it really gave me a good leg-up. The director was a Scottish guy named Brian Welsh and 'In Our Name' was one of his first feature films that he'd done but he didn't have any connections in Newcastle. Well the one thing that I have if I have nothing else is connections in all walks of life so we hit it off very well. The star of that film was a Whitby born girl named Joanne Froggatt who went on to become a major ITV star. I filmed the first part of the film in a barracks then the second part across the moors with a load of squaddies. The problem that Brian Welsh had though was he had a diminishing budget and he didn't have any squaddies and that was where I could help with my contacts. At the time I was running my Sunday football team so I told Brian that as long as they were paid expenses, I could rally up my troops and that was his problem sorted. In the end I got three footballers and three actors from my drama course from Gateshead college and the guys Mark Conder, Scott Carter, Grant Longstaff, Peter Brown, and Dom Clauzel did a great job.

Another problem for Brian was he needed a boxing gym scene but he didn't know anyone with a gym. I rang Davey Gregory who still had the old boxing gym in Felling and got that angle covered. Brian also needed a nightclub scene; well I was still working on the doors so I was able to cover that too. At the wrap party in December 2010, Brian Welsh stood up and told everyone how he couldn't thank me enough and that I was an absolute godsend to him.

Brian told me he couldn't have got through the film if it wasn't for me and asked if there was anything, he could do for me. I just laughed and said, "You can help me to get an agent".

Brian asked if I had spoken to Sam Claypole because if I hadn't then he would be happy to introduce me to her but he said he'd put a good word in for me first, it was exactly what I needed. Well true to his word Brian organised for me to go to Sam's office in January 2011 in Darlington. When I went along to Sam's office, I had a long meeting with her, she then asked me to read a couple of scripts from films she'd been involved with. At the end of it all Sam said that I was a little bit rough around the edges but she was willing to take a chance on me. What she meant was even though I had schooling qualifications in acting, I didn't have any credits and that's what matters in the industry. You have to have the credits to your name and that only comes with TV and film appearances. At the time I only had '55 Degrees North' and 'In Our Name' which wasn't a great deal. When Sam Claypole took me on it was a great relief to have an agent and that's where my acting career really began.

Over the last ten years or so it's been a lot of hard work and effort to get to where I am today and I have had a lot of knockbacks but I have never given up. A lot of it is luck and who you know not what you know.

I had been invited to the screening in London at the Grosvenor Hotel for the film 'Rise of the Krays' this was the first film, 'Fall of the Krays' being the sequel made by

Carnaby Films. I was invited to that opening as a guest and only because I was seen as a bit of a Kray expert plus, I was asked to take my friend Freddie Foreman along as well. In there we met the stars of the film and Fred and I did a few interviews which were great for the film's PR team. We didn't get a chance to meet the director Zack Adler that night but at 'The Fall of the Krays' premiere the following year I was introduced to him.

Zack came over and told me he wanted to thank me for bringing Fred along as it had helped with publicity and the film had reached number one in various charts. He thanked me and said, "If there's anything I can do for you" and again I said, "Well actually there is". I asked him that if there was any film that came up which he may think I was suitable for then could he consider me and I gave him by business card. One of the biggest problems in this game is finding people as good as their word but Zack certainly was. Within six weeks he rang me up and told me that he was going to be the director on the new 'Rise of the Foot soldier' movie and that he thought he had a little part for me, although I would need to go down to London and audition. In the meantime, he emailed me the script for the part he had in mind and asked me to tell him what I thought. The character I was to play was called 'Steamboat'. It was right up my street and it had a couple of fight scenes with the lead character Pat Tate played by Craig Fairbrass.

The casting was a few weeks later and I was told that day that I had the role. I had to head down a few weeks later to choreograph the fights and get measured up for wardrobe. I had to go to the famous Peacock boxing gym in South London to rehearse the fight scenes. That was the first time I met Craig and the other actors Eddie Webber and Andy Beckwith (from Snatch). Up and coming actor Josh Myers was also there. Within six weeks of Zack calling me I was on set filming.

On set its full of lights and is really hot. When you're watching a film, you don't imagine it looking like a battlefield with stuff everywhere. Then there's film directors and producers all over the place which the viewer never sees.

Me and Eddie Webber who was in the film 'The Business' got on really well on set, that guy is a consummate professional and it's great to work with someone like him when you're learning the ropes as I was. In the prison fight scene when Craig Fairbrass was belting Andy Beckwith, he ended up accidently smacking him for real on the fifth take and broke Andy's nose.

As soon as Craig walloped him, I could see straight away that Andy's nose was gone. Of course, with Andy looking like that it effected the whole shoot because he had to get rid of the black eye before we could continue. The best thing about shooting that film was getting to work with Shaun Ryder because I am a massive Happy Mondays' fan. That whole era of music from The Farm and The Inspiral Carpets around 1990/91 was my generation. Shaun Ryder had a nightmare with his script and told me he'd been performing for over quarter of a century and he could never learn the words to his songs so he had no chance of knowing what he had to say. After a few run throughs it became clear that Shaun was really going to struggle with his lines. In the end Craig and Zackary pulled him to one side and had a pep talk with him and the script for Shaun was made shorter which was great for me because I got a few more lines in the film. As it happens the scene turned out fine once Shaun calmed down and he got over his nerves. It was a real pleasure to work with him. We were sharing taxi's back and forth to filming. At times on our journey he would point out when going past Kings Cross all the back alleys where him and his bandmates had scored crack cocaine. Other times across London he was showing me where he nearly got shot and I was just listening with my eyes wide open. These days Shaun tells these stories for a living, no script needed.

He does after dinner talks and I can fully understand why he's flying with it because The Happy Mondays have a massive following. I told Shaun I was amazed he could even recall that stuff because he must have been off his head most of the time, Shaun just looked at me, smiled and said, "Yeah man I was". Fast forward twelve months from there when the film was out and doing well, Shaun came up to Newcastle with his band Black Grape and I was in the audience. Shaun had stuck us on the guest list with a few mates. When he was on stage, just before he blasted out a song he shouted, "THIS ONE'S FOR STEVE WRAITH MY CO-STAR IN RISE OF THE FOOTSOLDIER THREE, I FUCKING LOVE YA MAN" and I was like 'WOW'! For me to be in that position where I've gone along to pay and watch him perform, to the point where now he's dedicating songs to me blew me away. I hit a good run after ROFS3. I was back in London again for The Krays – Dead Man Walking, although I only had a little cameo role at the end. I was the one that put Frank "The Mad Axeman" Mitchell into the back of a van just before he was killed. I was actually a consultant on that too as I was invited onto the film by Jonathan Sothcott. I was on-set when that film was being made for the actors to pick my brains on certain Kray matters, it was a unique experience. When I went to the premiere there were five hundred people in the audience and among those were some famous faces. Alan Pardew who used to be Newcastle's manager was sitting behind me of all the people. We shook hands but didn't talk football. When it said the film was by Jonathan Sothcott and I was his consultant for it that was a real buzz for me.

I wasn't anything to do with the film 'Legend' which was about the Kray twins sadly but I was lucky enough to have been invited to the premiere at Leicester Square by Tom Hardy. I went along with my best mate Christian Simpson and Freddie Foreman again. That's where I met one of my musical heroes the one and only Morrissey who is a big fan of the whole Kray story. Jamie Boyle who helped write this book is the biggest Moz fan in the world and I think Jamie would have fainted if he'd have met him. When I met Morrissey, it was probably the only time I've ever been starstruck. I've met all my hero's such as Jonny Rotten, Paul Weller, the lads from Auf Wiedersehen Pet, people from Blake's 7 but Morrissey was a different level. To be able to have a chat with him albeit briefly was surreal. When I saw him I didn't call him Morrissey I called him Steven which I thought would catch his attention and it certainly did the trick, he was really very pleasant to me.

Other films I have been involved in include a science fiction film called 'Scintilla' and the hooligan film 'Cass' which was about my friend Cass Pennant. I played a Geordie hooligan in that with another of Jamie Boyle's hero's Frank McAvennie. I was also in 'Meet the Guvnors' with Cass Pennant, Carlton Leach and Barrington Patterson. I was in a scene with them which was supposed to be Wembley but it was actually filmed at Arsenal's ground The Emirates. Cass got me the part in that so you can see my point when I tell you it's all about who you know most of the time. The only problem I had with that was it was made by a company named Fulwell 73. Fulwell is in Sunderland and 73 is the year Sunderland won the F.A. Cup and the year I almost bit my grandmother's finger off if you remember from the beginning of the book. When I get down to their studios in London to speak with them about my part, I find out that their office is a shrine to Sunderland Football Club. I'm walking in this place in London looking at the seats and turnstiles from the old Roker Park and the walls are adorned with pictures of Sunderland legends such as Kevin Phillips and Niall Quin and I'm secretly thinking, 'BLOODY HELL'! I mean this was my idea of what hell looked like.

As I was walking around the office two guys popped up from around the corner and shouted, "STEVIE WRAITH WELCOME INTO THE BLACK CATS DEN". Of course, we then started talking football and the banter came flowing about how one club was better than the other and the kind of conversation ensued that you'd expect when a Geordie and a pair of Makems got together. I also got a chance to film at my beloved St James' Park in the film 'Goal.' I was cast as Fabien Barthez and got to play in goal at the Gallowgate end. It was surreal being on that pitch. During a break in filming I got a chance to take a penalty at the Gallowgate End too. I stroked it into the onion bag and just imagined what it would be like to do that on a Saturday in front of 52,000. Sadly, our work ended up on the cutting room floor as the director and lead actor were replaced and we weren't recalled for the reshoot.

They were great lads though and good to work for and the film still gets rave reviews today.

I've also worked on the other side of the camera as a producer on a documentary called 'Fred' about Freddie Foreman, you might have seen it on Netflix. I worked on that with Christian and Salon Pictures. Lionsgate distributed it worldwide. Another first for me which I am immensely proud of.

The Mrs still maintains the best bit of acting I have ever done was on the popular ITV detective series 'Vera' when I played 'Big Pete' a dodgy café owner who was using illegal immigrants as staff and only paying them in meals. In the first scene with Brenda Blethyn I am seen in the kitchen cooking and cleaning. 'Best bit of acting you have done that, you're never in the kitchen.' I could never get a big head living in my house!

Looking back at that part it was a big break and one of my more testing roles. I had to be on set at 7am that day so had gone to bed early. Unbeknown to me the script was rewritten and as I arrived on set I was handed the new script and most of my lines had been changed. It completely threw me and I was in a mild state of panic as I put my costume on. I was trying to learn the new lines as I was called to make up and then onto set. It was obvious after the line run that Brenda had the same issue as me and she kindly offered to do a few line runs with me until we were both happy. Lovely gesture that and the sign of a true professional.

So, what's the moral of this chapter? What should any budding young actor take from it?

Never give up! Always network and learn from the knockbacks because you will get plenty on the way. Stay true to yourself and practise your craft and don't accept second best. You never know it all. We are all learning from the moment we take our first breath till the day we die. The 7-year-old boy who dreamed of being an actor reached his goal. So, what's next? I'd love to be a villain in Coronation Street, or the Bond Villain. As this book goes to print, I have just landed my first lead role playing the part of Stephen Sayers. Who is he? Let me introduce you.....

22

Meet the Sayers

The First time I was to hear of the Sayers name was when I was working on the Planet Earth door around the late 90s. One night I was working when Joanne Sayers came to the door, she was John, Stephen and Michael's half-sister and she had a pair of trainers on but this was a nightclub, she wasn't dressed appropriately so she was never going to be allowed entry. Then she started saying, "Do you know who I am?" whilst pushing one of the other doormen.

Needless to say, she never got in but a few of the other doormen told me to keep an eye out for her because her family were rather dangerous. At the time the Sayers name never really meant anything to me and why should it, I was never in their world. From that day on I got to hear more and more about this notorious family whose stories are now embedded in Tyneside folklore.

When I was working the 'doors' the Sayers weren't the only naughty family in Newcastle so you always had to be ready to play the game on the door because that person you're putting out could be related to one of them. I made a point of being fair to everybody that came in the club and I never discriminated or gave others an advantage. If there ever was a problem with two sets of families in the club then I made sure both parties got put out in the correct manner. If ever I had to ban people then it was never for long periods of time so I reaped what I sowed on the doors.

When I started the doors all the Sayers brothers were in prison. John was serving his sentence for robbery, Stephen and Michael were also in prison for blackmail. I picked up a book by local author Stephen Richards and read up on the notorious faces that I was starting to encounter. It gave me a better understanding of what I was going to be dealing with.

Before the brothers got out of prison, I'd met their Cousin Tony Sayers when I was working at Chase on The Quayside around 1999. I got to know Tony well. I was the head doorman so when he popped in, I'd look after him by letting him jump the queue or by putting him and his friends in the VIP area. It was Tony who first said to me, "When my cousins come out I'll introduce you to them" and that was it. Tony knew I had connections with The Krays and had written a book so he thought it could be beneficial to both parties if we met. When the brothers got out, I got to meet them one by one, I first met Stephen and I found him to be a very pleasant guy if the truth be told. Stephen was very humorous for someone who had such a fearsome reputation. I got on with him really well. I could tell he was a genuine man. John Sayers was released next and Stephen invited me up to the Prince of Wales pub on the West Road in the city for his release party. There were a lot of influential faces from both sides of the fence that night.

I wasn't sure what John would be like. The way that the media portrayed him was a 'Godfather' like figure. He was nothing like that. He's an extremely polite guy who doesn't drink or take drugs. He's very intelligent, family oriented and one hell of a shrewd businessman. We got on well. By the time I met Michael I'd moved on to 'Sugar' nightclub door. Michael had his release party in there and I went along with Stephen and Tony. Michael is an incredibly well-educated man who speaks four different languages. He had done a lot of research when he was inside. It's not only different languages Michael's studied, he's also looked into the human body language.

After the success of my Kray book my ambition was to write a book on The Sayers family. I asked John and

Stephen on a couple of occasions but I received a polite No. They weren't open to the public spotlight until Donal MacIntyre did his documentary series in 2006. Donal was doing the series on hardmen/gangsters up and down the UK who had never had any previous television exposure so he chose Brian Cockerill, Wayne Hardy, Ian Tucker, Paul Ferris, Dominic Noonan, the Sayers family and Conroy who was from another infamous family in Newcastle. Donal sent a researcher up to Newcastle first to come and see me to ask if the Sayers would take part in it. When I asked Stephen, he told me it wasn't for him but he told me to come to The Mill Tavern which he ran on the West Road to speak with his brother John the following night. When I sat with John and told him what it was about, he listened, then he ripped the Donal Macintyre researcher's business card up when I handed it to him and said it wasn't for him either. I then went back to the MacIntyre researchers and told him the brothers weren't interested but that they wanted an indication of what it was about as they'd heard others from Newcastle were going to be involved. I had to make it clear that the Sayers name could not be mentioned and they agreed to this so I passed that message on to the family.

When that Newcastle based documentary was shown on national television in late 2006, Conroy was on there and what he said was crazy. I just thought the whole thing was embarrassing. Let's make something clear here, there's nothing positive to come out of a life of crime, so for him to go on national television smoking drugs, going into the local Chinese takeaway and saying they were Triads and then calling the Sayers family police informers was absolutely ridiculous. It made Geordies a laughing stock. The image of him making a curry in his vest shouting 'Stick that in ya Dockramentary' worked in my favour though.

Stephen rang me and asked to meet up.

At Blakes Café on Grey Street we had a coffee and he said, "Do you know what I think I'll actually now have my say, I want to do a book and I want you to write it." He had come to the conclusion that an unanswered lie becomes a truth and he was right. Conroy had basically come out and accused the whole Sayers family of being "Grasses" and if you throw enough mud it sticks but it was totally untrue. When you read through the transcripts that I've got of every interview that John, Stephen and Michael Sayers have done in custody then all you read is "No comment" apart from saying their full name and addresses at the start of the interview. The Sayers maybe many things but police informers they are not.

Although there was no longer a war on the streets between Stephen and Conroy it became a war of words. It became a cyber battle and Stephen won that. Paddy was posting several posts about Stephen when he was in prison with various accounts. He wasn't only having a go at the Sayers but he then started having a go at me. Stu Armstrong suggested a bareknuckle fight between Conroy and Stephen Sayers, Conroy's response? A Facebook post saying "I'll not fight Stephen Sayers but I'll fight Steve Wraith." I had to laugh. When Stephen came out he used his ace card with Conroy, I can't really go into specifics about it for legal reasons but we received a screenshot saying that Paddy had downloaded some images on his computer. Now whether he did or he didn't the screenshots saying he did were enough for Stephen to then go and post stuff which he did saying that Conroy was of a particular persuasion. What happened from that point was Conroy then contacted the police and got Stephen arrested and charged in a court of law with malicious communications.

Conroy made a five-page statement against Stephen Sayers which was the beginning of the end for Conroy. Once you make statement when you're in that world it's game over because no criminal will ever trust you again. For him to make a statement against his rival for as something as petty as a post he did then there was no coming back from that. These days it's believed that Conroy is living in a caravan somewhere in the countryside in the North East and no one has seen neither hide nor hair of him ever since. The crazy thing about it all was there was never any needle between the Sayers and the Conroy's, it was all in Paddy's head.

Even his own family have abandoned him I believe so that tells you all you need to know.

The book was eventually released. The Sayers 'Tried and Tested At the Highest Level' is a bestseller and into its third print. At the time of writing I'm working on 'Operation Sayers' the sequel which will be released in late 2020 and is about the many operations that the authorities have carried out against the family. The Sayers film is also in pre-production. Garry Fraser the two-time BAFTA winner is writing and directing the project and as I have already mentioned in the last chapter, I will be taking on the part of my friend Stephen on the big screen.

23

Trolls and the 'Green-eyed Monster'

Since the day I became a public figure I've always had to deal with trolls and cyber bullying.

Presently, in May 2020, I have just had to deal with some Troll on Instagram accusing me of having sex with young boys behind my wife's back. Jealousy in these cyber-bullies boils over sadly when they see people doing well in life. It doesn't matter what industry I've been in there's always a green-eyed monster that has got it in for me. The first real experience I had of it was a guy from London named Tel. This wannabe got jealous towards me because I'd ventured into the world of unlicensed boxing in London with Joe Pyle Snr and Jnr. The first hiccup I had with Tel was when he put my fighter Gary Firby in the same dressing room as his opponent on one of his shows. To cut a long story short when the two started talking and the opponent realised that Gary had had five professional fights the opponent didn't wanna know and pulled out. Leaving me and Gary travelling from Newcastle to London for nothing, not to mention the sixty people who'd all bought tickets who had travelled down on a coach to watch Gary too. I made sure me and Gary got paid but that was really bad organisation. I told Tel Currie exactly that and that was the turning point. Tel didn't acknowledge it then but he was keeping his anger for a rainy day because he wasn't going to be spoken to like that by me.

Tel was a guy who ingratiated into the underworld but they saw him coming and he was used by a lot of people because he allowed himself to be used. Tel was the complete opposite to me. I never pretended to be a hardman when in London with these people but he did. Tel would wear a suit seven days a week and be seen with your Roy Shaw's, Dave Courtney's and Charlie Richardson's of the world. What Tel did to me was really nasty and vindictive. It was him that started banding around the words Wraith and "Grass" in the same sentence. Look I'm just a straight-goer I'm not a criminal so how can I be a grass? I've never been involved in any crime so it was just ridiculous to tar me with that brush, I mean, what have I got to grass about? None of it made sense. I found out what Tel was doing and I've got proof of this because I've got the letters.

Tel sent letters to Freddie Foreman calling me a police informer and Fred showed them to me. He then sent letters in the exact same vein to Charles Bronson and Joey Pyle Snr amongst others. All the letters said, "Steve Wraith is a grass and we need to keep well clear of him as he's only in it for himself". In actual fact that's all he was in it for because Tel himself started writing books. I don't think I fully understood what Tel was doing until I started getting emails from the likes of 'Johnny Nash' telling me to steer clear of London if I knew what was good for me. I thought this was a bit odd. I had never met him. When I read the email back a few times I noticed it was the same tone and use of words as the letters that had been posted out. This wasn't Jonny Nash who'd emailed me, it was Tel pretending to be Johnny Nash threatening me. It was absolutely psychotic behaviour and it was utterly sickening. It all came to a head when I went down to a boxing show at Caesars in Streatham. I went down with Eric Mason who was a good friend of the Krays and he'd not long been out of the nick. I was sitting on a table with Eric Mason, Joe Pyle Snr, Roy Shaw and a few others. This event was a charity night for Charles Bronson.

Harry Marsden from Newcastle was also there and Kenny 'Panda' Anderson a good pal of mine and Godfather to my youngest daughter. Everything was going well until I saw Tel whisper in Roy Shaw's ear and with that Roy launches himself out of his chair and literally flies for me. Of course, drinks flew everywhere. When Roy grabbed hold of me my instant reaction was to push him back and by doing that Roy fell back onto the floor. I didn't go into this situation blindfolded so beforehand I'd tipped off a few of The Outlaws biking club who were all there keeping an eye on me. There was eight of them there watching my every move. The Outlaws told me they had my back so not to worry. As soon as they saw what had went on four of them came straight over to me and Eric and got us out of there.

As we approached the entrance of the building Tel appeared laughing, he then said, "That will serve you right you daft Geordie bastard". I then shouted something back at him so he threw a right hand which caught me square on the chin and I fell back into one of The Outlaws arms. Well that was the worst thing he could have done because the four lads from The Outlaws taught Tel a valuable lesson. I was then escorted out, then put on the back of one of The Outlaws bikes and taken to their clubhouse in East London.

After that you'd have thought the jungle drums had been beating because the word was out that Steve Wraith has had bother with the legendary Roy Shaw. People were saying how dare Steve Wraith push Roy Shaw over and that kind of thing. Dave Courtney was in America at the time but he rang me up saying, "God what have you done"? I then got a call from Joe Pyle Jnr telling me they were in Cheam and I had to go see them which I agreed to do. I'd rather get the situation sorted out then let it get out of control. I jumped back on one of the lad's bikes and headed across London.Both Joe's were there and they said, "Look Steve it was all bang out of order we know exactly what's going on"! I then supplied Joe Snr with the letters from Tel which I had taken down with me as an insurance policy in case something happened. Now they could see it with their own eyes. What happened after that was very simple. I was called down to Wimbledon a few weeks later to a sit-down with Tel and both Joe's. When I arrived at Wimbledon Station I was picked up in a big white limo and big Perry was driving. It was like a scene from The Soprano's. When I was inside the limo, I was sure that the locks were going to go down like in the mafia films. I was then taken to an Italian restaurant. I was dressed for bother if I'm honest. I hadn't gone down in a suit in case it ended in fisticuffs. I thought if I'm going to go down, I'm going to go fighting. I was travelling over three hundred miles and into London for god sake so I didn't know what I was walking into.

When Tel turned up, he arrived well over two hours late which was an absolute piss-take considering he was coming from Wembley and I came from Newcastle and manged to get there on time. Me and the Joe's had had a starter, main course and dessert waiting for him.

Ultimately, he turned up and because he was late, he wasn't in the Pyle's good books. Joe actually gave Tel a bit of a rollicking in front of me for taking the piss. Joe told him it was time for him to call it a day now with his anti-Wraith campaign or sort it like men in a fist fight. Tel then leaned over to shake my hand and I'll never forget the words he said, "Let's make some money together". I shook his hand for Joe but to be truthful I still felt like cracking him because of what he had done but that's just not my nature. The guy had caused me so much shit and now he thinks I'm going to work with him. Joe Snr actually sorted a few things out for me, one being with Roy Shaw but I'll touch on that later in the book. Tel and I never crossed paths after that. I do know that many years later he upset somebody else along the way, he got set about on his own doorstep pretty severely and he was never the same after that. Tel died around 2014, I was told he never recovered from the beating and died. I've also heard he hung himself so I'm not sure what is true. I don't like to speak ill of the dead and there's very few people I disliked in life but Tel was one of them. If he was on fire I.....well you know. The guy genuinely did me wrong for no reason and it's fair to say he could have got me killed out of sheer jealousy. It was Tel who ruined my relationship with Roy Shaw but once Roy realised what Tel's game was after Joe Pyle Snr and Freddie Foreman showed him the evidence, that's when Roy accepted the full picture.

Today my social media attracts a lot of trolls. Twitter has to be the worst. There isn't a day goes by that I don't get some sort of nasty abuse from these people that hide behind a computer. For years I used to reply to these people. Try to flip them and change their opinions. In some cases, it worked. These days I just block them. I used to sometimes kill them with kindness but now I don't have the time to waste on others negativity. I don't mind people having a go at me if its constructive criticism in a civil manner. I put my head above the crowd in many walks of life so I appreciate I am there to be shot at. I'm like marmite.

You love me or hate me. There are a couple of accounts on my twitter that both share Newcastle content for example who are not vindictive but are very clever in the way they manipulate the followers against me. Sometimes there's a bit of humour and I can certainly laugh at myself. However, they did overstep the mark by calling me a sex offender.

That isn't funny. It is slanderous. I pointed that out to them. I explained that my solicitor was aware and that I would not take the matter further as long as an apology was issued. The apology duly came. Trolling can get on top of you if you let it but you do learn not to let it get to you. You can only do that through experience and to gain that experience then you have to take a lot in the first place and I have. Will it ever end? Not as long as social media platforms allow people to set up multiple accounts with no credible ID checks allowing them to hide behind fake profiles.

Remember trolls are insecure people who get pleasure out of other people's misery, don't let them win. Do these people bother me? Let's just say the lion doesn't turn around when the small dog barks.... #winning

24

Villains

I know a lot of you reading this just don't get my fascination with crime and villains. It's simple. It's an interest I have away from my day to day existence. It's my form of escapism. I read a book as a child and I have walked through the book and come out the other side having met all the main protagonists. I don't regret it. It has actually helped me in life meeting these people not hindered me. I've never gone down that road, and I've never pretended to be a gangster. That's a misconception that many have of me. Why? Because I'm bald and have a bent nose? I like to wear a suit? I have many people in my phonebook of that persuasion? I have written and promoted books and events with them. Maybe. But I can assure you I am no super criminal that hasn't been caught yet.

In my book 'The Krays The Geordie Connection' I cover how I met all these people but I felt I owed it to the reader and some of the chaps to bring a few of their stories up to date.

Tony Lambrianou was part of the Kray firm and I got to know him through Charlie Kray. I first met Tony at Ronnie Kray's wake in Lenny McLean's pub 'The Guvnor' in 1995. I got on really well with Tony for the next nine years until his sudden death in March 2004. With my best friend Christian living in London he got to also know Tony really well and those two ended up working together on bits and pieces. Me and Christian ended up at lots of Kray parties in London. When Reg was alive, he said he was doing them for "Charity" but he would allegedly often take big slices of the profits for himself. With Lambrianou being a big part of the whole Kray journey, he was always invited along.

I got Tony to come up to Newcastle to support my own events when I was raising money for young Terry Moran who was injured severely with fireworks on Bonfire night. I raised £2,500 for Terry thanks to Tony making the journey because he was obviously the name people wanted to meet on the night. Tony then came up the year after in 1996 to do a similar event.

I always respected Tony Lambrianou for doing those things because he didn't have to do that. It was nice that I could give something back to Tony when my friend Ray Caan (RIP) went to a lot of effort to find Tony's mothers grave up here in the North. Tony's mother was originally from Consett and she was buried in Shotley Bridge near there. It was quite an emotional moment when me and Ray took Tony and his brother Chris Lambrianou up to see their mothers grave for the very first time. Elizabeth Lambrianou had sadly passed when both brothers were doing their 15 years for their part in the murder of Jack "The Hat" McVitie. When she died both brothers were refused permission to attend their mother's funeral and up until Ray found it they had no idea of her final resting place.

My relationship with Tony went from strength to strength over the nine years I knew him. It was a massive shock to everyone when Charlie Kray was arrested in 1997 but Tony was at the forefront trying to fund raise for Charlie. Tony then made sure Charlie's girlfriend Judy was looked after. Tony really stepped up for his long-time friend but of course Charlie's own stupidity sealed his own fate. Tony Lambrianou's death was completely unexpected. Me and Christian Simpson had only been out with Tony weeks earlier when he passed. Yes, Tony was losing a little bit of weight but he looked ok and he didn't seem to me that he had any underlying health problems so when I got the phone call to tell me Tony had gone, I was stunned. A couple of days after Tony's death my best mate Christian was asked if he would do the honour of looking after Tony's body where he rested at English's funeral parlour in Bethnal Green. Christian of course obliged but said he would like me to do it with him and the Lambrianou family were happy with that and I went along with Christian. I went down to London and took it in turns to look after Tony's body with Christian. When Ronnie Kray had died, I'd been in this similar situation in the same funeral parlour. I'd already seen Ronnie Kray laid out so I'd already seen a dead body before. When I went in to see Tony laying there my first thoughts were of how smart he looked but then again Tony Lambrianou always did look dapper. Tony was laid looking very peaceful and calm and any pain that he must have had had disappeared. Mine and Christian's job was really just to make sure that anyone wishing to pay their respects did so in the correct manner and were who they said they were.

One person who came to pay their respects was Johnny Nash from the North London family who are very well known. The Nash's always preferred to keep themselves to themselves and still do to this day, they are still a very well respected family too. I'd heard so much about Johnny but had never met him before that day and it was a real pleasure to meet him (You will remember Tel had pretended to be Johnny in email mentioned in last chapter). Johnny knew my name because I was friends with Eric Mason.

Christian had not only been asked to looked after Tony's body but also like Dave Courtney at Ronnie Kray's funeral, had been asked to take care of the security and had agreed. Christian asked me if I'd stand with him that day too and I told him I'd be happy to assist him. Because Tony's funeral was going to be such a big job the first thing we had to do was liaise with the police. Christian and I recruited a lot of people who were already in the security industry because this was going to be such a monumental day and of course there would be people milling about that didn't know Tony but had come out to pay their respects and those that just came for a nosey and to see who would be attending. Although we hired top security guards, we also brought on board people who were really close friends to Tony like Andy Hollinson, Andy Gravenor and Matt Leach. Those three especially stood up and were counted for their friend. 'The Outlaws' biking gang also came out in their numbers to ride along with Tony one last time. To many of us there that day Tony was our friend so we all wanted to give him the best send-off he could get. When I look back on that day now over sixteen years ago it was every bit as important and surreal as Ronnie Kray's funeral because it was a gangland funeral. It wasn't just the underworld that turned out, it was people from the showbiz and sporting world. Afterwards we all toasted Tony at his wake and we also raised a glass to everybody who had pulled together. Since that day I've spoken to Chris Lambrianou on many occasions and I know he's happy with the job Christian did and he can't speak highly enough of how he handled it all. All I can say is Tony left a big gap in everyone's lives when he left us.

Eric Mason was a great guy and he contacted me whilst I was writing 'The Geordie Connection'. One day I got a letter from Eric's girlfriend at the time, Maxine, who was running a pub in Manchester called 'The Hare & Hounds'. Eric was in prison at the time but she told me that Eric would like to contact me. Maxine told me Eric had a lot of information of when the twins came to Newcastle and he'd be more than happy to meet me when he got out from his latest prison sentence. When Eric was released, I decided to travel to Manchester to spend time with Eric and Maxine. Eric was a very dapper man, although small he was very stocky and although he had lived away from London for many years, he still had the Cockney accent. I'd read his book 'The Brutal Truth' but it wasn't until I spent time with him that I realised what a life he'd had. Eric Mason was the last guy to be birched and the last guy to receive the cat of nine tails in the U.K. Inside Eric's book was a picture of him with the Krays in the Dolce Vita club in Newcastle so not only did he know about the Krays going to Newcastle, he actually went with them so it was great to finally have a chat with him to find out first-hand what really happened. From that point me and him really hit it off, we had a photograph taken together which I put in my book.

Eric sadly passed in February 2012 aged 82. He had so many great stories to tell and they weren't all just about the Krays. Was Eric a close friend of the Krays? Yes, he was but was he as close as some? Then no he wasn't. He had a relationship with the twins but I have to say he was let down by them when he was set about by the Richardson gang and left with an axe in his head. One of the people Eric was really good friends with was Jack "The Hat" McVitie so when the twins killed poor Jack his relationship with the Krays was never going to be the same again.

I'd put Eric Mason in the same bracket as Micky Fawcett, somebody who had a really good story to tell. Eric Mason was a proper villain there's no doubt about it and that showed when he was still getting banged up into his 70s and 80s. Eric was "At it" all his life and he made a few quid out of it. Eric was smarter than most of people in that game though and he knew how to invest his money. He was definitely a ladies man too and I'm godfather to one of his kids who he had in his 70s! Eric Mason liked to party and even used to come up to Newcastle for a night out. I took around twelve lads down to one of his pubs in Manchester to one of his getting out parties. He always had a cheeky glint in his eyes and liked to cause some chaos for a laugh. I got to know Eric's son Jeff Mason quite well and today I'm putting together his dad's final book with him. Eric was writing it in prison and he was sending me the notes. It will be a lasting tribute to Eric. Eric spent his final days in Blackpool where he moved to from Manchester as old age was catching up with him. In the end when he passed Eric's mind wasn't what it was, like with most of these old villains. I went to the funeral, it was on a very miserable grey rainy day. I was very sad to see Eric go. He was great company and good fun to be around.

Bruce Reynolds, the brains behind the great Train Robbery, was another old face I got to know. I got to know Bruce through the twins and other various criminal faces. When I met Bruce, I met his son Nick also who was a very influential musician in the Alabama 3. Nick was also a great sculptor who did the 'Cons to Icons' sculptures of people like Roy Shaw, Frankie Fraser, Freddie Foreman, Bruce Reynolds and Dave Courtney etc... After meeting Bruce a few times we ended up swapping numbers.

I tried to bring the 'Cons to Icons' tour to Newcastle because our city wasn't renowned for our art at the time. I had this idea of bringing it up to Tyneside but unfortunately the insurance was ridiculous to cover it. I even spoke to a good friend of mine who'd recently won the lottery and he said he was going to put the money up but at the last minute he pulled out, this was really embarrassing for me. In the end Bruce and his son Nick realised it wasn't my fault and they knew I'd been let down. That whole experience didn't put me off trying to get Bruce Reynolds to the North East because he wrote a book in 2004 called 'The Autobiography of a Thief: The Man Behind The Great Train Robbery' so it was my chance to do a launch in Newcastle. Waterstones in Newcastle hadn't been open long and were doing book signings with the likes of 'Mr Nice' Howard Marks, which I went to do security for. I arranged for Bruce Reynolds to come up to Newcastle Waterstones and I started promoting it, this was pre-social media days really so I had to rely on the papers. In the end we'd agreed this book signing for a Thursday night and Nick and Bruce would come and stay at my flat in Felling slumming it Geordie style. The sad thing is that when they came up the Journal and The Chronicle papers had incorrectly printed the wrong date, they put it in on the Wednesday so Waterstones had a load of people turning up on the wrong day. When Bruce sat down to do his book signing of course about six people came which was another massive disappointment for me. It wasn't all bad because when Nick was up we had a good drink.

Looking back, it was bizarre that I had one of The Great Train Robbers staying in my little pad. At the time I was working on the door at Sea Nightclub so I got the chance to take them out on the Quayside. I did take Bruce on a tour of St James' Park which I have done with several ex villains over the years. I kept in touch with Bruce until he died in February 2013.

Sadly, I was abroad when Bruce passed so I didn't get to pay my final respects to the brains behind one of the greatest robberies Britain's ever seen.

Paul Massey the Mr Big of Manchester was another I got to meet. Paul was very good friends with Conroy and Paul Ferris. One memory I have of Paul Massey was when I was on the door in Tiger Tiger and he was in town with Conroy. At the time I was the head doorman and as I started my shift, I realised there was holy hell going on. Everybody in that bar was on red alert because you could feel there was something in the atmosphere that wasn't right. Conroy usually didn't venture into town but this night he came with Paul Massey. This eventually got back to another crime family from Newcastle who weren't very happy that Paddy had reared his head. As I was on the door this well-known man came up to me and said, "Have you seen Paddy?" By this time, I'd realised he was in my bar but I turned around and said, "I've just started work and to be honest I've not seen him yet" which I hadn't. Then the well-known Tyneside man said, "Take my watch because if I see him, I'm gonna get this sorted" and I just said, "Right no problem". Obviously, this was the last thing I wanted to happen in my place of work. I walked up to Conroy and Paul Massey and we exchanged a few pleasantries. Paul told me we had a few mutual acquaintances and there was just small chat in general, then Conroy said, "Right Steve we're just about to go" but I said to give me five minutes, he then went, "Aah right ok". He knew what was going on outside or what could happen with members of this family from Newcastle. Cards on the table I did Conroy and Paul a favour because had they gone out there then there would have been one hell of a situation on my door. I essentially stopped world war three kicking off in Newcastle that night. I didn't know Paul Massey although I knew the strength of Conroy though and it wasn't going to end well for them that night had they went out any earlier. To be truthful I did what I did to protect my bar, customers and my job. I've since seen the main guy who was looking for Conroy that night and he knows what I did and respects my reasoning behind it. Paul Ferris, who I've now got to know really well, speaks very highly of Paul Massey and it was very sad to see the guy murdered outside of his family home in 2015.

I've known Charles Bronson for twenty years but that was his former name so I've got to call him Charles Salvador as he is now. Once I was drawn into an argument with Charlie and it ended up with him not being happy with me. At the time Charlie had fallen out with his then manager Stephen Richards and he didn't know which way to turn. I was told Charlie wasn't very happy with Stephen Richards and was asked if I could help him out by Dave Courtney. I acted as a middleman really and went to meet Mr Richards. Charlie wanted me to get some of his belongings back and to sever all ties with him on his part which I did. After eight weeks of helping Charlie out he then asked me if I wanted to be his manager and I accepted this offer. This was the year of the millennium and I was now looking after all his affairs, but it was difficult having to rely on letters back and forward to be in contact with him. In those days Charlie wasn't having many phone calls and a lot of the issues me and Charlie had in those days was due to communication being lost in translation. Tel, who I mentioned in the last chapter, was also in his ear at the time stirring the pot. Me and Charlie ended up having a big disagreement. He then went on to have a go at me in one of Tel's books. Luckily, we managed to patch it up and I think he knows I'm somebody who has always been there for him. He just had to stop listening to the anti-Wraith brigade out to cause trouble for me. Over the last year or so Rod Harrison has been very close to Charlie and has been somewhat of an advisor to Charlie and its Rod who's gently nurtured mine and Charlie's relationship back to the peaceful one it is today. I've always championed the causes Charlie was behind and pushed many of his books and today in 2020 I'd say me and Charlie are even closer than we were in the past. These days I often visit him in Woodhill, Milton Keynes. I speak with Charlie every week and to be honest he's more interested in what I'm doing, what I'm wearing or where I'm sitting. I'd like to think that one day that man will be free. It's going to be a long road as he's still on the closed unit. He's wiser now that he's getting older and it's really down to when he starts mingling in with other prisoners and how that goes, I think that is going to be a key factor as he has been locked up for 45 years now and a lot of that time he's been in isolation. How is Charlie going to deal with inmates spiced off their nuts? It's going to be difficult isn't it!?

Having met Charlie a few times now I know he's in good health. The guy's still monstrously strong and to some prison officers he'd be very intimidating. The prison where he is today, Woodhill, is really supportive of him. The governor is a fan of his if you like and he's willing to give Charlie a chance to change. I'm happy to say at the moment he's following all the guidelines and he's keeping himself to himself. There's still a long way to go but Charlies is on the right road at the moment.

Regarding 'The Wee Man' Paul Ferris, I'd always wanted to meet Paul and I'd read Reg McKay's books on him. I was a big fan of the way Reg had written those books on Paul as well. I think from my perspective Paul Ferris was the last big British villain I'd yet to meet. It was through Scottish photographer Brian Anderson that I got to meet Paul, Brian had often mentioned me to him so Paul was aware of me anyway. It wasn't until the making of Paul's feature film on his life 'The Wee Man' that me and him got together. At the time of meeting Paul Ferris, I was writing for Loaded magazine which is a lads' mag as a True Crime correspondent and they wanted an interview with Paul because of his film being released. I saw this as an opportunity for me to finally hook up with him. The magazine that I was working for told me to keep it film based which I did but I always felt I'd be coming back to Paul at a later date, although I wasn't sure why. I did that first interview with Paul on the phone. When we finally spoke, I would say he was very guarded and didn't give much away. Everything I asked him was met with short concise replies. Just enough. To be honest when I finished that first interview with him, I thought I might struggle even getting my full word count for the story but I did in the end. Around one month later the article came out to the public and I got another phone call from Paul but this time he hadn't withheld his number. Paul was ringing me up to say that he'd read the article and he just wanted to thank me for doing what I said I was going to do. What he meant by that was that I'd not stitched him up like some writers do, I'd stuck to what he had told me and not embellished anything so I'd won his trust over.

About one year later on from then I was going to Glasgow to record an advert with Shameless actor Jody Latham for Brian Anderson. Brian was launching a new True Crime magazine. It was when I was up that time that Brian told me he had been with Paul Ferris and he wondered if I fancied a meet when I was up next, to which of course I replied yes I'd love to. After that we set a date for a couple of weeks later. I got on the train up to Glasgow and I met Paul in this plush restaurant. That day we had a good couple of hours together talking about everything such as Freddie Foreman, The Sayers, who he'd spent time with in Frankland and then football. Paul's a massive Glasgow Celtic fan so we had lots in common. I actually tried haggis for the very first time.

That day me and Paul got our photograph taken. I asked if he had ever thought of doing another book. Paul replied, "Not really like but what's your thoughts?" I told Paul I'd read his books that he had done with Reg McKay but now that he'd passed had he ever thought of doing a tribute to Reg? Paul looked at me and just said, "Let me get back to you on that" and never said another word about it that day. Six weeks later and the deal was done, Paul loved the idea that we were going to pay tribute to someone that helped him so much in his life.

Paul and I came up with the title of, 'Unfinished Business' which is how he saw it. Me and Paul then worked tirelessly for the next eighteen months on it, going over his life story with my former business partner. When interviewing Paul, I had to keep him on track and I'm sure he won't mind me saying that. With Paul you could be talking to him about something and then he could just go off in a totally different direction. Apart from that Paul was great and his stories were marvellous. When I had it all typed up I didn't want anything to be in 'Unfinished Business' that was in his three other books with Reg McKay because I knew I was going to be judged against them. My co-writer, who I was working with on the book, was going to have this massive job of making mine and Paul Ferris' notes something completely different. He ended up doing the book like a murder board you see in those detective films. He had a load of bits he had to fit in with the correct times and dates all over his office.

In Paul's book I would say the main story was the police corruption by Strathclyde Police. That was the one thing that Paul wanted to get across and it's what the end product was.

'Unfinished Business' sits nicely today in the collections of 'The Wee Man's' four books.

Mad Frankie Fraser was another one I met around the time Ronnie Kray died. At the time I met Frankie everybody got on in the gangster world and everyone was friends. This was before the likes of Frankie fell out with people such as Dave Courtney and Freddie Foreman and at that time Charlie and Eddie Richardson were even talking to each other. I do recall one time going into the casino with Dave Courtney and Christian. Dave was messing about on the roulettes for a bit then we walked upstairs and into an office where there was Joe Pyle Snr, Joe Pyle Jnr, Freddie Foreman, Mad Frankie Fraser, Tony Lambrianou and Roy Shaw so it was really quite surreal to watch all these villains together. Maybe I was a little bit starstruck more than anybody else with little Frank because this guy was the real old school who'd served forty plus years in jail. This guy had his history with the Kray's and the Richardson's.

The one thing I must say about little Frank was he was always very polite and had bags of humour. I got to know Frankie a bit at the Monday club at the Carlton which was in Elephant & Castle. Frankie really was well ahead of all the chaps as he was the one who started doing the books and documentaries first and he was even taking part in crime bus tours! Mad Frankie Fraser was probably the first celebrity gangster of that era. Of course, the shit really hit the fan when he started calling Dave Courtney a "Police informer." At the time Dave was going through hell with this former bent police officer Austin Warnes. Frankie was often putting things of that nature on his website and of course

Dave was then having to react to it like Stephen Sayers did with Conroy. All this caused a bit of a gulf in the underworld and people then had to choose sides. Even though me and Christian weren't even criminals we still had to take a side, obviously although we liked Frankie it was Dave who was looking after us so it was a no-brainer. After all that everything was forever awkward. I did have one wild night out in London linked to Frankie which I'll tell you about. Me and Christian finished our security job one night and we ended up going to The Ministry of Sound. We then left there and we went to a place called The Leisure Lounge which was some sort of after club place. You could go there at 6am and finish at 9am. Still to this day I have no idea where it is. At the time I used to be guided around London by other people but these days I know where I'm at. Anyway, me and Christian were in this Leisure Lounge and for some reason we ended up with Frankie Fraser and his other half Marilyn Wisbey. Frankie pulled me aside and said, "Marilyn wants to stay out but I'm off home so can she stay with you and Christian?" Of course, we reassured Frankie his Mrs would be looked after by us and she stayed out with us. Basically, we stayed out together from the Saturday to the Monday. Marilyn even came back to the girl's house who I was seeing at the time to watch telly because she just didn't want to go home. Looking back, it was crazy but it's what you do when you're young isn't it?! By the time me and Christian dropped Marilyn back off it was 48 hours later, god knows what Frank thought. I got to know Frankie's sons David and Patrick. It was through them that I eventually got Frankie up to Newcastle to do a talk. It was funny because when we did this night 'An Evening With Mad Frankie Fraser' Jamie Boyle the author of this book came.

Jamie paid £10 to have his picture taken and he noticed that Frankie was quietly whispering something about him to one of his sons with a slight sneer. When Jamie asked one of his sons what was so funny, he was told, "Dad said you could do with going on hunger strike!" That's what Frankie was about though and he had very dry humour.

I can't do this villains chapter and not mention my old friend Dave Courtney who I've got a lot of time for. I first got to know Dave from visiting Reg Kray. Dave was on a few of the same visits as me using other people's prison VO's so that Reg would have an audience. This was mainly at Nottingham and Maidstone jails because both were very slack. On some occasions Reg had potentially twelve people visiting him and most brought bottles of Scotch in amongst other things that they shouldn't. It got to the point where all the screws would let Reg put all the tables around together and Reg would hold court with his different visitors.

I've always got on really well with Dave. He's never changed in thirty years. Dave's loud, loves being the centre of attention and he's funny with it. His clothes are unique, some would say flamboyant.

When it came to Ron's funeral in March 1995 that's when it all changed for Dave. Dave was then the centre of the world's media and there was no going back to his old life. Dave that day employed me to look after Charlie Kray at the graveside as Ronnie was lowered into the earth.

From that day at Ron's funeral I've kept in touch with him. I used to spend a hell of a lot of time at Dave's house when I was younger at various parties when him and his ex, Jennie lived together in Woolwich. Dave had a pub over the road from his house called 'The Albion' and we would spend a lot of time in there. I would kip at Dave's quite a bit when I did a bit of debt collecting for him. Dave has come up to Newcastle on several occasions and he's given me some invaluable advice over the years. The best advice he ever gave me when I was living in London was, "Go back to Newcastle and be a big fish in a small pond." Now I know many who would take that as quite an insult and say I was being snubbed but I know Dave was doing it with the best of intentions. Dave told me I had potential to do well in life but if I stayed in London I would be swallowed up and he was right. On this planet and after my parents and family I don't think there's anyone as proud of what I've achieved as DC is. Every time I see him he tells me exactly that and its heart-warming to hear. Me and Dave almost share the same birth date barring one day so we always get together every February for a good old knees up. Me and Dave might not speak for six months but when we pick the phone up it's as if we spoke to each other just the other day. A lot of people don't really know the real Dave Courtney but I do and I can tell you all he's a genuine guy who'll do anything for anyone if he could. If you want me to sum him up then the guy has lived his life the way he wanted to and who can blame him for that! He's also the funniest man I've ever met in the flesh, 100%. He's also very clever and over the years he's reinvented himself when he's needed to. Today in 2020 Mr Courtney is almost a pensioner (sorry Dave I had to get that one in HA) but his journey is far from over yet. I know the guy has his critics but don't we all....

25

Another fall out with Roy Shaw and the Ex from Hell

I found out about Roy Shaw the same as everybody else and that's by reading the books.

With me knowing the Krays they would often mention Roy, particularly Ronnie Kray who knew Roy very well, and as I was at many of the Kray functions it was always going to lead me into the same company as Roy eventually.

When Ronnie died in March 1995 his death brought all the old faces together such as Lenny McLean, Buller Ward and Nosher Powell among others. Subsequently Lenny McLean went to Ronnie's wake but Roy didn't because he didn't like McLean. Even though the fights had been and gone almost two decades before, the beef was still there between the two legendary fighters.

I never really had a great deal to do with Roy and if I'm going to be totally honest, I was always very wary of him because of his reputation. Roy, even at his elder age, had a tremendously strong physique still with a real aura of menace about him. When you looked into his eyes they had a really scary look about them and you could tell he didn't trust many people if any. I just always felt with Roy that he would be capable of kicking off at any given moment and if that happened there wasn't a lot anybody around could have done about it.

Roy for me had an incredibly unpredictable nature. This was a man who'd had the liquid cosh and electric shock treatment in Broadmoor and other mental institutions. If anybody clearly had the devil in his eyes it was Roy Shaw. Anybody who could fight off a dozen screws or break out of prison cells isn't going to be completely level-headed so I was always on my guard with him.

I'd gone to Dave Courtney's 40th birthday bash, February 1999 in Essex at one of Dave's friend's house. The one thing about Dave Courtney is the guy really knows how to throw a party and on that particular night I was there with my best mate Christian among other faces such as Howard Marks and Freddie Foreman. That evening this stunning blonde-haired woman had caught my eye, she'd been making eyes at me most of the evening. At the time we'd all had a couple of drinks so everybody was merry. I'd had a chat with this woman and we ended up kissing. I gave her my number but she never gave me hers because she said, "I'm not going to get involved with you because I'll hurt you," but I told her I wouldn't allow myself to be hurt. I woke up the next morning and never gave her another thought and to be honest I'd forgotten all about her until a fortnight later when I got a phone call and the caller said, "Hiya Steve do you remember me from Dave's party?" It all started coming back to me then. She then said that she had a place in Sheffield and did I fancy going to visit her for the weekend, I thought nothing ventured nothing gained and I had nothing planned so that's what I did. I organised cover for work that weekend and I jumped on the train to South Yorkshire and she agreed to pick me up. It was weird because before I got there, I couldn't quite remember what she looked like but when I got there, I was pleasantly surprised although she was much older than me, 11 years in total. She picked me up in this black BMW and took me around the streets of Sheffield. When we arrived at her home it was like one of them 'WOW' moments because she had electronic gates and this huge drive and this luxury 6-bedroomed home. I thought god this is me definitely landing on my feet here I can start planning my retirement. Together me and this woman had the most amazing weekend and did what couples do. On the night I left I just said to her, "Why do you always wear that baseball cap?" Because the only time she didn't wear it was when we were in bed. It turns out she wore it because she she'd had surgery on the top of her head. She then lifted her hair to show me where she'd had reconstructive surgery. When I asked what had happened, she started crying and I comforted her. When she got herself composed, she went and got some pictures which she showed me which were pictures of her with some horrific injuries. It turns out she'd been beaten up by her ex-partner. She'd had to have her face totally rebuilt which is the same total tosh she told Roy Shaw a little while later except she told him I was responsible for those injuries but I'll come to that. Anyway, going back to my weekend date with this woman everything was great or so I thought. Our relationship blossomed for the next few months and she even came home to Newcastle to meet my parents. I went to meet her family too and got on with them all and the age difference between us was no issue. This woman seemed to have a lot of money but I never really questioned where she got it from, she always told me she was divorced and it was her settlement. When I was with this woman of my dreams, or so I thought, I was living in cloud cuckoo land thinking I can now give my job up and concentrate on becoming a full-time author. Before I got with this woman, she'd been dating Charlie Kray and she even owned one of Charlies old 1960's cars which she had in her garage. She was a woman who liked to go around dating all the old faces that's what kind of person she was. She also dated someone in a well-known British '90s band. When I wrote to Charlie Kray to let him know I was dating one of his ex's he sent me a letter back saying she was a lovely girl and I had his blessing. I then spoke to Freddie Foreman and Joe Pyle Snr who said the same. At that point all the signs about this woman were positive so I thought I should maybe do the honourable thing and ask her to marry me, looking back I couldn't see past the end of my dick really. I proposed and she said yes, then she told me she was pregnant although I never saw any scan photos. I just believed everything she told me because I was blown away in this whirlwind romance. As if being pregnant wasn't enough she told me it was twins! How gullible was I?

Everything was going great until one weekend when she came up to Newcastle and we had this blazing row. Her mood swings were horrendous but I just put it down to her being pregnant. Every time I would go near her, she pushed me away. I'm pretty calm in a row and I think that was frustrating her even more. Her aim was to try to cause as much chaos and mayhem as possible as if to say look what this guy's doing to me but I didn't do anything. It all ended by her locking herself in the bathroom and shouting that she just wanted to go home so I just told her to sod off because I'd had enough by that point. She then got in her car and left and I thought that was it, I never expected to see her again and god I wish I hadn't if I knew what was still in store for me. With the woman now back in Sheffield and the engagement off the next thing I thought I would hear, if anything at all, would be from the Child Support Agency I thought. After the argument I didn't ring her because I hadn't done anything to have warranted her treating me like that and kicking off in the manner that she did. I never heard a thing from her for two weeks until I got a call out of the blue saying, "Steve I miss you and I need to see you." I told her I was in no mood to be getting the train down to Sheffield but if she wanted to come to Newcastle then I'd speak with her. To cut a long story short she told me how sorry she was and that she'd been taking Prozac which had shattered her moods. I fell for her bullshit hook, line and sinker and I went from not giving a damn about her anymore to agreeing to go on holiday with her.

As a way of saying sorry this woman told me she was going to take me away abroad and that I didn't need any money because she was going to pay for everything. She then booked a two-week holiday for us both in Greece and she wanted me to go down to Sheffield so we could both fly from Manchester Airport. One of the things she specifically told me was that I didn't need to bring any money because everything was paid for in the five-star hotel we'd be staying at. We boarded the plane together and off on holiday together we went. I didn't go skint as I took a little bit of money and thank god, I did with what was about to ensue.

For the first couple of days the holiday was superb and we were both in love as much as we'd ever been with each other, that was until we were holding hands walking around this market when she turned around, looked me in the eyes and said, "I've never loved you, I was never pregnant and I'm married in America so fuck you" and then she walked off and left me. Well I was just stood there for five minutes like, eh? What? It turns out that she'd planned the whole thing as some sort of weird revenge. She then got in a taxi but as I was stuck in a foreign country I had to follow her and I got in the other side of her taxi even though she was telling the driver not to let me in. I had to tell the driver that we were engaged and this was just a domestic argument. On the drive to the hotel we didn't speak to each other. Inside the apartment she then gave me both barrels in the context of, "Go on fuck off back to your scummy shit life in Felling among your alcoholic mates" I was speechless, how had it come to this! She took madness to another level but again I didn't react. All I knew was I needed to screw my loaf on here and luckily, I'd brought a mobile phone with me and I called my good friend Paul Donnelly to tell him the full horror story. I asked Paul if he could pick me up if I got back to England and he assured me it wouldn't be a problem. Paul was one of the lads who played for my football team so at least that problem was now sorted.

I went out for some fresh air to be by the pool to gather my thoughts on this horror story but she had followed me wanting more arguments and by the time I'd got back to the room I just piled all my stuff into two carrier bags because I didn't even have a case, the case we went with was hers. I then went into the safe to get some money for a taxi and a flight but just as I was doing that, she came running shouting, "WHAT ARE YOU DOING YOU BASTARD YOU'RE ROBBING ME". I told her I wasn't robbing her but that I needed some money to get to the airport as she clearly didn't love me so I needed to get home but that's when she went to attack me, I just grabbed her two hands and pushed her on the bed. As I've pushed her onto the bed her hand hit the pebble dashed wall and had cut her slightly and she started smearing the blood all over her face. Then she screamed, "I'M GONNA TELL THE RECEPTIONIST YOU'VE TRIED TO KILL ME." I was just in disbelief of what I was hearing. It's funny now twenty years on telling the story but it wasn't at the time. I took my engagement ring off and flung it on the bed and told her she could tell them what she wanted. She then ran off crying and locked herself in the bathroom. It was then I started to panic thinking I could be arrested at any time because she could say I've done god knows what to her but I clearly hadn't.

When I got downstairs, I regained my composure and asked for them to call me a taxi which they did and I managed to get to the local airport. When I got to the airport it turned out that there were no flights to England and that I'd needed to get another taxi to another terminal, this was all draining what little money I had and I still had to pay for a flight back to the UK.

I had to get another taxi on the way to this airport and when I got there the place was ready for closing. I found a girl who finally spoke English and she told me that the next flight wasn't until in the morning so now I was going to be sleeping rough for at least twelve hours.

She also told me that the flight wasn't going anywhere near Newcastle but it was going to Luton but I thought fuck it, that will have to do. I then rang Paul again and told him he wouldn't be picking me up from Manchester but now it was Luton and thankfully he said that was no issue. That night I had to do a "Tom Hanks" and I slept on the airport floor but I didn't sleep much because of what had happened at the hotel. I was sure the moment I arrived in Newcastle I was going to have the police coming for me. The whole experience was awful I felt so drained. When I arrived back in England, I'd literally spent all my money, I was down to the last pound because at customs on departure I had to buy a bag for £40 as I was only allowed one piece of hand luggage and I had two carrier bags. I was just thankful to be on British soil.

I've never been so happy to see one of the lads when I clapped eyes on Paul at Luton Airport. I'm forever grateful to Paul Donnelly for doing that and helping me out in my worst hour.

The follow up from that though is where the fall out with Roy Shaw started because that woman started seeing Roy after we split up. Her first move when she got back from Greece was to get herself recorded coming back off her flight with her arm in a sling for her little cut on her hand, she'd obviously got someone in on this with her to build it all up for my downfall. Why would anyone need to film her getting off the plane? She wasn't a celebrity.

The big error she made was she told somebody who at the time was also causing mischief for me, today this person has changed their ways with me now, but at the time this woman told this person about her plan. The person she told then left messages on my answering machine saying what was going to happen and that I was going to be stitched up to look like some sort of animalistic woman-beater. Thankfully with that message the whole story of me beating this woman up well and truly fell to pieces. That voice message her mate left was like a smoking gun at the crime scene. Although it wasn't nice to hear what the plan was, I was smart enough to send it to the likes of Freddie Foreman and Joe Pyle Snr for it to sink in and prove I hadn't done anything. When they listened to it, they both said they could hear quite clearly that I hadn't done anything wrong. Both said I had their backing but from now on I needed to think with my head and not with my dick. I just needed to solve the issue with Roy now.

By now Roy had obviously seen the pictures she had shown me of her major face surgery and been told that I had done that to her. You can imagine what Roy Shaw now thought of me. I have to say from that moment on it made it very uncomfortable for me at events and funerals but I still went. Of course, I didn't want a confrontation with somebody like Roy Shaw but I wasn't going to stop going to these events for something that I hadn't done. I thought if I stop going to these things then it looks as if I'm admitting guilt. I did hear on the grapevine that Roy was going to do all sorts to me although I never had a threat directly from Roy. It was all hearsay from the likes of Tel among others. I guess the big test was always going to be Charlie Kray's funeral in April 2000. Although I knew one of the hardest unhinged men in Britain wanted to snap me in half, I always felt ok because I had the backing of men like Freddie Foreman and Joe Pyle Snr because those two knew the truth. When I got to Charlie Kray's funeral I didn't go and do the security as I had done for Ronnie's, I just went as a mourner because I was close to Charlie. Although I went to pay my respects to my friend, I was very well aware that I had this issue with Roy hanging over my head. I had to count on strong people to help me out if anything happened. Although Dave Courtney also knew about what had gone on, he was a little bit wary but he did invite me to his house on the morning of the funeral. I went to Charlie's funeral with Ian Freeman and Ray Caan (R.I.P) and we all chipped in to get Charlie a diamond geezer shaped wreath. I told the lads that it was probably inevitable I was going to have a situation with Roy Shaw. The lads said it was fine and they still wanted to come along but what I did in my own wisdom was separate myself from them when I got down there. If it was going to happen to me, I didn't want the people I was with to get it from Roy also if that makes sense and I didn't want people fighting my battles. I went down to London and I put my faculties in the hands of the gods and let fate decide the outcome.

I thought if Roy does decide to flatten me then its him who's going to look the mug and I'll just be the one trying to stand back, that was my philosophy. When I was at Dave Courtney's house it was full of cameras as he had a documentary team filming him. Dave had hired these vintage cars to get to English's funeral parlour on Bethnal Green Road were Charlie was at rest. As I got to the church I was on my own away from my mates for obvious reasons. As I looked up, I saw my ex-girlfriend there stood glaring at me but she was with another fella and he wasn't Roy Shaw to my great delight. She'd moved on to another guy and he was also staring at me.

It was no surprise after my relationship with that woman when I found out she cheated on me with a major well-known Hollywood American actor. She also did a kiss and tell story to the tabloids in 2004 about a former Premiership football star. To this day I'm not even sure if Roy Shaw even went to Charlie's funeral but if he did, we didn't cross each other. As I looked over at my ex and her new fella, I was getting daggers thrown back at me from the pair of them. The new fella was then staring at me like Nigel Benn looking at Chris Eubank and I was just like, 'god grow up mate you don't know the half of it', I pitied him and what he probably had to look forward to being with that bunny boiler.

When I came out of the service Bruce Reynolds and his son Nick had a lovely red Rolls Royce there on the day and

152

asked me if I wanted to jump in with the pair of them. They both knew of the issues I could be facing that day. We made our way to Chingford Mount cemetery in Essex which is around five miles from Bethnal Green. Once Charlie was buried, I got back in the motor and went onto the wake then back to Dave's house in South London and we toasted Charlie's passing. The whole day had gone really well from my perspective. The biggest disappointment about it all though was when the writer Stuart Wheatman wrote Ian Freeman's book a little while later. There's a chapter in there saying I'd asked Ian Freeman to go down to protect me which is a complete fabrication of what really happened. I've since told Stuart about this not being right and I found it really demeaning. Anybody who was there knows I distanced myself from the people that I was with. I certainly didn't ask anyone to fight my battles as I would never do that. With Roy not going out with the girlfriend from hell anymore peace was once again restored.

I started to realise over the years that Roy's mental state had started to deteriorate and that he didn't actually remember who I was. To him I was just a name who'd cropped up with ex-villains from time to time or when Tel was mixing it. My one saving grace was not having any photo's together with that treacherous woman so she couldn't show him what I looked like maybe. I think a lot of the time when he was angry with me, he had no idea what I looked like. It wasn't until that boxing event at Caesars in Streatham, as I told you earlier in the book, that Roy even clapped eyes on me for the first time. One of the nicest things in it all was the year before his death in 2011 I finally sat down and had a discussion with Roy and had my say about what had happened over the last twelve years. I was at the film premiere of 'The Killer Bitch' at Leicester Square. Roy by then was a shadow of the man who wanted to rip my head off a decade earlier. Roy's clothes were hanging off him and he would get confused a lot so he needed people around him to look after him like Dave Courtney etc...

I'd never really got to speak with him properly until then so I finally got the chance to say to him that I hoped he realised that none of those things I was accused of years before were true. Roy also realised that Tel calling me a police informer was also utter crap. Roy had had his head filled with this rubbish by two people who had nothing but bad intentions for me so it was really emotional for me when Roy stared at me and just said, "I know Steve, I know" and put his hand on my shoulder. For me that meant so much and it was nice because that was the last ever time I saw Roy.

I did go to Roy's funeral with Freddie Foreman and Christian Simpson. Again, we all chipped in for a nice wreath for Roy. Tamer Hassen the actor, Jimmy White the snooker player and Bill Curbishley the manager of The Who were there paying their respects. I saw Roy's only son Gary Shaw that day and I had a chat with him. It was a sad way for Roy Shaw to go. Roy was a hell of a man and a man's man. At the time I was writing all the gangland stuff for Front Magazine and I wrote Roy's obituary for it which was an honour.

26

The Ugly Side of Football

As a Newcastle United fan, I've seen some great games home and away but at the time of writing I've still not seen us win a trophy. I have also seen and experienced the ugly side of the game. Hooliganism. When you think of the era I grew up in, following football was rife with football hooligan issues. I've seen football violence at its worst through the mid 1980s when all English clubs were banned out of Europe. One of the first times I ever went to a football match at Hartlepool there was a riot on the pitch between the rival Darlington fans so I knew what the bad side of football was about. I remember the 'Sack the Board' campaign in the late 80's when fans would run on the pitch to demonstrate and after the game head round to the players entrance to sing 'sack the board.' I was once photographed on the back of the Daily Mirror holding my mate up in the air as he burnt his scarf. I got a belting off my Dad for bringing shame on the family.

Growing up and going to the Newcastle games myself football violence was never very far away, especially when I went in places like 'The Farmers Rest' at Haymarket which is no longer there. It was in there that I really became aware of these guys who would go to football matches to fight for a hobby! The away games were a laugh. If I wasn't in the back of a mate's van with a crate of beer in those days then I was on a bus full of mates heading up and down the country. Worst places I visited were West Ham and Millwall. The West Ham trip in the eighties saw me and a few of lads being chased around Upton Park by some locals. We got back to our bus and as the driver pulled away our back window was put out showering people in glass. Luckily nobody was hurt but we had a cold journey back North. At Millwall the walk to the ground was really intimidating. You would have mothers with kids in prams shouting and spitting at you as you approached the ground on the aptly named Cold Blow Lane. The crowd there were mental chucking coins and spitting at you. Pure venom. We got hammered on the pitch that day and a few of our lads were picked off on the way back to the bus. No broken window that night though so that was a bonus.

When I started running my fanzines commenting on Newcastle United, I became a target for many of them. Now they all knew who I was because I was popping up on TV and Radio and commenting in the local papers. The first run-in I would have with one of these people was outside of St James' Park and it was over one of my fanzine editors Rob Blaylock. Rob used to stand outside of the ground as one of my five fanzine sellers. For whatever reason on this particular day Rob had upset one of the firm. I was walking towards the ground to see Rob to collect the leftover fanzines and pick up the money when all of a sudden, I could see him having a bit of a confrontation. Then I saw two people punching him from behind and him going down to the deck and the fanzines and takings all go flying. I was actually with my dad but we got over to pick Rob up off the floor and ask him what had happened. Rob told me that it was over nothing and he'd basically been assaulted for no reason. Rob told me who they were so I took it upon myself to find out who these people were and that's when a situation developed. With me doing my fishing it was only then that I became the target because they'd viewed me as butting in on something that didn't concern me when I had become vocal about what had gone on. Over the next few months, the bad feelings towards me were festering within the firm when I was at home and away games. If ever I was at away games I would be followed and be under intense scrutiny from these people. Then the threats started coming, I would have messages getting sent back to me of, "We're gonna do ya" and others of that nature. Sometimes I'd be at matches and I'd receive a push from the back and other digs of a similar nature, all just trying to intimidate me. The firm in total had a number of around two hundred and now I was on their most wanted list like Osama Bin Laden with the F.B.I. I shouldn't have opened my mouth was their philosophy and now I was going to pay the price.

When England played Northern Ireland and David Kelly scored but the match was abandoned after 28 minutes there was an infamous flag at the game. It was an England flag but it had Wallsend on and that was where the trouble happened, so when The Chronicle rang us up to ask my opinion on it. I told them it put Newcastle in a bad light and it was sad to see that type of behaviour. The fact that I'd made such a comment didn't enhance my popularity with the anti-Wraith brigade among the firm and it only poured fuel on the fire. Word got back to me saying I had better watch my back because of my actions.

It didn't stop my love of Newcastle and I still went to the games but I had to become extra vigilant. It all came to a head at an away game at Goodison Park in Liverpool. Before the game I was standing in a bar called Arkles on Anfield Road and I'd nipped to the gents, as I did, I was followed in by some of the lads. I was then told I was in bother to put it mildly and told to get outside as I was going to be "Done". I was completely on my own so I walked out to face the music when unbelievably I bumped into more of them. It was like a scene from Michael Caine's film Zulu and I was surrounded. I just had this thought of, 'I'm totally fucked here what do I do?' I had a bit of an argument with one of the leaders but no punches were thrown. Of course, with voices raised a Liverpool bobby walks over and says, "Have you got some problems lad?" I didn't need to even say anything because it would have been blatantly obvious to Stevie Wonder what was occurring. Now the rest of the lads were giving me the death stare as if I'm now some sort of supergrass on top of what they already hated me for. As the police were giving them all a grilling I nashed across Stanley Park and into the ground. Lucky doesn't come into it! Now I'm viewed as someone who'd been to the law but that wasn't the case. To be quite truthful, of course that police officer was my knight in shining armour and it was like some huge scene in a film where someone's life gets saved at the last minute. What happened in Liverpool wasn't going to go away. All that happened was that my execution was postponed for another day, like some death row prisoner who'd won a stay of execution until the next hearing. Even today when I see one of the lads who was there, he constantly goes to me, "You grassed" but I didn't. There's no paperwork. You weren't arrested. There was no trial. I suggest you read up on what that word 'grass' means. I didn't know the police constable was going to appear from nowhere and stop me getting a good hiding. If you want the truth, I was happy he did and out of 1000 times it couldn't have happened at a more precise moment again. I was as relieved as anyone would have been if they'd been surrounded by ten angry GBH merchants. The guy calling me an "Informer" would have been relieved if he'd have been in the same situation. What did he want me to do have a fight with ten people? Just let them hit me?

On another occasion not long after I was supposed to be going out to my local 'The Swan' in Heworth, I got a phone call. My mate had his foot in both camps if you like and he told me not to even bother coming! When I asked why he told me there was a mob in all waiting on my arrival. To cut a long story short I'd been set-up by a so-called friend who'd tipped them off where I was going to be. He was supposed to be a pal and I've never spoken to that person since.

At some away games I'd be literally surrounded like the time I arrived at a ground at 2.55pm to take my seat and when I looked around there was five of them behind me. What was worse was when I looked to my left, one of them was sat next to me smiling. Can you believe that, out of a three thousand allocation! For the whole game I had people having a go at us from behind, not to mention my new best mate next door. I was sat there all the way through that game listening to, "We're gonna get ya outside" and I was like, "Guys just watch the match!" At the end of the match I managed to give them the slip amongst the crowd heading home. Another close escape.

At another away game at Queens Park Rangers at Loftus Road in 2009, which was the season Chris Hughton got us promoted, I had another skirmish. For that game I was offered a VIP ticket in the ground. Newcastle won 1-0 by a Peter Lovenkrands goal. I was actually given the tickets by Nicky Butt for looking after him on the doors. I took my best pal Christian who is Freddie Foreman's godson. When Peter Lovenkrands scored, in front of us was an elderly gent with a young boy around 6 years old and they started jumping up and down. Stood next to them was this pissed up middle-aged cockney bloke in a Stone Island coat that started having a go at this old fella and the kid shouting "FACKING SHAT YOUR MOUTH YOU GEORDIE MUGS". As he's shouting his mouth off this fellow Geordie turned around and tells the drunken Cockney, "WHO THA HELL YA PICKIN ON YA COCKNEY PRICK?" Me and Christian are just standing there and I'm thinking, 'keep ya mouth shut Steve keep ya mouth shut' but as I'm trying to keep out of it the boozed-up guy turns to me and says, "And I know you're a fucking Geordie as well ya shouldn't even fucking be in here!" I don't think he'd even heard me speak so I'm sure he had a radar for spotting Geordies. I just told him there wasn't any need for it. I said, "I didn't even jump up and down when Newcastle scored!" Then I told him that the people who he was targeting was an OAP and a bairn so he should have known better, well as soon as I said that he blurts out, "AAH YA WHAT, WHAT YA FACKING GONNA DO" and he's then jumping up and trying to get over the seats to have a go at me along with one of his mates. If that wasn't bad enough, I heard a load of noise behind me and it was more angry drunken Cockneys. I'm not kidding you there must have been at least thirty of them all dressed in Burberry and Stone Island looking for mine and Christian's blood. This mob then started jumping over seats trying to get to us. At that point I'd just bought a cup of tea and that went flying. I knew at that point I had two options, stand and take a beating or run and jump so I chose the latter one. I then literally took a running jump, catapulted myself over three rows of seats and landed on two lasses, I'd managed to cut my head on landing but that would have been the least of my worries if the firm and gotten hold of me. Again, like at Everton I was saved by more guardian angels this time it was some stewards who came over to pull me to safety because they'd seen what was going on. I'd just left this melee of people which was about to turn into a free-for-all. I was then frogmarched out to safety and walked towards the proper Newcastle end down the side of the pitch and as I'm getting closer, I'm greeted by a ripple of applause from the Newcastle fans. All you could hear was, "HE'S HERE, HE'S THERE, HE FLIES THROUGH THE AIR STEVIE WRAITH, STEVIE WRAITH". It was fucking hilarious because a few of my mates had seen what went on. Then word got to social media that Steve Wraith was now a football casual like something out of the film I.D. It was my mates in the Newcastle end that started the song off thinking it was hysterical. It must have looked like I'd incited a riot but I was just so relieved I didn't have Dr Martin prints all-over my forehead. Someone actually took a picture of me being ushered by the QPR stewards in orange jackets.

A few years later I was approached by Mark Mennim to do a book about his time as a football hooligan in the firm, I was happy to talk to him as all the bother had died down. We met for a coffee and he said that he wanted to do a book and he'd been told I was the man for the job. Mark's nickname among the firm was 'The General.' I knew him as he was area manager in the pub game for The Sayers. Mark was a target for most of the media and even the authorities which led him to being arrested on more than one occasion. He had been stabbed by a mad Turk to the point he was carrying his guts around in his hands on one away trip.

What became apparent with Mark was that it was going to be incredibly difficult to do the book because he was useless with times and dates. Mark could remember fighting on the terraces but he couldn't remember who it was against that type of thing. I told Mark that we'd started so we had to finish so I started talking to some of the other members of the firm (the ones who'd speak to me anyway) and we managed to fill in the blanks with some fabulous input from the others who apart from Mark Mennim all remained nameless. The book in total was an amalgamation of around forty different people's stories. I met some people and had a few pints with them and took notes. Others emailed me. Others who wanted to remain anonymous posted stories to me. The book went on to be a massive success and it still sells today. It had stories from some of The Bender Squad, NME (Newcastle Mainline Express) and The Gremlins which were all different sections of Newcastle firms. That was three generations of football hooligans from the 70s, 80s and 90s.

The book is full of stories told through the voice of Mark Mennim and it was fascinating to do. Some of the military precision that went into some of the brawls you'd never expect from these people. I got to understand them more. Why they do it. They see it as fighting for their city.

Defenders of the City if you like and I understood that to a degree. I could never condone their actions but I understood it. What I tried to do with the book was not only give them a platform to right the wrongs written about them in other books but a chance to cement their place in our social history. There are so many books out there i.e. West Ham, Chelsea, Millwall, Middlesbrough etc but many of them are filled with lies and those lies over the course of time become truth because they're the only books the general public have to read.

I'd like to think that the one thing I achieved on the Newcastle hooligans behalf is that I set the record straight. Newcastle's firms didn't always win which I found refreshing, especially The Gremlins who were happy to tell me a story about the time they all went on a train journey wearing Kappa tracksuits only they got off at Birmingham station to get chinned because they were all wearing the same gear they stood out like a sore thumb to the rival supporters, so they got straight back on the train and came home again.

Sadly, some just see me as a parasite who has made money off their endeavours. If I hadn't done it then someone else would have. They can't say I kept the project a secret. I went out to see them all prior to the book being written. There was a frank exchange of views with some but they all accepted that I was going to write the book regardless.

There were around a hundred people at the book's launch night at Cosmic Ballroom. The lads there knew the book was done with the right intentions and loved it. When the book came out there was one guy who'd done absolutely no work on the book, incidentally it was the guy I'd had trouble with in the past and I'd put him out of venues too whilst doing the doors. This same guy assaulted my brother in the street one day for no reason. As I say this guy did nothing with the book whatsoever but he thought that he was owed some money from it. On the eve of the book launch I received a text message off him saying, "You ducking better give me some ducking cash out of this", I don't know if the F button was broken on his phone or he was averse to cursing but what also followed was, "I'm going to get some ducking people at ya ducking door if you don't ducking pay us". If you don't laugh, you'll cry in situations like that. I then had to make some phone calls to others saying, 'look this guy has got nothing to do with the book so why is he texting me at stupid o'clock?'

As I've already said in the book, I'm not a violent man. I'm linked to a lot of major faces of British crime but I've never once picked up the phone to use any of those connections. What pleasure is someone going to get out of battering Steve Wraith because I'm not a fighter? I've received one punch in all the time I've been doing this and that was through mistaken identity. Some kid punched me in The Bigg Market but I was more concerned about having a black eye because I had an acting job the next day. I found out the culprit and I actually got an apology from him. He said he was off his head on cocaine and he thought I was someone else.

I don't worry when I go out, it's never stopped me going out in the centre of Newcastle, although some folk can be dangerous, especially when in large numbers and full of Dutch courage or Columbian courage! Often when I've met these people by themselves it's a different story as there isn't anyone to egg them on. The guy demanding money from me for a book he had no part in, I put that down to jealousy, he didn't want to see me making money out of their stories. If that guy wanted to do the book then why didn't he do it? This relentless hassle is sadly part of my life. As we were putting this book together one of the firm had a 'pop' at me on Twitter which six of the lads sent me a screenshot of. I responded to it on my Twitter account and their 'Whatsapp' group which is 200 strong went into meltdown wanting to know who the mole was. One of the top boys then rang me to tell me not to be concerned and to give him a bell if things got out of hand. I appreciated that. He didn't have to do that.

After the hooly book was released I was approached by a member of the Seaburn Casuals (Sunderland FC hooligans) to do their book but I politely declined the offer for obvious reasons.....

27

BNP? Not on my Watch!

Politics for me is one of those subjects that you should never really speak about in public, a bit like religion I suppose because its nobody else's business. If people do find out then they tend to hold it against you. The same can be said about football especially if you live in the North East because it can end in arguments and much worse. With regards to politics, it's a big thing, whichever party is in power get to make such huge decisions for our country I consider it to be a really important issue. For me, I was brought up in a house full of conservatives. I wasn't someone who was politically motivated so it was something I never thought I would fall into. I've always voted since the day I was allowed to and I have always told people that my vote is between me and the ballot box.

I originally voted Conservative. Things changed when the poll tax came in. I started reading into politics more and I turned away from the Tories. Rather than waste a vote I started to vote Liberal Democrat in the General Election. Locally I chose to vote Labour mainly due to the fact that they were the only party who would have somebody local running for election. You would see other parties pull a candidate in from another area to run for your ward just so they could be seen competing for the seat. Ridiculous really. Who is going to vote for a stranger from another area to represent you as councillor? You can be really naïve when you're young about the whole thing unless you're brought up in a really political household.

I ended up running for council in 2003/04 when I was living in Woodlands Terrace, Felling which was the first house I bought. I was lucky enough to get on the property ladder at an early age. When I sold the Post Office to concentrate on my career on the 'doors' I spent my money on buying my first bachelor pad. As a twenty-something it was important to be near the pubs and my Sunday football team. Anyway, my local elections were coming around in 2002 and I remember getting a knock on the door. To be honest I never really answered the door because I couldn't be chewed after being at work all day. It turns out this knocker was quite persistent and wouldn't go away so in the end I got up and had to answer it. When I opened the door to my surprise, I found a skinhead wearing a donkey jacket, Dr Martins holding a bulldog on a lead who said he was from the British National Party. He then asked if he could count on my vote and tried to hand me a leaflet which I took but I told him I was having my tea and closed the door. As I was sat in my flat looking at this leaflet to be honest it really annoyed me. I have a lot of friends from different cultures and to have the BNP knock on my door, well I was incensed. I didn't think I would ever feel that way about politics. From there I decided to go online that night to read up on political parties and what I should and shouldn't know. At that moment I certainly didn't have any ideas on becoming a local councillor. I had enough going on working on the doors and I had a good income and what I thought was a good life, I certainly didn't want to be sitting in boring council meetings. At that time in the Felling area at elections Labour were comfortably ahead with Liberal Democrats coming second, but now the BNP were coming in and trying to upset the apple cart. I was a member of the local Conservative club in Heworth with my dad and my grandad.

I never ever went to meetings, the only reason I ever went into the club was because they had a great snooker table. I went along to the club and I got pointed in the direction of a guy named Paul who lived locally to me. Paul was the local Conservative rep and he told me he'd pop to my house and see me for a chat. Paul was really approachable and an all-round nice guy. He told me he'd happily take me on as a member but I'd need to pay a subscription and come along to the meetings once a month at the Conservative club in Low Fell. Paul told me the party were always happy to have new blood and asked me why all of a sudden did I want to be involved with politics. I just told him that honestly, I didn't know but that I had the BNP around my flat the other week door knocking and it disgusted me. I told him I'm against any kind of racism big-time and now I wanted to make a stand, even if I lost but could at least split the vote it would all be worth it.

Paul liked what he heard from me and I didn't realise why he was so happy until I went along to my first meeting. Paul took me along to the beautiful old building in Low Fell and it was literally like walking onto the film-set of Cocoon. Every single member was an OAP sitting around in their best gear. All the best china was out for the buffet which I found bizarre.

Basically, it was all very serious and there was a person up on the stage making some sort of speech. She reminded me of an even older version of Margaret Thatcher if that was possible.

The speaker was very posh, you could tell she shopped at Sainsbury's or Marks & Spencer's. The speaker was reading out what the Tory head office had sent them and about Conservative visits in Newcastle and saying how we all could be involved. The first visit was from Michael Howard a few weeks later who by then had climbed his way up the ladder of the Conservative party. I went along to see Michael Howard and I had a chat with him. Michael thanked me for my support and said it was good to see a younger face in the Newcastle branch. Like a lot of things in my life it was a bit surreal because I'd often watched Michael Howard on the telly making decisions for the country alongside Thatcher. I started thinking I must now be alongside this chap in the trenches. I had to remember that everything that was happening around my newfound position, I was in it to fight the BNP only.

The local election was on the horizon and I was told that I'd need to do a leaflet drop of around 5,000 fliers. Although I had zero chance of getting in I still had to come up with some proper policies. I worked on the flyer with another young volunteer Daniel. All my friends thought I was crazy for doing it in the first place. The policies I came up with were simple. Cutting down on crime, better street lighting and penalties for people who were letting their dogs foul on the pavements, those kinds of basic issues. I managed to pull together a pretty substantial introduction piece and subsequently all my policies were on the leaflets. Getting out and putting them through people's doors was no problem because I'm used to walking because I don't drive. Paul did suggest that one way of getting people onside in Felling was to hand leaflets out on a Saturday afternoon. I've got to be honest I was a little bit hesitant about that because it was a Labour area, also a lot of people were beginning to know who I was by then from other things I was doing. I knew if I was going to get some stick then this was going to be the time it would happen. It's a good job I'm made of tough stuff and I have got skin like a rhino. At the time I was also doing the doors so I wasn't particularly worried about anyone physically attacking me because I was used to that kind of thing. I thought as long as I could back up my policy then I could do it. So, one Saturday afternoon I went along to Felling Square and stood outside Barclays Bank with my 2,000 leaflets. Talking on the street with people was interesting. Some of my mates came past on purpose to take the mick, some people laughed in my face when I tried to hand them a leaflet. It wasn't all bad though because a few stood and asked me what I would do if I got in and what would I change? I've got to be honest though the vast majority said I wouldn't dream of voting for the Tories and called me, "Tory scum" which is what I expected. I was prepared for it and that's what I got.

Some people who were extra abusive to me I had to tell them I was only doing it because the BNP were running. Most of my hecklers were BNP voters.

After handing out leaflets most of the day I was thankful that I didn't have to do that again, I'd done my bit. When it came around to the election process and the counting that was an experience itself. I'd seen it on TV. Up this neck of the woods it's always done at Gateshead Leisure Centre. When I was there the first thing I saw was the BNP guy who'd been to my house, he even had his bulldog with him. From my perspective I was just happy to be able to do what I set out to achieve. Needless to say, I didn't get in but I did split the votes although the BNP still got in ahead of me. Maybe if I hadn't have stood then the Conservatives wouldn't have got as many votes. As far as I was concerned they didn't get in front of me without a fight. I stood up for what I believed in which is what I always do.

These days it's something that gets constantly thrown at me by the trolls. If you're on my Twitter and you've seen the comments saying, "You bald Tory nonce" then that's where all that comes from. Although it was a long time ago it still gets dug up and it's not something I'm ashamed of. I'm glad I did it and I wouldn't change it even if I could. Most think to vote Conservative is a sacrilege but I did it to take a stand, I was always going to be an easy target in Gateshead though because it's predominately a Labour area. I fully understand the hatred the Tories get from a lot of these mining towns because what Margaret Thatcher did during the miner strikes was unforgivable.

Today I'm very good friends with a lot of Labour politicians, is it something I'd go back to and would I run as a Labour councillor? I think I've got a lot to offer but at the moment I don't have the time on my hands to give, but I wouldn't rule it out for the future. I'm certainly community minded and since then I've gone on to do school governor work as well as voluntary work with Gateshead council to help rejuvenate parks or put Christmas lights up.

I'm very much a guy who'll happily give up his time for free but a lot of people don't know about that and probably wouldn't believe it either.

28

Bringing Unlicensed Boxing to Tyneside

I've always been a big fan of pugilism from a very early age. After football, boxing was always my second love. The real draw came from the 1986-89 era when 'Iron' Mike was demolishing the heavyweight world scene. When I left school, I started training at Dave Gregory and Glenn McCrory's gym in Felling in St Patrick's Church. The gym was a proper old school gym, damp ceilings, paint coming off the brickwork and the place stunk like a boxing gym should do. Training in there at the time was world champion Glenn McCrory, Billy Hardy, Danny Moir and a guy called Terry French. I would be circuit training but at the same time looking over in awe at these top fighters. Originally, I went along just to keep fit because I was playing Sunday League Football.

I did the boxing training for a couple of years and I thoroughly enjoyed it. Around midway through the first year Bernard O'Hagan asked me if I'd like to do a bit of sparring, I told him I'd have a crack at it. Although I was never a fighting man, I've always enjoyed trying to indulge in the skills that boxing brings. I also loved being around the fight scene which I still do to this day. So, I got in to do a bit of sparring with this kid my weight and I'm having a dance about, I was trying to put into practice what Bernard the coach had been showing me.

I was good with the punching side of boxing but I struggled with the footwork which was required to be an elite level fighter. The way the coach showed me just never seemed natural.

Even when he turned me southpaw it wasn't any better so I stuck as an orthodox. The first round went without incident in the sparring and I thought it was a doddle, that was until my opponent dropped a huge right hand straight on my nose in the second. I didn't go down but I saw stars. If you think of when Tom & Jerry see stars when they've hit each other with hammers in the cartoons then you get my drift. I was totally blowing by the third round and at the end of it I thought, I'm never doing that again. I didn't enjoy being punched in the face I've got to admit and I never sparred again.

I used to love watching Terry French who was the Northern Area champion at the time.

Although I never wanted to be a boxer, I did get myself involved with the unlicensed scene first and that was through my London connection Joe Pyle Snr. I used to get invited to a hell of a lot of events down there with the big crowds at Caesars in Streatham. At first, I was just invited down as a guest. Among those big boxing functions, it was really a who's who with faces such as Dave Courtney, Roy Shaw, Charlie & Eddie Richardson, Freddie Foreman, 'Mad' Frankie Fraser and Eric Mason who would all be there together on tables of ten in their dickie bows. This would have been around the early 2000s and it was a great opportunity for me to watch and learn. When I was training back in the Atlantis gym in the Felling which is where Viv Graham trained before he was murdered, I'd got to know Gary Firby quite well, he'd been training around the pro scene and even had a handful of fights under the BBBofC.

Gary had been to jail and when he came out I had started training with Gary because I wanted to bulk up with working the doors. Whilst training with Gary I got to some great levels without taking any steroids which is something a lot of doormen relied on. Over an 18-month period I went from benching 40kg to 120kg and that was doing four reps. I've never been as strong as I was back when I was training with Gary and I started putting weight on. Back then though my diet wasn't as good as it is these days. When I was on the 'door' I'd be constantly getting free pizza's and burgers at all times of the morning which isn't good for anyone.

Gary Firby knew because he had a criminal record, he couldn't go back into the pro game which was a real shame because he was good enough. It was then that I said to him, "Why don't you come and fight down London for me?" Gary then came down with me on one of Joe Pyle Jnr's shows just to watch to see what it was all about and he loved it. Boxing in front of 2,000 people and most of them villains was right up Gary's street. I had a word with both Joe's and I told them about Gary Firby and that he could bring probably over fifty ticket sales with him and that's where Gary "The Geordie Connection" Firby was born. Gary fought on a few of those shows and even fought for the Guvnor belt which he won on points and Roy Shaw presented him it. Gary did well beating Welshman Steve Yorath and even gave away five stone. He then lost his title to one of Joe Pyle's big prospects Sven Hamer and that was the end of our journey in London.

I was then approached by a guy named Phil Riley who told me he was thinking of setting up unlicensed boxing in Newcastle and he needed someone to promote it and would I be interested? I told Phil thanks for asking me but I didn't really have the experience in boxing but I thanked him all the same. In the end I agreed to meet him because the Riley's are cousins to the Sayers and Stephen had called me to explain this.

I met Phil in the bar Pacific in Newcastle and we had a sit down together. Phil told me we wouldn't struggle to find the home fighters to put on the show and he would provide the away fighters and everything would be above board. I told Phil that day I'd give it a go and that's what I did. The first unlicensed show I would stage was at Felling social club and Gary Firby was on that bill. Top of the bill was old pro world title challenger John Davison having a farewell fight against Rob Newbiggin who was flown in from Miami for the fight. Later Newbiggin would change his sex and become a woman. We only had a capacity of 400 in the venue but I did 500 tickets so the place was absolutely jumping. John Davison got a fantastic send off and he even mentioned it in his autobiography which was nice.

Over the next few unlicensed shows in Tyneside I attached the Bubble Foundation UK within Great North Children's Hospital to it so it was all for a good cause. I learnt so much from those shows and they only grew so I had my pick from local fighters. I would always be loyal to my guy Gary Firby and he made sure he was on every show I would be involved with. I even did one at Gateshead Leisure Centre which held 1200 people and it was a sell-out. On that show some of them weren't even boxers but just local people wanting to have a scrap. The whole thing was a great money maker for all involved. Around that time a guy called Spencer Brown from Blackpool set up the EBF (European Boxing Federation) so that gave us a bigger platform and more importantly insurance. I would have to liaise with the police and local council so it all went to plan.

In that time during the eight years of promoting the unlicensed boxing I was learning my craft for the professional game. In the end I left the unlicensed shows as there began to be too many copycats and everybody started doing it. On my shows I would use EBF opponents but what many of the copycats were doing was putting Geordies against Geordies which I didn't want to do. I didn't mind if there was a title at stake but putting two local lads against each other was only going to bring crowd trouble and it wasn't long before it followed. When you put a bill on of sixteen contests with thirty-two local lads it ended up in riots and brawls breaking out. Sadly, I had a stabbing outside one of my shows. It was linked to some long-running feud with two families and it all escalated. I then had a show where girls from Sunderland were fighting people from Newcastle. I had around twenty people getting stuck into each other at ringside within touching distance from me and I had to jump in with Ray Simpson to break it up. Of course, then somebody phoned the local paper and its all-over The Evening Chronicle 'BOXING EVENT ENDS IN BRAWL' so I started to get sick.

I could say I went out of unlicensed boxing on a high but I'd be lying and I went out on a low on a St Patrick's Day bash at The Lancastrian Suite. With it being Paddy's Day I thought it would be funny to hire two dwarves dressed as Leprechauns and let them box each other. When I eventually saw the dwarves that I'd hired I noticed that one of them looked like Eric Gates who used to play for Sunderland, well you know what I did next don't you, yes I scrapped the Leprechaun suits and put little Eric in a Sunderland kit and the other in a Newcastle kit. It was the funniest thing I've ever seen and Phil Riley who used to referee the fights was such a big giant of a man so when the dwarves where running under his legs when he was breaking them up it just added to the laughter. The whole thing was classic comedy and people just couldn't believe what they were watching.

I have to say that looking back on the white-collar business Gary Firby was my most loyal fighter and I'm still good friends with him today. Me and Gary go back a long way and it would be fair to say I built my unlicensed career around him and he went on to become 'The Guvnor.' Gary has been up and down the country and fought them all, only he hasn't had the exposure as folk like James McCrory. Gary will fight anyone and its only as recently as early this year that he got in the ring Friday night and boxed with gloves, then Saturday he had a bareknuckle fight then on the Sunday had a blindfolded contest. Three fights in one weekend.

He keeps announcing his retirement but he has had more comebacks than Frank Sinatra!

29

The Noble Art

I became involved in the professional ranks by going to one of Glenn McCrory's amateur shows. At that time Glenn had a stable of top Cuban fighters and it was he who suggested that I get into the pro game because he had seen what I had been doing in the Unlicensed game. At first, I thought he was just making small talk as we sat at the table at ringside. Then another North East boxing legend Billy Hardy chipped in saying, "You should Wraithy you should."

At the end of the day I fell into the pro game because I was sick of the troublesome unlicensed game but I still needed a boxing fix so it was a natural progression. After surfing the net and reading up on a few things I applied for a BBBofC licence, contacted the Northern Area council and went for a meeting with them. In the old days the meetings were held in The Roker Hotel in Sunderland on a Sunday morning so off I went. When I arrived all the usual North East council members were there like, Fred Potter, John Jarret, David Venn, and Reg Long. I sat waiting to go in like I was back in Argyle House waiting outside the Headmasters office. When I was called in I went into this huge room and every licence holder in North East professional boxing was there i.e. Phil Jeffries, Tommy Conroy and Mal Gates.

I had to stand and tell them all a bit about myself and then take a few questions. It was all basic stuff and if there's one thing I am good at it is standing in a room and talking. After the questions I was asked to leave the room for a couple of minutes. David Venn then asked me to come back in. He spoke on behalf of the area council and told me that they'd be very pleased to have me on board. The outcome was that I had to get my application form stamped and pay my £10,000 into the BBBofC, what? £10,000 nobody told me about needing to pay that kind of money it was news to me. The large sum of money was for a deposit so that if one of my shows went "Tits up" I could cover it.

I walked out of that meeting utterly deflated. For a start I didn't have £10,000. Did I know people who had that kind of money to borrow, of course I did but I didn't really want to lend that large sum of money from anyone so I walked away for another twelve months and went back to the unlicensed circuit. It wasn't until I met a guy named Dave Tweddle who I'd met socially, Dave and I got on really well, in fact he'd been to support a lot of my boxing talks.

For some reason when me and him were out, he turned around and said, "I'll pay the ten grand for you if you'll pay us it back in your own time". I then set a target and I paid David back within three years. I told Dave that even if I didn't make 1p on the boxing he'd have his money and it was a gentleman's handshake and that was that. When I made a profit on a show i.e. £500 here, £600 there Dave got it sent to his bank account. I'll always be thankful to Davie Tweddle who's a building contractor from Ashington and I'm friends with him to this day, not to mention he's a fellow Freemason.

I've got to say that Phil Jeffries plays a huge part in my story because he was an established promoter. His son Tony won a bronze medal at the 2008 Beijing Olympics. Phil did nothing but encourage me and help me along and he knows the fight game inside out. Phil at the start told me that me and him should do a show in Gateshead together and that he'd put his name to it, that way there was no pressure on me and I could see what it was all about. Me and Phil did the show together and I did all the running around. I found the whole pro-boxing game easy and it wasn't any different to the white-collar business. The only thing wrong with the boxing in that aspect is the financial side of things. You just don't make the money in the professional game. You won't know this unless you've been in the trade but it's a shock to the system when you find out what it's all about. I got out of the unlicensed game because I thought it's only a matter of time before there's a death in it and we'd all be tarred with the same brush, but there was far more money in the unlicensed game than professional ranks.

Going into the pro game your rewards are not financial they are your fighter's achievements.

At the time I arrived on the scene there wasn't many promoters in the area. Yes, there was Phil Jeffries but by now Tommy Conroy had taken a backseat and Hartlepool's Gus Robinson by that point had sadly passed. North East boxing in my opinion was in a slump with the exception of Phil Jeffries. Before I came along there hadn't been a show in Tyneside for a long long time and it was my dream to reignite the flame.

When I started the late Ronnie Rowe from Birtley was a great voice to listen to. Ronnie told me what boxing was about but he warned me that financially it was going to be hard. After speaking to some proper Northern boxing faces, I started to get a feeling for what it was all about. When you watch my early press conferences (on YouTube) all I'm saying is our aim is to find the next world champion from the North East. That's all I set out to achieve. I wasn't bothered if I got hold of that fighter, all I wanted to do was kick start the boxing game and get everyone talking about it. Eight years on we've got Eddie Hearn, MTK and Frank Warren doing shows up here. Fighters like Lewis Ritson and Tommy Ward are only steps away from world title contention. Middlesbrough's Joe Maphosa is going to be another star who's been on several of mine and Phil's shows. Joe Laws is another who sells between fifteen hundred and two thousand tickets on shows for fun.

In the early days Sedgefield's Bradley Saunders was my first big fighter. He was signed to Frank Warren but he wanted to put him on in the North East. I promoted a show named 'License to Thrill' in 2013 and he was top of the bill at Gateshead Leisure Centre. That show was in association with Francis Warren. As a promoter you have to pay for the venue hire, posters, tickets, ring, doctors X 3 which equals a minimum of £1500 alone for the doctors.

Then you've got timekeepers X 2 (for a show over 8 bouts), referee (2 if over a certain amount of fights), food, boxing whips, seconds and security so all in all you're looking at kicking on for £6,000 expenses before the bell rang. If I can walk out with £500 - £1000 profit at the end of it all I'm over the moon. Bearing in mind that's eight to ten weeks work. Professional boxing pays absolute peanuts and you just can't make money on these shows. The only way you can make money on those shows is if you've got good sponsors and I've been very lucky over the years, folk like David Tweddle, Lee Barr and Portland Consultant Engineering, Aka and LA Taxis, Jacob at Ideala, Cheryl and Adam at Grosvenor Casinos and others have been a god send and without them I'd have been completely snookered.

When I started doing pro-shows in the North East it gave Phil Jeffries the incentive to do even more shows and between me, Phil, Eddie Hearn, Ronnie Rowe and Frank Warren at the time there were up to eight shows in the North East a year. Local fighters if they stayed fit had the chance to have six to seven bouts a year and if you do that and you're good enough you're putting yourself in contention to move onto better paydays. The arrival of Matchroom and Eddie Hearn in Newcastle has a lot to do with the recent boom in the North East. So how did it come about? One of my mates Danny Cox knew Eddie quite well. His late Dad Tommy set up the breakaway darts organisation the PDC and Eddie's Dad Barry threw his financial support behind it and the rest is history. Danny called Eddie and told him that we were keen to meet him with regards to boxing in the North East. He invited us to a presser at the Grosvenor hotel in London and said he would meet us beforehand. We arrived on time and bumped into a few faces including Scott Quigg and Johnny Nelson. Eddie arrived and came over to say hi. He suggested we grab a coffee in Costa downstairs. The next 20 minutes I went into overdrive telling Eddie about what we were trying to achieve and how we were going to do it. I didn't stop to breathe. He smiled nodded and told us to continue doing what we were doing and that he'd be in touch. We swapped numbers and that was that. We headed back to Newcastle buzzing about the meeting and Eddie was as good as his word. A few months later he gave me the opportunity to help stage a show with Matchroom. I worked on it with Ronnie Rowe and Lewis Pendleton from Fighting Chance and it was a big success.

From then it went from strength to strength with the shows getting bigger and better. I got the chance to arrange the local undercard for Antony Joshua's big fight in Newcastle. I managed to get Mal Gate's fighter Anth Nelson on the card fighting for a Commonwealth Title. He ended up topping the bill and winning the title! Boy did we celebrate that night.

The reason that MTK and Matchroom are still coming up to the North for shows is because of the hard work of the likes of Mal Gates, Imran Naeem, Neil Fannan, David Binns, Gary Barr and Pete Shepperson. The trainers are the unsung heroes in the boxing world. They train fighters day in day out and sacrifice their own spare time to help fighters achieve their goals. They deserve the credit from the North East Fight fans. Mal Gates and Pete Shepperson are my best mates in boxing. Not far behind them are the whips Andy Wilde and Spud and Ginge Woollatt who make the shows run like clockwork. The House seconds such as Colin Innes and Paul Charters are vital too as is Natalie Hubbard who films all of our shows and gets me from A to B. One name I can't fail to mention is Frankie Hutchinson who is always at local shows getting signed pictures of fighters. If you go to Frankie's house, he's got a room put aside with cases upon cases of information about every fighter that's ever lived. The guy is fanatical with his love for boxing and he is also a real loveable character.

Out of all the fighters I've managed Billy Snaith from Ferryhill is really special to me. Billy told me when he signed for me that he wanted one warm up fight and then he wanted to knock Daniel Cope's head off in a Northern Area title fight and I was like, WOW! I told Billy at least I know what the plan is. Billy told me he was going to train with Jeff Saunders Snr and we set off on this golden journey. Billy told me that once he won the Northern Area Title that he was retiring. Within twelve months we had a warm-up fight then we had him in a ten rounder for a challenge belt and then we made the Cope v Snaith fight on my show and Billy did what he said he was going to do, beat Cope and then retired.

I'm currently looking after Ellis Corrie, Lawrence Osueke, Anth Ornsby and Shannon Bowe.

Ellis is a welterweight and only 22 and has won and defended his Northern Area title in fine style and is one to watch. Lawrence is Light Heavyweight and had a faultless start to his career but has faltered at the time of writing fighting at English title and British Title Eliminator level. Anth Ornsby is one for the future but has started well whilst Shannon Bowe is my first female fighter and I am looking forward to watching her progress.

People ask me what my best night in boxing has been so far, well It will come as no surprise for you to hear that it involves Super Flyweight Anthony Nelson from South Shields.

Mal Gates and I worked hard to put on a show in 'Nella's' hometown of South Shields. It was a homecoming for me of sorts having been born there. We staged an English Title fight there against Terry Broadbent which was a great bit of matchmaking by Mick Marsden. 'Nella' sold over 1500 tickets that night. The place was bouncing I had a Northern Area title on the undercard too with John Green fighting Peter Cope. 'Nella' was outstanding that night and won comfortably. The photo of me Mal and 'Nella' is pride of place in my office. Like I said we aren't in pro-boxing at our level for the money but for the memories.

I keep saying I'm stepping away from boxing each year but I haven't managed it yet. Today in 2020 I'm still very active as a promoter and a manager. The line from the Godfather sums it up I guess, 'Every time I try to get out, they pull me back in.' But I wouldn't have it any other way.

30

The Superstars

Ricky Hatton, Marco Antonio Barrera, Anthony, Joshua, Tyson Fury, Nigel Benn, Conor Benn, Chris Eubank, Steve Collins, Frank Bruno, George Groves, Carl Froch, Billy Joe Saunders, David Haye, Roberto Duran, Jake La Motta, Mike Tyson, Floyd Mayweather, Shannon Briggs, Micky Ward, Thomas Hearns, Sugar Ray Leonard, Brian London, Robin Reid, Joe Calzaghe, Joe Bugner, Larry Holmes, Roy Jones, Riddick Bowe, Evander Holyfield and Joe Frazier are several boxers I've done 'An Evening Withs'. I've even done one with Eddie Hearn. I'm sure there's many I've forgotten and if I have its purely by accident. If people think I've done all of those and made millions then they're sadly mistaken.

For example, I went into the Roberto Duran night £5,000 down and if we hadn't had a good auction, I would have lost money on that night. People forget that when I do these functions, I have to hire venues, pay staff, buy food etc and those nights I put on are all about taking the risks that are involved in business. I am a risk taker of that there is no doubt.

The first night I ever did was in 1995 for my football team and the whole thing with QFX cost £500, today in 2020 I've just put Floyd Mayweather on in Newcastle and that was a five-figure risk. If something like that all goes Pete Tong you could be looking at re-mortgaging a house or wiping out your savings. If it does go tits-up I'm the one who's got my name signed to that contract. I personally came into the event business when the recession hit so it was the worst possible time to set up. Many years ago, I've sat in

184

sportsman's dinners that have seen signed Mike Tyson shorts/gloves going for £3,000 - £4,000 - £5,000. Today you can buy something like that for £150 all day long. Those poor buggers who paid all that money years ago must be thinking 'god almighty there goes my investment'!

Over the years I've had to duck and dive and learn the tricks of the trade. I've enjoyed working with the boxing legends because first and foremost I'm a fan. I'll never forget in my youth I would go into this bar in Gateshead which was called 'The Fleece' on Gateshead High Street to play pool and inside it was full of top signed memorabilia. The owner of the bar had met all the top boxing stars and I remember thinking, god I wish I could meet all these people, well twenty-five years later I've done it.

Chris Eubank was completely different to anyone I've ever met before. I first met him in The Grosvenor Hotel, London. When you watch Chris Eubank on television you would be forgiven for thinking it was all an act, forget that because that's actually him 24/7. After our meeting me and Chris had a gentleman's agreement and the date was put in his agent's diary.

The date was set for five months in advance so it gave me plenty of time to promote and sell the show. The event itself sold pretty well and it wasn't a struggle. I would speak with Chris regularly to keep him updated on the whole situation. Chris would even ring me from time to time and we'd often exchange emails so on the actual day when he turned up and didn't even know who I was it really threw me. I was like "Chris, I'm the guy you've been speaking to for five months" and he was like, "Oh yes". How to make someone feel completely unimportant wow!

Chris turned up late to the event itself. He was supposed to be there at The Lancastrian Suite at 7pm sharp. Chris didn't even get into Central Station until 7.45pm. There was never any sense of urgency when he was sat there sipping orange juice totally oblivious that I had hundreds of people wanting to meet him as he strolled around in his own time chilling out. I had to say, "Come on Chris we do need you on stage now so people can see you." I told him we had to do the photographs first but then he came out with, "Oh can we not do the photographs last?"

I told him "No we always do the photographs first." When Chris was on the stage before I could even introduce him, he grabbed the mic and started a speech saying how unwell he was and he had a bit of a cold. I was like for god sake this is a complete nightmare because it's the last thing people have paid to listen to. After around forty minutes of whizzing through the photographs Chris then turned around and said, "I'd like to go to the hotel!" Well, I was dumbfounded. I thought 'he's getting paid X amount of pounds and he's now wanting to go back to the hotel!' In the end I had to get my driver to fly him back to his hotel. I sent a member of security with him as well so we could keep close tabs on Chris in case of anymore hurdles which may occur.

When Chris arrived in the hotel on this Friday night, Newcastle were playing Chelsea the next day and the London team were stopping in The Hilton Hotel where Chris was staying. My member of security told me as they were going into the lift Jose Mourinho came out and as he saw Chris, he offered to shake his hand and Eubank blanked him and walked straight past him. My security guy then went upstairs to wait outside of Chris's room whilst he did what he had to do. When Chris was in his room, he was changing his shirts then came out and asked my security guy Lee Devlin to help him with his cufflinks. By the time Chris had done what he was doing the food and the auction had finished and I was constantly on the blower to my security guy asking where Chris is and how long they were going to be? Chris literally got back to the venue ay 9.55pm and he'd hardly been there all night. Finally, Chris then stood up and gave one hell of a talk. He gave one hour and I have to say he was one of the best speakers I've ever had. Chris was that good I didn't really need the compere. Chris was one of the most difficult people I've had to deal with but he totally redeemed himself in a professional and articulate manner which only Chris Eubank could. The feedback I got from my customers was that it was the best function they'd ever been to. I've only had that twice. Roy Jones was the other one on the two occasions I had him in the North East.

The first time I put Roy on he'd literally just retired and was a huge name in the world of boxing. When Roy was over he wanted to go to some allotment to view these Cockerels because he had a big fascination with these birds. You can imagine my face when I rang one of the lads from the agency James Ward to ask where he was with Roy only for him to say he'd be a little while longer because Roy wanted to go to some chicken farm. I asked, "Are you joking me my events going to run late"? I had to lump it because this is what Roy wanted to do. In the end I've had to join them in this chicken coop all suited & booted, not to mention it had been raining and it was all muddy. Roy's then stood there saying, "Aah man these birds are amazing man" and I'm just thinking 'yeah, yeah Roy'. Eventually I got Roy to the venue about 15 minutes late. I thought it was going to be a disaster but it was anything but. Rather than babble on with pre-questions Roy just stood up and said, "What do you guys wanna know?" 150 people in the audience just battered him with questions all night and it was breath-taking, Roy did 90 minutes when he was supposed to only do one hour.

I've done three evenings with Roberto Duran and the only downside to that is that he doesn't speak English he has a translator. Everybody knows the infamous story about Roberto Duran knocking out a horse so what he did was he used one of the guy's in the audience as an example to show him where he hit it. After that everybody in the audience wanted the same picture of Roberto posing with his fist on the exact spot that he knocked the horse out.

The Raging Bull Jake La Motta was 91 when he came over to do 'An Evening With' on one of my shows, his wife was 44. His wife built it as 'The Lady and the Champ' on social media. She got up on the top table along with Jake and she was helping him with the Q & As and the first thing she said was, "If you're wondering, it's me who gets on top". The whole room went silent in shock, no one was expecting that!

Another fighter I got towards the end of his British tour was Evander "The Real Deal" Holyfield and because I got him at the very end, I found Evander very dour. I don't think I got the best out of Evander as the answers to the questions weren't great.

I'd have to say I got Tommy Hearns on a bad time also as he seemed the same.

The complete opposite can be said of Shannon "The Cannon" Briggs though. I thought all this "LET'S GO CHAMP" was going to get right on my nerves but actually the guy was fantastic throughout. I found Shannon that good that I even travelled to Sunderland so I could see him again. Shannon wanted me to go out for meals with him and wanted me to be part of his whole British experience. Shannon always remembered everybody's name and got on really well with my number two Natalie Hubbard.

There are other people who I found to be amazing to work with and I have a great deal of respect for because they were all very genuine and two of those are both the Tysons, The Gypsy King Tyson Fury and Iron Mike Tyson. I got Fury booked in to come to St James' Park just five weeks after he had beaten Wladimir Klitschko. It must have been around a fortnight before the event when I got a call from someone at the football club telling me that they now couldn't host Tyson Fury at the club because of what they considered to be homophobic comments that he had made recently. The person on the other end of the phone told me that the club had committed to a scheme to help stamp out homophobia within football and couldn't be seen to have such a figure in the premises, which I fully understood. Tyson hadn't made these comments maliciously it was his religious beliefs and he's as entitled to them as anyone else is. What it did leave me with though with fourteen days to go was the huge headache of finding a new venue. It's not easy to find a new place to fit two hundred and fifty bums on seats at such short notice but I managed to get a place at 'The Hyena Comedy Café' which was close to St James' Park, what a relief that was.

It was a really nice touch to be able to present Tyson with his IBF belt as he hadn't received it up until that point, I have Eddie Hearn to thank for that. Tyson came up with his lovely wife Paris and at the end of the night he asked me if there was a good Indian restaurant in the city I told him there was one named Akbar's and I told him where it was, only Tyson insisted I go with him and join him for something to eat and it was on him. I spent the next four hours with Tyson and his wife. Looking back, I could see then whilst I was listening to Tyson that he was going through something. Tyson opened up to me on a few things he was struggling with now that he had reached the top of his sport and everyone knows what happened after that so I don't need to go into it. I'll never forget Tyson saying to me though, "Steve I'm probably going to struggle with all this fame and money because I'm just a traveller." It was difficult to watch him have a breakdown so publicly after that, I really felt for him. It reminded me of what I'd seen with Gazza. Since then Tyson has always kept in touch with me, only a few years ago he came up to Newcastle for Christmas. He stopped off at Harry's Bar and he rang everyone he knew in the area (including me) and bought everyone a pizza and paid for their drinks. He's a really genuine guy.

I gave Mike Tyson a copy of my first book 'The Krays, The Geordie Connection' and a documentary when I had him over the first time and when he came back over for the second time he came over to me and shouted, "STEVE MAN" then told me how much he enjoyed the book, he thought it was great. Mike was utterly fascinated with the twins and had even reached out to Reggie when he was alive. When he came over the following time I was just going into the pro game and he gave me some invaluable advice. Mike told me the boxing world was full of sharks and to trust nobody.

Ricky Hatton is very much cut from the same cloth as Tyson Fury and he's done a lot for me over the years. I still get hilarious snapchats from him at strange times in the morning which never ceases to make me smile. I'm happy to call Ricky Hatton a friend.

I got on well with Carl Froch and his nemesis George Groves although it was hard to do both of them. What I mean is if you sold one set of supporters a ticket then those people weren't really interested in going to the others night and vice-versa. I got on tremendously well with Carl's brother Lee Froch. I've got to be honest in their day I was Team Froch. Carl was an incredibly good speaker and I don't know if he's ever mentioned it but he knocked out George Groves in front of a sell-out crowd at Wembley (laughs). Carl and George Groves played the game well for the fans.

I was lucky enough to get Joe Frazier before he died which was just three months after my show. My lasting memory of Smokin' Joe was nothing to do with his amazing talk that night but his hilarious behaviour backstage. Every so often Smokin' Joe would be sat smiling, signing things and taking pictures when all of a sudden totally randomly he'd blurt out, "WHO LET THE DOGS OUT" whilst doing a bit of shadow boxing. This was a song by the Baha men at the time.

Unfortunately, I never got to meet Joe's arch rival Muhammad Ali because I came into the event business just after his last tour so I only missed him by months. The other big regret I have was not meeting Sir Henry Cooper, I actually had him booked in to come to Newcastle but he died before it took place. Henry would have been great for me as a boxing fan but to also get his angle on the Krays, it wasn't meant to be.

Floyd "Money" Mayweather wasn't a nightmare but his security team were. Floyd was such a massive event and easily as big as Mike Tyson. Floyd as a person couldn't have been nicer and I'm glad it went well because he was one that I'd have had to definitely remortgage my house for if it had gone wrong!

When I set up the room for Floyd his security would then come and look at it and then say move that table and chair back because it's going to get in the way of the champ, then another guy would come down and tell us to put it back as it was. There were so many silly little pointers which they felt needed to be addressed like why there was wires taped up or concerns that the champ might fall over this that or the other from his team. You don't need that type of hassle but that's what you get from these kinds of people.

With Mayweather in town I had many of Newcastle United's players wanting to meet him among others. What annoys me about these events is people do think I'm literally making fortunes off it. Then there's the people who think they should get something for free because they know me. I'm just the same as everyone else and I've got to make a living. What I don't like is arrogance and I don't like people walking in unannounced. It's like that when you write a book people want a free book even if they have no intention of reading it. If you want to come to my events but you can't afford it but you think you can help me moving forward, I don't mind you ringing me up to tell me this is your boxing idol, you're struggling and you'll never get this chance again. If I can help you I will but the ultimate fact here is I'm running a business. I can't afford to pay for people who can't do anything for me and just expect to be there. I've fallen out with people over this before because its pure arrogance on their part although they'll remain nameless. Usually it's the people who've got money as well who don't even need to do that and it's embarrassing. I'm hoping a few will read this and take note.

Getting back to Floyd Mayweather and the issue with Nando's, it was just a nightmare and I'll tell you why. When I do these events with the big stars, you're usually working with the exact times to be precise. I was told the champ would be there for 6.30pm and he'd be leaving at 9.30pm on the dot. If the photo and food are slow or the auction overruns then that's going to run into the golden time with Floyd. We were told the champion doesn't wait for no man so that's the kind of thing you have to be aware of when you take on such a huge name. One of Floyds specific requirements was that he wanted hot mixed chicken options and it had to be just out of the oven when the champ got there. From my perspective 6.30pm is the time I'm told he's going to get there but he doesn't arrive until 7pm and so the £190 I'd spent on Nando's is no good. Floyd's head of security has one bite and like in Goldilocks and the Three Bears when the porridge isn't warm enough, he says it's not good enough for the champ to eat. I was then told that the champ needed more Nando's so I had to send out two former Northern Area Champions Paul Charter and Colin Innes to the Metro Centre for more Nando's. It cost me £380 in Nando's for "The Champ." I suppose the bonus was I had a loyalty card for Nando's (laughs).

The big boxing names weren't my only big events because I've had my share of world footballing stars too. One name I have to mention who was as big as any star in the football world was Paul Gascoigne who I've known since 1988. Drifting away from the evening withs for a minute the first time I met Paul was in Newcastle's great F.A Cup run in 1988. I'd been pushed out of the queue and I never got a ticket. It was for the game against Wimbledon in the fifth-round tie. I was 16 years old at the time and this might sound crazy but I was told that Gazza's home number was in the phone book. I went through the phone book and there was three John Gascoigne's in the book. After ringing the first two I was told wrong number, I rang the final one and it was only Gazza's dad John who answered! "Hiya who is it"? John says, I ask if Paul is in and when he asks who is it I tell him it's Steve his mate. When Paul came to the phone I must have been a stuttering wreck and I think I blurted out that he didn't know me but my name was Steve Wraith, I was 16 years old and I'd been pushed out of the queue and didn't get a ticket for the Wimbledon game, with that he's just said, "Right ok I'll meet you outside the club shop at 12.30pm on the day of the game". Right enough I turned up outside the club shop and there were around seven other kids waiting. Gazza pulls up in his motor, opens the window and looks at his list of paper and calls a few names, one of them being mine, "Steve there's ya ticket son" and then he was off! Gazza actually still remembers this to this day. Paul was always doing stuff like that for people.

When Paul has done my 'evening withs', I've had some good ones and some absolute shockers! There is no in-between with Gazza. I've had Paul Gascoigne at his best and I've had him at his worst. In 2010 I had a night planned at The Lancastrian Suite with Gazza, his pal Jimmy 'Five Bellies' Gardner and Joe Allon as compere with me just being the promoter. Unfortunately, Gazza fell out with Jimmy just before and they still haven't spoken to this day. Sadly, they fell out over a newspaper article.

In the build up to our event Gazza had his biggest breakdown. Paul overdosed on the drink and the drugs and it finished up with him going to see Raoul Moat holding four cans, chicken and a fishing rod. The most bizarre thing of it all was when I went to do the deal with Paul I went to meet him in a restaurant in Jesmond called Francesca's. On that day Gazza pulled me to one side and said, "I've been watching the news do you know that Raoul Moat?" Gazza asked me this because he obviously knew I worked on the doors with him so he must have had an inkling. I told Gazza I'd worked with Raoul at Planet Earth Club. Gazza then asked me what he was like so I told him and never thought anything of it. About 5.30pm that night I was getting ready to go out and do a talk-in with Joe Allon when I received a phone call from a very pissed up Paul.

"Steve, Steve everyone's left us everyone's left us" he kept saying. I told Paul to calm down and that I'd ring Jimmy 'Five Bellies' to go and see him. I rang Jimmy but Jimmy was at work in a bar and couldn't go to his best mate's aid. Jimmy did tell me though that he'd give Paul a ring to put his mind at rest so I thought that was that. Later on that night I was in Cramlington with Joe Allon doing the football talk-in and I was also working with John Beresford and Kevin Ball. At the interval we went into the bar where everyone was having their pie & peas when across the room on Sky Sports News on a large screen it read, 'Gazza has arrived in Rothbury to visit Raoul Moat' well you could have knocked me down with a feather. I turned to Joe and said, "I can't believe it because he was asking me about Raoul this afternoon." The event that I had planned for Paul was set for the October and the Raoul Moat incident happened in the July of 2010. About one week before Paul's night his agent rang me to tell me he'd fallen off the wagon spectacularly and told me we'd be lucky if Gazza made the night at all because he was in such a state. By now Paul and Jimmy 'Five Bellies' had had their falling out so he was now off the show and it was just Paul or what was left of him. It was obvious because it was all over the media, what had happened with Gazza and the show had a few cancellations tickets wise. His agent eventually told me not to cancel it and said we'd play it by ear and that's what happened. With two days to go I got a call from Paul's councillor in Bournemouth to say he'll 100% be there and his councillor will be escorting him. Paul turned up on the night and he did the best show I've ever seen him do in his homeplace of Dunston. Sadly, Paul fell out with his agent because we had in the small print written in the contract that if ticket sales had been affected by Paul's behaviour then there would have to be a deduction in Paul's fee. It turns out Paul's agent hadn't told him so when Gazza was paid, he wasn't best pleased. From our perspective we did the right thing to cover us but that's when I got a bit of stick off Gazza saying we'd ripped him off but it was all above board. After all that I've seen Paul, been there for him and been on the phone to him constantly at times when he was at his lowest. When I was on the door, I would often get phone calls from other doorman saying, your mates in can you come and pick him up? Even though I don't drive I've gone and had him picked up when nobody else would or I've had taxi's picking him up. By god I've had some comical moments with him though like when he was staying at Freddie Shepherds apartments and he'd lost his key fob so I've had to give him a hog up. We must have looked like two burglars. One time he had to stand on the wheelie bin and he'd had to climb in through the window.

I've always been there for Paul so when he attacked me on social media it was a real kick in the balls. Although I believe karma will get you in the end, I also believe that if you do a good turn for somebody then it comes back. The reason Paul personally attacked me I believe was because I had announced a show with Peter Beardsley and Paul Gascoigne in 2017. The show was again at The Lancastrian Suite and it was a sell-out, then I'd had yet another dreaded call from Paul's agent revealing that he'd fallen off the wagon and he definitely wouldn't be doing any show. I cancelled Paul but what I didn't want to do is cancel Peter so I let everybody know Gazza was off and that we'd refund 50% of the tickets. We must have lost around fifty sales but the night still went ahead. You know by now that I'm a man who doesn't like to be beaten, I still wanted to do Peter and Paul together so I went for it the following year at the same place. Again, it sold out and I got another phone call, you know what's coming next don't you, the call said Paul wasn't in a great place. Now I never received the news this time from his agent it was a close friend of Paul's. The agent was quite the opposite and, in my opinion, he was bothered more about making money. The agent then told me quite bluntly that he wasn't wanting to pull Paul off the show and that he'd be there. From there I had a feeling what to expect so I told Peter Beardsley to brace himself and sure enough the inevitable happened. Paul turned up and he was very drunk and there was a suspicion that he was under the influence of other substances too. I knew I wasn't going to get the best out of Paul. I suppose it was a good job I was tipped off because I knew what to expect. The sensible thing I did was to invite one of Paul's best friends who used to be a policeman and who Paul trusted implicitly as my guest to support him. I can't deny or paper over the cracks about that evening and it has been well covered in the media. The whole night was a car crash and Paul wasn't even coherent enough to have been on the stage in the first place. Paul unbelievably got through the photographs and from my perspective we got there in the end. I received a lot of criticism over the whole episode but ultimately as a promoter what was I supposed to do in that predicament? Look, Paul Gascoigne has to make money and doing that is the only way he can earn a legitimate honest living. People have said to me that I was using someone who was mentally ill and an addict to make a profit but that's Gazza's only way. The fact of the matter is sometimes you get him on a good day and sometimes it ends like that I'm afraid. It was after that night that Paul had a go at me via Twitter. I immediately complained to his agent as a matter of urgency saying it needed to be removed because it was damaging to me, my brand and I'd done nothing wrong. What I will say is some of the things that happened on that night have never come to light and never will. What needs to be remembered is that I'm only doing my job. I love Paul Gascoigne a lot because I've never forgotten what he did for me when I was a young football crazy lad. I've got a lot of time for him and I always hope he can stay fit and well and that he can battle and be victorious over his demons. I'll always be there for him but would I ever manage him? Then no has to be my honest answer.

Regarding many other people I've met doing the sporting nights I could fill a book on that subject alone. Everybody's favourite Geordie Alan Shearer I have to mention because he's one top guy and he's great at doing events. He's arguably Newcastle's greatest ever player. I've also gotten to know Alan and had a lot of good times with him over the last decade. I've done the most events with Alan in the North East and even raised £54,000 for his charity when I staged Newcastle Legends against Manchester Legends at Kingston Park.

Peter Beardsley was my hero so to start and do events with Peter was special for me. Peter at first did a lot of work with one of my fellow promoters so I dare say it took me that bit extra to win his trust. I have a lot of time for Peter and he has some great stories about his fantastic career. In 2019 I managed to do an evening with Peter, Kevin Keegan, Chris Waddle and Terry McDermott, I was like a kid again walking into St James' Park for the first time with my Grandad Green in 1984. I think I must have done 'an evening with' with the full squad of 'The Entertainers' now. Tino Asprilla is one of my favourites. I've had more nights out with Tino than business project meetings. Tino isn't a money grabber, if he comes across to Newcastle then it's for the craic. Tino is loved in Newcastle and when he first arrived in Tyneside

1996, he arrived wearing this great big pimp looking coat. We actually managed to sell that iconic coat for £2,000 on the promise that whoever was buying the coat had to have Tino at their home for tea, which he did. Tino ended up going for tea in the posh end of Newcastle, Darras Hall. In the end me, Tino and his translator went along for some tea. The buyers ended up getting the coat framed and signed. It's sad because the two charity games we had with Manchester United and Liverpool that were a few years apart he came over but he couldn't kick a football anymore. Tino struggles playing but I'm happy to say is still the life and soul of the party. I must say he still has horrendous fashion sense.

David Ginola wasn't keen at first to do 'An Evening With' but I did manage to persuade him to do it. David gave up his own time to go around the children's wards at the local hospital which wasn't even in his contract so that just shows the measure of the man for me.

Les Ferdinand I have to say I personally love. Les was the No.9 before Shearer but he's just a thoroughly lovely man who could never do enough for me. Les has a massive affiliation with the area.

For a brief spell I got involved in the Darts world with Danny Cox and we put on some great exhibition matches in England and Scotland involving players such as Phil 'The Power' Taylor, Adrian Lewis, and Raymond Van Barneveld. I had a trip to Finland too for a tournament when I was briefly involved with the Scandinavian Darts Corporation.

It isn't only sporting figures I've been involved with. I've dabbled in music too. I did security for Robbie Williams, JLS, Peter Andre and Jordan to name a few. I also minded stars such as Keith Lemon, Johnny Vegas, Joe Brand and Sir Michael Parkinson. I have also worked and promoted two of the biggest names in the SAS Chris Ryan and Andy McNab.

I really had fun managing a local indie band named The Longsands. They started coming into Tiger Tiger playing acoustic when I was the head doorman and I loved their music. I asked the singer how they weren't getting anywhere because their music was tremendous. To cut a long story short the guys got messed around by a few managers and they came to me and asked if I would be interested in managing them? I give it a go putting the full Steve Wraith PR train behind them. I'd learnt a lot about promoting myself and we got along well together.

Together we raised their profile massively by using my connections. I got 'Mr Nice' Howard Marks to do a video for them as well as getting them onto the hallowed turf of St James' Park just before we beat our beloved rivals Sunderland 5-1 on Halloween. The Longsands played on the pitch in front of 52,000 fans singing their own version of The Blaydon Races for the teams to come out to. Together we released not one but two hit albums. It was through my connection with The Longsands that I got to meet other bands such as 'From The Jam' which included Bruce Foxton who I had mimicked as a kid and Rick Buckler. They loved The Longsands and invited them on tour. From there they were involved with Ocean Colour Scene who took them on a tour too and it was soon building and building. Getting them on Radio 2 with Bob Harris for forty-five minutes was an all-time high for the band. When The Longsands split I'd already set up a relationship with the 02 Academy so it was great for me moving forward. I think my greatest PR stunt for The Longsands was when I got Mike Tyson to have a game of conkers with Trevor Cox from the band and the press filmed it. Trevor came up with the idea. The Longsands from Cramlington meeting Mike Tyson isn't a big story but The Longsands having a game of conkers with Mike Tyson is. It was my job to convince Mike Tyson that not only does he have to pose for snaps with fans and do a talk but now it's in the small print that he has to have a game of conkers. It's on the internet still to this day and we all made money from the newspapers with that silly story. We even had press from New Zealand and Japan wanting to cover the story, it went global. That story alone led to other things like going to other bands houses doing challenges. The Longsands followed that up with a trip to Ricky Hatton's house to play a game of darts. The band also had an egg and spoon race against the Ashes winning cricketer Steve Harmison on a beach. Another member took on former Celtic player Frank McAvennie in a mini-golf game, the team had a game of 'British Bulldog' against the Newcastle Falcons rugby team and we filmed them all.

The band got some marvellous publicity from those things. Another good bit of PR for the band saw us emulate the Sex Pistols infamous boat trip down the Thames where they played live on deck before being pulled over by the police and arrested. I mentioned the idea of hiring a boat and going down the Tyne to the lads Ian, Gaz, Paul, Trev and Stan and they laughed at first. Once they realised I was being serious they started looking into the practicalities. Ian's brother Alistair said we could make it work and I set about booking a boat through 'Riverside Cruises.' We booked a couple of guest speakers for the trip too like former ICF hooligans and now authors Carlton Leach and Cass Pennant and the tickets sold out in no time. The only thing we could not book was the weather but we could not have asked for a better day. A few of my good mates including Dave Beaney, Danny Coggins, 'Singe' and Neil Jackson came along too and it was a great buzz seeing tourists photographing the lads from the quayside as they belted out their greatest hits. I'm pleased to say the police didn't arrest us that day but I had achieved another dream and got the band a bit more recognition.

Over the years I've worked with other names such as Big Country, The Farm (who got me on stage to sing Altogether Now), Glen Matlock, Bad Manners, Toyah, Hugh & Cry,

T'Pau and I've even brought QFX back in 2020 but this time to a venue that was a bit bigger than that function room at the Portland in 1995. I have interviewed a few of my heroes too such as Rick Buckler and Bruce Foxton from the Jam and the legendary manager of 'Oasis' Alan McGee who has become a good friend.

I have really enjoyed the challenges I have set myself and despite all the hard work that goes into putting these nights on I have had time to enjoy some of them.

31

Are You 'Steve Raff'

I have always lived with the philosophy on the door that if someone says they're going to do something to me then nine times out of ten it's not going to happen. I forget how many times I have been told that people were coming to shoot me but it never happened. It's the quiet ones you have to be concerned about.

Whenever I've heard people with serious reputations have wanted a word with me it's been easily sorted out. This is because it's usually caused by someone else stirring the pot. One night I was working on a door in Newcastle and the company who I was working for lumbered me with someone they were desperate to get rid of. This guy had a lot of experience working the doors, far more than me, so right away he wasn't happy that he was working under my supervision. You can see where this story's going can't you!? This guy felt belittled, I could see his point, I'd have been put out if it had been the other way around but it was nothing to do with me. This guy used to be the head doorman at his other place so he didn't like being off the front entrance, so when I asked him to go check one of the other entrances he came out with, "Who are you to tell me what to do?" The only thing I could respond with was, "I'm the Head Doorman and in charge of you for the evening!" As soon as I said that the guys pushed me but as he's done that the manager of the premises came out and witnessed the full thing. I'm sure the company only put him on my door for the night so he'd lose his temper and they could get rid of him. The manager said he wasn't having this on his premises and sent the guy home straight away. He asked me what had happened but I didn't really need to explain as he had seen the whole incident. I then had the bosses of the company coming to pay me a visit wanting me to make a statement. By then I knew what was going on and I told them I wasn't happy because I knew I was being used to create his exit strategy and I wasn't comfortable with it at all. I was then told that if I didn't make a statement, I could lose my job. In the end I put a statement in but I insisted that I would work with the guy moving forward at any venue. I made it clear I had no issue with the guy. I had to go to his hearing but it didn't make any difference because the guy got binned. When the guy got the sack, he blamed me, unbelievably he said it was all my fault. The guy then went to work at another club in the city ran by another security company. The guy who runs that company lives down South but he was seriously heavy duty and when he was mis-informed as to why this doorman had lost his last job, he labelled me a grass. It doesn't take a scientist to work out what was going to happen. Now fast forward a year and I'm on a night out in the city with a well-known family and the family who I was with insisted we all go to the club.

Unbeknown to my company and unbeknown to me this particular trouble causing doorman is working at this club. As we all approach the door out comes my old mate. As soon as the guy spots me, he says, "He's not getting in" whilst pointing at me. Now the family who I was with on that evening don't take no for an answer which puts me in a right predicament. The bouncer wouldn't budge with his decision and the family who I'm with say, "If you've got a problem with him you've got a problem with us!" In the end I just said its ok I'll go home, but my friends from this well-known Tyneside family said, "No, no, no, you're not going home or anywhere else, you're going in" and I was forced in. The outcome was that I went in but I had the most uncomfortable evening ever. I've never been so paranoid sitting in a venue as I was that night. Truth be told really, I was fine in the premises because of who I was with but it was after that the real problems began.

A few days later I received numerous phone calls from this heavy-duty character and he was seriously pissed off. "Are you Steve Raff..." he said as he went into one before he hung up. He was annoyed because he thought I had turned up with members of this well-known Newcastle family on purpose to gloat which wasn't the case, I didn't even know he worked in there. After a few threats from the security boss by phone I turned my phone off and made a cup of tea, Winston Churchill said a cup of tea makes everything better. I'm drinking my cup of tea by now and I'm giving it some serious thought about what I should do? I rang the people who I was out with on that particular night and their advice was to just invite this heavy-duty boss up to Newcastle for obvious reasons. I thought I cannot do that; violence won't solve this and that's not me. I don't want to be in this situation in the first place let alone make it worse and start an all-out war. Again, fast forward six months and I thought it had all blown over. I know where the bouncer works so I'm going to stay away from his door.

I went to this charity event down south for two well-known gangsters, one had died and one was on the way out so it was for his family, everyone was suited and booted and there were some seriously big heavy lads there you wouldn't want to mess with. Then as the night was going great and we were watching a tribute video I felt a tug from behind, when I turned around there was this gentleman stood behind me and he said, "Are you Steve Raff"? to which I replied "No". Again, he glared then once again repeated, "Are you Steve Raff because it says you are in the programme?" Then it hit me, I'd forgotten I'd done a little piece in the programme and there was a picture of me to go with it. I said, "Look my names Steve Wraith not Steve Raff at least get my name right please!" As soon as I said that he tried to go for me but all the security had clocked the tension which was building up from him and they asked him to leave. At that time, I had no idea what was going on but at the same time I was trying to think of where I'd been called Steve Raff before then it clicked. It was all beginning to make sense. This guy was the heavy-duty security boss and I couldn't believe it. I was that puzzled I'd actually deduced that it could be one of the QPR fans who were annoyed I'd jumped rows of seats to avoid a beating from them. I didn't have any idea. By this time Dave Courtney and Joe Pyle Jnr had seen what was going on so they've come straight over to ask if I was ok. Well the penny dropped when those two explained to me that heavy duty guy was seriously fucking heavy duty and what in the name on god's green earth had I done to upset such a man? I told Dave I honestly hadn't a fucking clue. At that precise moment I had no knowledge of who he was so I wasn't lying. That was until Dave told me that heavy duty guy did security and looked after a chain of clubs up and down the country. Well in that chain there was one club only that he looked after in Newcastle and that is when I suddenly put it together like an episode of Taggart. Now I was faced with the problem of rectifying the whole messy affair.

A few days later it had all blown over until on the fourth day and my phone rings and again I'm being called 'Steve Raff'. Not only was it heavy duty guy but its heavy-duty guy telling me he's driven to Newcastle and he knows where I live. Well there is only one thing to do in an intense situation like that and that was to follow Sir Winston Churchill's advice and make a cup of tea. As I sat drinking my magic cup of tea, which supposedly makes everything better, I knew I was faced with another slight problem, the person who I was with in the club in Newcastle when bouncer guy wouldn't let us in was locked up. I could have rung him because he knew the full story so he could have explained to heavy duty guy because this fella who I was with was a face so heavy-duty guy would have taken his account into hand and respected his word. I knew there was one more person I could ring who was also there that night and a bit of a face but the only problem was he was usually stoned by this time of night. 'Fuck it' I thought, in desperate times it leads to desperate measures so I rang the other person who I was with that night and you guessed it he was that stoned he couldn't even think straight let alone move. After a bit of hard work of talking to my stoned buddy he did remember the whole story of what went on but said that was ages ago. He told me he knew what to do and he'd ring me back in twenty minutes. I tried to point out that this guy was on his way to see me now so the situation required a little bit of urgency. Then my stoned mate rings us back and says, "Right my heads clear so this is what we're going to do" then he told me in detail what his meticulous plan was to hasten what may have been my sad decline. My stoned mate had rung heavy duty guy and told him what really went on, he then told me that I had to call heavy duty guy myself to give my side which I did. To cut a long story short the full episode was put to bed without one drop of my blood being spilt which is always a bonus. Not only that, but heavy-duty guy offered me a chance to meet him that night for a night out to put the past behind us. Now he knew the complete story he knew it was all a misunderstanding. He told me he was prepared to accept my word and that my good (stoned) mate had vouched for me. He told me that now he'd heard the proper story it all made sense. I put the phone down, breathed a sigh of relief and stuck the kettle on again.

32

Llambias

Derek Llambias was the chief executive at Newcastle for a period of time. He resigned on June 19th 2013 after a five-year reign. When Derek came in, to be fair he tried at first to ingratiate himself with the supporters. Derek worked alongside Lee Charnley who's now managing director at the time of writing and John Irving who was in charge of the financial side of things. The three of them worked together as a team behind the scenes. At first, they gave away free tickets in the VIP section to introduce themselves to certain fans who ran fanzines or high-profile groups or websites. They did this to try and influence supporters, I was one of them and I was chosen because I was doing the very first Newcastle United podcast called Toon Talk. I would broadcast once a week from my home. Llambias invited me along with Steve Hastie from NUFC Fans United. My first invite was to go along to a game in The Sir Bobby Robson Suite in the corporate area where you would get free food and drink before watching the match in the director's box. At first with Llambias it was all small talk, he was sussing us out. He said all the right things. Asking how can we make the match day experience better for fans and telling us that communication with the fans was the key and they got that. I didn't speak to him a lot. I was much more interested in listening to him for obvious reasons. My first impressions were that I didn't particularly trust him or believe what he was saying although I couldn't put a finger on why I felt that way. After listening to him that night I felt it was a waste of time for supporters. I felt whatever we said or did it would not matter and that it was simply a tick box exercise. Steve Hastie and the other fanzine editors came to the same conclusion as myself.

I knew the ship at St James Park was about to hit rocky ground. Under Ashley and Llambias people have been constantly unhappy with the way the club has been run i.e. lack of investment in players etc... and if we did find a player half decent then it seemed like the club was only interested in bigging that player up so we could sell him to make a profit, our club shouldn't have been about that. It never seemed to come into it that perhaps we should have been keeping hold of those great players to build a team around them for us to try and get somewhere. In mine and the majority of others opinion it was all just about getting the turnover and promoting his sports brand globally. All Newcastle fans wanted was a bit of hope and maybe a chance of a little bit of success like any other football fan but under the Ashley/Llambias cloud we felt like all hope had been removed. We were stuck in limbo and Llambias was a big part of the problem. Before Llambias arrived at our club in 2008 we knew very little about him. I did a bit of research and I found out that he was a casino owner and with Mike Ashley's love of gambling you can only presume that's how the two met, although I could be wrong.

When the fans first turned on Ashley/Llambias the fans held banners saying, "GO HOME COCKNEY MAFIA" the straw that broke the fans' backs was bringing another Cockney, Dennis Wise, in above Kevin Keegan who ended up leaving the club and winning a huge pay-out at a tribunal. The London press had a field day saying that we hated cockneys!

It couldn't be further from the truth. Some of our best ever players have been Cockneys, Rob Lee, Warren Barton, Les Ferdinand and Gavin Peacock to name a few. Our fans were never anti-Cockney we were anti-Ashley/Llambias.

When we were relegated in 2009, we bounced straight back up the following year. The key players in bringing us straight back up were Joey Barton, Steve Harper, Alan Smith and Kevin Nolan. I became good friends with Kevin and his Father. It was Kevin Nolan who invited me to the promotion party at The Diamond Inn, Ponteland near the airport. It's in the posh affluent part of our city. I invited along a few of my close pals. We got there early and headed upstairs to the function room. We were first there so I bought the first round. Within twenty minutes the place was jumping with Newcastle United players along with all the backroom staff. Chris Hughton the manager then came in with The Championship trophy.

The trophy was then put at the back of the room for people to get their photo taken with it, everyone was in a great mood. Mike Ashley then walks in with Derek Llambias. He went straight up to the barmaid and handed her his credit card, "Tonight's on me" he said. The lads burst out laughing realising that I was the only one who would be buying a round that night.

It really was a cracking night and the best night I've ever had in the company of Newcastle United's players. There was around two hundred people there and the night lasted from 7pm to gone midnight so can you imagine how much Mike Ashley spent that night! Mike must have spent easily the wrong side of five grand which is peanuts to him.

When we got our hands on the Championship trophy me and my pals unscrewed the top of it, signed a bit of paper and stuck it in the top of the trophy with the date and our names on making our own Geordie time capsule. In 100 years time someone will open it and go 'who the hell is Steve Wraith, Chris Liddle and Dom Clauzel!' That night was great for a number of reasons and one of them was Joey Barton. He got up to sing Deacon Blue's Dignity. It was the song that the team played before every game because they knew they'd let the fans down the season before with the relegation. Joey getting up and blasting out Dignity was a hair standing up on the back of your neck moment. Joey also sang Geordie Alouette which is a hilarious Geordie song. Joey was the star of the show that night.

About half-nine there was a little break in proceedings where all the food was brought out, things like curry and rice so it was time to take a break from the entertainment. It was at that moment that I saw Mike Ashley standing alone at the bar which was unusual because him and Llambias had been inseparable all night. I'd had a couple of drinks so I thought I'd introduce myself to Mike and off I went. I told him I'd been a bit of a critic of his over the years but I wanted to shake his hand and say congratulations on promotion. I also asked him what his plans were for the future. To my recollection Mike thanked me very much for my honesty and then he told me he ran the football club like a business. He said he wasn't there on a day to day basis he left that to Llambias. He said at the start of the season he'd have a look at the team then would decide where he could improve.

Mike Ashley is clearly an intelligent man and a good business man but, in my opinion, not when it comes to owning and running a football club. Llambias reappeared like Count Dracula at midnight in a puff of smoke and he wasn't looking very happy because I'm talking to Mike. He then intervened and said, "Steve, Steve this isn't the time for this" in an extremely rude manner. When Mike was talking to me, he'd been tucking into a chicken curry but as he'd been eating, I watched Mike spit out this bit of grizzle and stick it on the side of his plate. As Derek came back, I noticed he picked up the wrong plate, which had been Mike Ashley's and he started eating this bit of crap that Mike Ashley had spat out which was funny to watch and of course I said nothing. I knew that Llambias was somebody that didn't like me and I was sure that we would clash again.

The following season we just ended up in the same situation again. We didn't get relegated but we continued the policy of buying cheap players from the continent. If they were a success then we shipped them out for a profit and repeated the process. It was soul destroying as a supporter. Ashley seemed happy to float above the relegation places in 16th or 17th in the Premier League and go out of the cups early. As long as we stayed up then he would get his TV money and free advertising for his brands. In the end I became a constant thorn in the sides of Ashley/Llambias especially on social media. Twitter is a vicious playground for NUFC supporters and if things are not going well at the club then it explodes with kneejerk reactions and opinions. We have all been guilty of it at times, maybe slating a player/s or ranting against the owner or having a pop at a journalist for daring to disagree with what we think. I was actually involved in a twitter spat with the club in 2012. I had heard a few stories from good sources at the club of player unrest so I tweeted: "Heard that the rumours of player unrest are allegedly true and that reluctance to buy has upset certain players," I then tweeted: "It's a shame because after last season we should be building on the success and we just haven't. It's all about saving money. As a club NUFC look set up for a fall again. Threadbare squad and alleged player unrest is a recipe for disaster."

Amazingly somebody at the club decided to attack me via the official account. It didn't take a genius to work out who it was…they tweeted "Here we are again, @stevewraith attempting to disrupt the club with unnecessary negative comment. Would have thought league success and a return to European football is worthy of positive comment. Trying to undermine the club's good work is a weak attempt to unsettle a positive, strong and spirited squad."

I really couldn't believe what I was seeing. The media soon picked up on it with Simon Bird running the story in the Daily Mirror. Another embarrassing moment for our owner and co.

After the twitter spat with the club, I started to realise how powerful social media is and I started becoming more and more active on there about the club.

The problem with Llambias is that he didn't understand that the club is the biggest thing in most people's lives in Tyneside and to some nothing else matters. Over the years things moved on and several managers chopped and changed. We even ended up with Alan Pardew (another Cockney) as boss. If Alan Pardew was chocolate, he would have eaten himself although I didn't campaign to get Pardew out. Pardew was the ideal manager for Mike Ashley because he was a yes man. There's a fact that can't be ignored and that is that Pardew was the last manager to get us into Europe which meant he was Ashley's most successful under his awful reign. During Alan Pardew's time at the club he did a special Q & A with John Carver and Derek Llambias in the Moncur Suite at St James' Park. I got a phone call from my mate John Harvey to ask if I'd like to go along to St James Park. I told John I'd come but I didn't think I'd get in because certain people at the club didn't like me. I told him that if they saw Steve Wraith there they'd panic. John said I should go because he knew I'd ask a sensible question. I reassured John that I'd be there as long as he put me on the list.

If they know I'm going at least Llambias & Co have got the opportunity to say no before I turn up.

I turned up at this function all suited and booted and many different people came up to me shaking my hand, many businessmen who've been to many of my events and it looks like I'm in for a good day. Five minutes before its due to start Alan Pardew and John Carver walk in, John actually stops to shake my hand and off he pops to take a seat. Then Llambias walks in and looks at me then walks off, only to stop and turn around to see if his eyes are telling him the truth that he's just seen me. It was like something from a Tom & Jerry cartoon. As soon as I could see

Llambias staring over I could see the cogs in his mind think, 'what the fuck is Steve Wraith doing in here?' It was as if he'd just seen the anti-Christ and all the colour from his face poured out of him within seconds. I could see Derek had marched over to Sharon the Corporate manager and I could lip read him saying, "What's Steve Wraith doing here"? I'm just sat smiling but thinking, 'I know what's coming'! I asked my mate John who had invited me if he had seen Derek's reaction and he said he had. Rob Armstrong also looked over to me and nodded his head in acknowledgement that he'd seen it too. It looked like Derek had tried to get Sharon to hoy me out but she wouldn't so if he wanted me out, he was going to have to do it himself. Llambias then marches over with a face full of thunder and he blurts out, "What are you doing here?" I told him that I was a guest of one of his corporate clients.

"Can I have a word with you?" Which sounded more like a demand rather than a question. I moved to one side and again he says, "NO, what are you doing here?" I told him again that I was a guest of one of his clients but then he came out with, "You shouldn't be in here" and I just said 'ok'. Then he says to me, "You'll never be corporate" as if I was some kind of poor boy like Oliver Twist standing there with no shoes on. I then asked him if he was asking me to leave and he confirmed he was. 'Ok Derek' I said and I put my hand out but he wouldn't shake my hand and I just calmly walked out. As I walked out loads of people had just witnessed what had happened because Llambias made it some big altercation even though I remained calm and polite. As I walked out Lee Charnley and John Irving were walking in and I just said "See ya lads" and I was off. I've never commented on it before today but of course Twitter did its thing as people had seen it with their own eyes. All he achieved was to embarrass himself and the club because it went wild on social media with tweets such as 'Steve Wraith's been kicked out from the football club' etc. I never had any further discussions with Llambias after that until he left in the summer of 2013. There's no doubt that Derek kicking me out backfired on him big time because of the backlash that followed.

My final run in with Llambias was a strange one. One day I got a phone call from Sir John Hall, the former owner of Newcastle. Sir John has become a good friend of mine along with other members of the Magpie Group such as Malcolm Dix and John Waugh. When he owned the club, we clashed a few times on TV and Radio but he always respected my views and could understand my passion.

"Steve I've got some gates you might be interested in"? I asked him what gates they were and he told me that when the ground got redeveloped in the 1990s, there were some gates at The Gallowgate end. I said, "The old St James Park gates?" He confirmed it. Then he told me, "I've just found the buggers" like it was a set of car keys (laughs). When I asked him where he had found them, he told me that they were in a field in Wynyard and asked if I wanted them? Sir John went on to say that he felt awful because he accused Freddie Shepherd of taking them and getting them melted down for scrap because Freddie was in the scrap metal game. Freddie went to his grave denying it in reality Sir John had just misplaced them.

"Anyway, Steve are these gates any good for you?" he asked. I told Sir John to leave it with me and let me speak with a couple of people. Bearing in mind I'm at loggerheads with the club and this wasn't long after I'd just done the coffin walk which backfired massively, I'll tell you more about that in the next chapter. Well now I'd had another brain-stormer thinking that if I could get these gates reinstated at the ground it would be a statement because these gates symbolise everything that was once good about Newcastle United. Ashley had just renamed the stadium at this time to so what better statement could fans make then to place some gates outside the ground with the name St

James' Park on them. If I could get permission from the council it would be great for the fans. I flung the idea around with Steve Hastie, Neil Mitchell, Zhara Zomorrodian and Bill Corcoran from the nearby Irish Centre.

Graeme Cansdale from 'Mike Ashley Out' was also involved and we started looking at how much it would cost to get these great big gates picked up and cleaned because they had been lying in a field for some time. The cost of moving and renovating the gates (6k) was ridiculous due to the size and weight of them but we had a few irons in the fire and were going to approach local businesses and start a crowd funding page.

Somebody somewhere leaked this information to my sparring partner Llambias and he wasn't happy. He thought that the gates were the club's possession and he wanted them back. After an exchange of letters backwards and forwards between Llambias and Sir John our former owner came up with a great plan. He betrothed the gates to me and the fans and told Llambias that he would now need to deal with us. I wish I had seen his face when he read that letter

Our plans of course had been to put the gates up across the road from the ground behind the Gallowgate as a form of protest towards the regime. The gates were to be open too so that fans could walk through them. We then hit another obstacle this time with the council who insisted we use their surveyors and contractors due to health and safety issues regarding insurance should the gates collapse on any one moving forward.

John Irving from the club, unaware of the issues we were having contacted a few of the others involved and we agreed that they should go and meet with the club to discuss our plans for the gates. I decided not to go on this occasion. If the truth be told I wasn't keen on the club being involved in the project. The outcome of the meeting saw them offer to take on the job and refurbish them and have them positioned. It wasn't what we had set out to achieve.

Our aim had been to have the gates open and adjacent to where the Alder Sweeney memorial now sits. In the end the gates were put up against a wall on Barrack Road with a plaque which said that the gates were a symbol of the club working with fans! They were up against a brick wall which we felt as if we had been banging our heads against since Ashley took over so I can see their point. If anything sums up Ashley's time at our club then it is the positioning of those gates....

Prior to Llambias leaving the club in 2013 Steve Harper asked me to arrange his benefit match. The club weren't going to give him a testimonial so myself and Ashes legend and Newcastle Fan Steve Harmison wrote letters to the club to put the pressure on asking for them to change their mind. It also seemed that the club had very few contact details for any ex-players because under this regime they had tried to eradicate the past and had fallen out with many legends.

Despite protests by Llambias and others Steve stuck to his guns and allowed me to be involved and we pulled in an all-star team that night to face an AC Milan squad. We raised over £300,000 as over 51,000 packed into St James' park to see the likes of Shearer, Ferdinand, Cole, Pavel, and Tino don the shirt at the ground for the last time. The lads invited me into the changing room that night which is something I will never forget.

My relationship never recovered with the club after that. They chose to snub me when they unveiled the plaque for the late great Joe Harvey at the Gallowgate End which I had actively helped raise money for with a big event at the Lancastrian Suite in Dunston called the 'Mackem Slayers' that featured derby day heroes. I co-promoted the event with Danny Cox and handed the Fairs Club a donation of £5000 towards the £10k costs of making the tribute.

Bill Gibson from the Fairs Club wanted to invite me to the unveiling and drinks reception but was told by club officials that I would not be welcome. I still took a walk up to the ground to see Bob Moncur and John Gibson pull the cord. I was proud to have been involved.

33

The Truth Behind The 'Infamous' Funeral March

In my lifetime, and not just with Mike Ashley, I would say there's always been a battle against the owners of the club. Going back to when Stan Seymour Jnr was at the club our fans used to call it, "The family silver" we had the reputation of not spending money on new players and that we were a selling club. When you fast forward a bit to Gordon McKeag it was the same. With McKeag there was a huge campaign to get him out as well. Then Sir John Hall came in with the Magpie group and took over the club. Saying that, when Sir John was at the helm, we had the best team in our club's history as we had a devastating attacking side which could ravage any defence in Europe with Kevin Keegan in the managers dugout.

We were runners up twice for the Premiership title in '96 and '97 and were losing FA Cup finalists in the nineties too but like everything in life what goes up must come down.

I would say that from the early noughties after Sir Bobby was sacked Newcastle United has been on the decline. Because of that the infighting amongst supporters has become common place as people share their views on various platforms. First it was fanzines and message boards. Now it's social media. In my time as a supporter I have lost count of the different fan groups that have come and gone. United Supporters For Change, NUFC Fans United, NUSC (Newcastle United Supporters Club), and of course NUST (Newcastle United Supporters Trust) are a few that spring to mind. Then there's the Twitter accounts who think they have influence because they have 500 followers and are getting 20 likes on each post. We actually have the most loyal, passionate, intelligent fans, but try to lead them or advise them? Well as the Geordie Dentist AKA Neil Mitchell said 'It's like herding cats.'

Getting back to the groups. Firstly, United Supporters For Change in the late eighties and early nineties were well organised and did exactly what it said on the tin. They helped change the club by protest which led to McKeag and the board selling their shares to Sir John Hall and the Magpie Group.

The Newcastle United Supporters Club was set up in the early 2000s. I actually went along to their first meeting at the Tyneside Irish Centre with 300 other likeminded souls. I didn't want to be part of it but I was happy to support it. Some of the people behind that supporters' group were running other fanzines and none of them particularly liked me although they would always say hello to my face. Quite often I would hear the things this group of people were saying behind my back. I never quite understood the animosity maybe they thought I was trying to get involved and takeover but I can assure you I wasn't. They never really made any major waves but the interest shown in this group was to lead to a more powerful entity.

The Supporters Trust spawned from NUSC and as an organisation has more power as the club has a duty to meet with a Supporters trust. I had some good friends involved in the Trust at the start but infighting again saw those people stand down. There were question marks over the financials with the trust and accusations levelled at key individuals behind the scenes. They eventually got their house in order and I sat on the committee in 2018-19 season.

NUFC Fans Utd was the splinter group set up by those who had left the trust. The brainchild of three good friends of mine Neil, Zhara and Steve. The idea behind that group was very simple. There would be a meeting once a month at the Irish Centre and all fans groups and fanzines would be invited to meet up over a pint and discuss matters that fans wanted to raise that month with the club. It would be an umbrella group that would simply communicate with the club.

People turned up that night from 'True Faith' and 'Mike Ashley Out' and other groups of a similar nature. The atmosphere was quite tense because of various fallouts with certain strong opinionated characters in the room who, to put it mildly, didn't get on. The meeting was chaired by Steve Hastie who spelt out what he wanted everybody to do. Steve said he wanted us all to meet once a month and that if anyone had any issues with any other supporters kicking off with each other than we should settle it here and now. Steve's meeting was a good chance for the baying blood thirsty crowd to get their views across in a civilised manner and if anything needed carrying over to the football club then this was our chance. Of course, with things like this you're not always going to get everyone agreeing and that's what happened. I liked the idea of NUFC Fans United because there were no roles and no governors, but it was clear that others did not share my enthusiasm. Despite the negativity over the years a lot of good things have spawned from that group. We were involved in the campaign for 'Safe Standing' and myself along with Steve Hastie held a demonstration of 'rail seating' in 'Number Nine' bar which club officials and the press attended. The Newcastle United Foodbank initiative was also set up by the likes of Steve alongside Bill Corcoran and Colin Whittle.

The Mike Ashley Out group were a good bunch of lads. Very covert to start with but once they broke cover, I got on well with them. Their focus of course was to get the owner out of the club by any means necessary and if they had to use unorthodox techniques then so be it. Several ideas were thrown around at these monthly meetings of NUFC

Fans United and one of them was that we should do a funeral march outside St James' Park. This had been done at previous clubs many years ago and even abroad. Our beloved neighbours in Sunderland in 1973 when they beat Leeds United 1-0 in the F.A cup Final did a funeral march on the pitch to rub salt in the wound and say that Leeds Utd had died that day at Wembley. The longer the funeral march talks went on the more the NUFC Fans United members warmed to the idea. A coffin saying R.I.P on it would certainly get the headlines in 2012 which was exactly our aim.

Now I know a lot of people think that because I was the Reverend who led the march, I must have organised it but I didn't. Everybody thinks that it was another Steve Wraith PR stunt but I cannot take the plaudits I'm afraid. It was actually the 'Mike Ashley Out' groups idea and the NUFC Fans United group gave it their full backing. It was Graeme Cansdale who knew someone who worked in a funeral parlour so he arranged to borrow a coffin as well as organising the pall bearers. It was Steve Hastie who sorted the route with Northumbria police because he had to get permission for the march. Graeme Cansdale also wrote the speech which was then run past all our group members so everybody agreed it was ok. With a day to go before the protest the guy who was asked to do the vicars job pulled out so this is where I came into it for the first time. Nobody wanted to don the cassock so they came to me and asked if I would be interested in doing it, a few others piped up saying, "You're an actor Steve why don't you do it"? After a bit of persuasion, I said yes. I had been involved in pulling it all together so why not! I rang my friend Glyn who at the time was reverend at St Andrews as well as the club's resident clergyman and asked him if he could kit me out. He said he would as he supported what we were doing.

The following day we met up at the Strawberry Pub and at the agreed time set off from the pub with the coffin. I led the procession behind the Gallowgate then up Barrack Road. We did the march on a matchday so all the worlds media i.e. The Sun, The Star, The Mirror etc where there flashing their cameras. There were around 1,000 fans on the march itself and we made a hell of a lot of noise. I remember seeing the ex-Newcastle player Olivier Bernard walking past and he stopped and shook my hand, I even gave him a cheeky blessing. We stopped at the gates where I read out the prepared sermon in front of the world's media.

After the march myself, Graeme Cansdale and Steve Hastie all gave several interviews which turned out not to be just national, but global exposure for us. After the protest walk, I took my gear off and went into the match and thought nothing more about it. It wasn't until I came out of the game and I started checking social media that the circus show began, most of it hatred for me and everybody involved. We had done the march to highlight our annoyance at the way Ashley was running the club but fans were saying that we had embarrassed them.

Looking back today, I have to say yes it was a fabulous idea and it got us some huge exposure but it did backfire on us all. The coffin stunt was repeated by the Mike Ashley Out group and others when a pay day lender was revealed as our strip sponsor. Graeme Cansdale dressed up as 'Willy Wonga' and jumped out of the coffin. Of course, because Graeme and I look alike it was me who got slated on social media for embarrassing the fans again. I was nowhere near the march I was doing a talk in at 'The Number Nine Bar' with Joe Allon that day. Going back to the first march I actually got a message from Mike Ashley's sidekick Llambias which read, "Mike just wants to congratulate you on your protest today, you all did well". Was that tongue-in-check or was it because we rallied up so much PR he was tipping his hat and saying touché, I'll let you decide. What that taught me was that no amount of protesting was going to get rid of this man. He revelled in it because it was giving him free PR for his Sports Brand globally. I would never protest on the streets against Ashley again.

My relationship with Sir John Hall, Malcolm Dix, John Waugh and the rest of the 'Magpie Group' really grew from this period too. Malcolm invited me onto various committees. I joined 'Sport Newcastle' helping raise funds for up and coming sports stars in the North East, and became a trustee at the Tyne Theatre and Opera House. Over the years Sir John Hall has invited me to Wynyard Hall for special meetings with the Magpie Group where we have chewed the fat about the club. His passion is infectious and his knowledge in business second to none. I have a lot of respect for him. Our last get together was at Nine Bar at St James' where we raised vital funds for the Newcastle Foodbank where he met fans and spoke about his regret of selling the club to Mike Ashley, Hindsight is a wonderful thing.

34

Pavel Was a Geordie

Pavel Srnicek first came to Newcastle in 1991 when Jim Smith signed him. He was extremely raw and would wear tracksuit bottoms whilst playing. He was your typical continental keeper at the time, unpredictable, and always coming out of his box like a sweeper. Many fans would cover their eyes when a cross went into the box in case he flapped at it costing us a goal. With hard work and games, the big man improved though. He settled quickly on Tyneside with his family, made good friends and was an integral part of our promotion team in the 1992/93 season. Lee Clarks brother that day had knocked up a t-shirt for Pav to wear on the end of season lap of honour. It was the words of the song that the fans had been singing for him during the season. 'Pavel Is a Geordie.' A legend was born.

At first there wasn't any real connection with me and Pavel, I was just a supporter who loved watching him play and sang the song about him like everyone else. Like all of the team from that era of 1992 -97 I would get to know Pavel quite well. I was still working on the doors in Newcastle city centre in many of the bars which the players would frequent and I would look after them on their nights out. Pavel would always stop and speak to me and we got on well.

It was in 2007 when I started off doing the football talk in events with ex-player Joe Allon. I had been working on a North East football magazine called 'Players Inc' with him and Andrew Brewster which was a big success. At first, I was told the mag wouldn't be a success but as soon as anyone says that to me it makes me more determined to stick two fingers up and prove that I can make it work. I remember a guy going on Radio Newcastle from the mag 4-4-2 saying our project will never work but 20 odd issues later it was still selling. The mag was averaging around 1,000 copies a month which wasn't bad going. So, we decided to launch the events side of the business. Me and Joe managed to get ex-players from Newcastle, Sunderland, Middlesbrough, Hartlepool and Darlington to do regular columns in the magazine so it made sense to try and get the lads work on the after-dinner circuit. We even had the referee Dermott Gallagher doing bits too. our biggest signing was 'Melchester Rovers' Player Manager 'Roy Race'. I had contacted the company that owned the copyright for the fictional character and made them an offer to replicate the comic strip inside the magazine. The deal was done and we got worldwide publicity which saw me appear on 'BBC Breakfast' to talk about the deal.

Pavel left Newcastle in 1998 but did return for a short spell almost a decade later. Me and Pav got back in touch properly when I arranged an anniversary game in the October of 2011 between Newcastle United legends v Liverpool legends in a charity game at Kingston Rugby Park in Gosforth. Pavel played in goal and we got beaten 4-1. Tickets were £10 and £5 for children. We ended up with 10,000 people there and raised over £40,000 for several registered charities. The whole event turned out to be a massive success. For the last five minutes of the game Pavel came off and I played in goal for Newcastle. I have a great picture of me and Pavel cuddling when we're swapping shifts and we really became great friends from there. It was Kevin Keegan's last managerial job and I was his last sub! Makes a canny question when I'm doing a NUFC quiz!

After the game Pav and I exchanged numbers and I told him if he ever wanted to do any footballing functions then to give me a call. Pavel ended up calling me the following year which was 2012 to tell me he was coming home to Newcastle. On his first visit he said he wanted me to meet his close friends. Joe Allon and I met Pav at Osbournes in Jesmond. He introduced us to a guy named Dennis Martin who had looked after Pavel when he first arrived in the U.K. He was with another guy Lorenzo who ran a restaurant in Jesmond, also a close friend of Pav. I got on really well with them and everyone in Pavel's circle. Denis asked me if I'd be interested in helping Pavel get some work whilst he was in the UK. I didn't need to be asked twice.

After working on Players Inc for a few years I went my separate ways with Joe and Andrew. It was my decision. I just felt it was time to set up on my own. There weren't any fallouts as some have suggested between me and the guys. I told the lads there and then I would be setting my own company up. I told them if they wanted to continue to run the company that I was completely fine with that but I was going to leave. The lads in the end decided to disband the company. When I set up Wraith Promotions, I kept Andrew on as a designer and Joe on as a compere. I took advice off a good friend Andy Naylor who was great in PR and it was him who first told me that the name Steve Wraith was becoming a brand. He told me that although I couldn't see it, he could. He pushed me into calling the company Wraith Promotions although I wasn't too keen, at the time it worked and the public got used to hearing about Steve Wraith Promotions. I'd always been invited to events but I found that when I changed the name it led to me getting more invitations to dinner-dos and charity events. I was even getting more calls from local businesses from people wanting to book players.

In 2013 Pavel was visiting Newcastle again. We had a talk in booked at a local football club. Dennis picked us both up and drove us there. As we reached the venue and Pav got out of the car Dennis said that Pavel wanted to have a chat with me at some point.

The evening was a big success and as we headed out to the car Pavel asked me if I'd consider being his football agent. He said he had been thinking of asking me for some time and that Dennis agreed it was a good idea. I did not need asking twice. We met up at a café in Newcastle a couple of days later to sign the contract. John Gibson from the Evening Chronicle was there to witness the occasion and to interview Pav about his career.

Although he enjoyed doing the talk ins Pav in his heart of hearts wanted to come back to Newcastle United as a goalkeeping coach. He wanted to be able to live in the UK again so he would need work to be able to do that. So, I made a few calls to people I know in football fishing for jobs for Pav. I spoke with Jim Montgomery at Sunderland who was a good friend of Pav's to see if he knew of any vacancies. Pav was that desperate to be back in the North East that he'd have taken a job at Sunderland!

Working for Pav in the football world wasn't what I was used to at first. Yes, I could talk about football and watch football daily but this was a whole new ball game for me, pardon the pun. As my work for Pav progressed, I approached him with the idea of doing a book.

Pavel told me that it had crossed his mind although there were a few hurdles that were stopping him. I asked him what was worrying him and he said, "I don't think I'm popular enough Steve." Pav also then said that there's things in the book that he wouldn't be able to put in from his personal life i.e. his marriage separation which was obviously a very personal thing. Pavel told me if he did a book, he would have to touch on that so he wasn't so sure about the whole scenario. He had a few issues with Kevin Keegan too which he knew he would need to mention and he wasn't sure how that would go down with the fans.

I discussed with Pavel how it all worked and I introduced him to a journalist/writer named Bill Scott from The Northern Echo. On meeting Pav, Bill said he would be happy to write

Pav's book and would even travel to the Czech Republic so the deal was done. Bill would stay with Pavel for a week when Pav was working as a goalkeeping coach at Sparta Prague. The book was written and then published through my company Mojo Risin'. The book was released in December 2015 and Pav was heading home to launch it.

It will come as no surprise to fans to hear that Pav called Newcastle home. I had a full week of work for him with the likes of ITV, BBC, Sky Sports News, Radio Newcastle and Five Live all wanting interviews. Pav was on every single network talking about Newcastle and his time here and his new book 'Pavel is a Geordie.' At the end of the busy week we launched the book at a packed out 'Tyneside Irish Centre' and me, Pav, Bill Scott, Natalie Hubbard, Tom Sweeney, Lorenzo, Kev Drew and Dave Thorpe From the Back Page Shop and Dennis Martin all got together and went for a Chinese buffet meal. On that night, before he left, for some reason Pav wanted to walk up to St James Park just to look at the ground. So, we parked the car up and had a walk over so that Pavel could stare at the famous stadium. It was a dark night but I took a photo of Pavel stood outside the ground, unbeknown to us both that would be his last visit and the last photo at our ground.

After Pavel had been to see the stadium that evening, we all gave him a big hug and off he went. We were never to see Pavel alive again. Days later I was to receive a phone call from his friend Dennis and he sounded distraught. Dennis had called to tell me that Pavel had collapsed back home in the Czech Republic. Dennis said he didn't know the full story; it was difficult to get details. It turned out that Pavel had gone out for a run but collapsed not far from his home. As more details circulated it came out that he was only 800 yards from his home but also only 800 yards from the hospital. It was minus 10 the moment Pavel fell to his knees clutching his chest just 200 yards from his mother's house. It's said he was found approximately 20 minutes after he collapsed which is a tragedy considering it was broad daylight and he was that close to a busy hospital. He could have possibly been saved if he was found sooner. Pav fell into a coma. It's unexplainable that a man who was only 47 years old and who was as fit as he was could die like that. The guy didn't really drink or smoke and wasn't into drugs. Pav was still very active as a goalkeeping coach at Sparta Prague so he was still training 4-5 days a week.

Pavel Srnicek collapsed on December 20th and lost his life on December 29th. Pavel was on a life support machine over the Christmas period which as any father will know when you have two young kids, it's a very hectic time. I was trying to give them a special Christmas but because I was Pavel Srnicek's representative as well as his friend it was my duty to keep people informed. Many people who wanted information naturally came to Pavel's agent. At that time, I was getting phone calls from every single worldwide news network which for me was really awkward. What I mean is that I'd just done a load of PR work with Pavel for his new book, which was out there now, and now I couldn't bring myself to publicise his book anymore because people would have thought I was being a lowlife trying to make money from a guy on deaths door.

I got permission from his family to put together a statement for the press because they couldn't speak English but at the same time I was in bits over Pavel myself because we were great friends. I became the link to the press for the family which was a massive relief for them. It wasn't only the press I was dealing with on a day to day basis, I started getting messages from all the Newcastle players, ex-players and management. Alan Shearer, Shay Given, Tino Asprilla, Paul Bracewell, Terry McDermott, John Beresford, Steve Howey, Gavin Peacock, Lee Clark, Liam O'Brian, Kevin Scott, Scott Sellers, Barry Venison, Brian Kilcline, Tommy Wright and Kevin Keegan were all texting me daily for updates on their old teammate which was only natural as the football team were like a family. My days were taken up with trying to reassure all these people whilst also not wanting to give them false hope. As we got past Boxing Day, I was more hopeful that he would survive because every day was a bonus or so I thought, that was until I had a chat with my mam who was a nurse.

My mam was clued up on what was happening because that was her profession and it was only then did I realise the full picture and that he wasn't going to pull through. Mam basically prepared me for what was going to happen. I know Pavel's family certainly weren't prepared for the worst and it was an awful period.

On December 29th I received the dreaded phone call telling me that Pavel had died. I was so upset as a fan and a friend. Not only was he my favourite goalkeeper that had played for Newcastle but he was a really warm lovely person. It had been such a privilege to be his agent. I prepared a statement with the family and with a distraught Dennis and then sent it to the worlds' media. The news broke on the yellow bar on Sky Sports News. Former Newcastle United Goalkeeper Pavel Srnicek Has Died. It sounds daft because I had sent them the email but I could not believe what I was seeing!

Pavel's funeral was in his home country and as his agent I would need to attend. Dennis was liaising with the family and he asked me if any of the Newcastle United players would attend so I had a ring around. Steve Harper and Steve Howey were both available and wanted to come. Natalie Hubbard who works for me and had been a good friend to Pav wanted to come too which was a brave decision as she hated flying. There were seven of us in total that travelled to see Pavel laid to rest. Making up the seven were Lorenzo, Dennis and Tom Sweeney. The press dubbed us the Srnicek Seven and had asked us to send back photos and a diary of events so that they could run stories in the local press.

Pavel's hometown was a very dark and bleak place but the welcome we all received in his village was outstanding. When we were over in the Czech Republic, we saw the spot where Pavel had fallen and there were candles lit and flowers put down which was a really sobering sight. It was only then that it really hit home how unfortunate the events of his collapse had been because somebody pointed out where his house, his mams house and the hospital all were. They were all a stone's throw away, so then my mind went into overdrive and I started thinking of conspiracy theories because I just couldn't understand for the life of me how nobody had seen him for twenty long minutes in the daylight. We went into Pavel's mothers house and all his family were there and they had a video on of Pavel's career playing with Czech music on, it was an incredibly emotional time. Everybody was drinking the local drink, which is called Slivovitz, I think it's some kind of fruit brandy and it was absolutely awful. Me, Steve Howey and Harps were knocking it back but trying not to taste it. There was a lot of tears that day that's for sure. There was a lot of talk through broken English, broken Czech, broken Geordie and drunken Geordie and all of Pavel's old Newcastle United tops came out.

After his mam's house we were all taken around to Pavel's home and it was exactly as he'd left it. Pav lived there on his own. You could see the plates he'd left on the side from the meal that he'd had. It was weird to walk into someone's house who had just nipped out for a jog expecting to come home but never did. The heating was still on timer, you could picture him coming home after a day's work and putting the telly on. It was as if I was going around a museum of Pavel Srnicek it was so bizarre.

There was easily a thousand people plus at Pavel's send off. Some of that number were the famous Czech Republic players such as Pavel Nedved, Ludek Mikosko, Karel Poborsky and some of the Czech F.A. Pav's funeral lasted three hours and when we came out the media were waiting. The Srnicek Seven all wore Pav's football tops as did his brother as Pavel was lowered into the grave not far from his home. The wake was more like a wedding reception in a small hotel and we all had a good singsong and again we were all made very welcome. Its somewhere that I will go back to at some point to pay my respects, I've just got to. I think us seven owed it to the Newcastle fans to represent them in saying goodbye to an adopted Geordie. Pav was one of us.

When I got back to Newcastle the first thing I did was get in touch with the lads such as Alan Shearer, Shay Given, Rob Lee etc to say that we needed to do some kind of memorial for Pavel. Everyone agreed it was a fantastic idea so that's what we did. The next thing I did was to go see my mate Glyn at St Andrews Church to put the idea of a memorial service to him and tell him it was a chance for the fans to show their respects and share their grief. At the time there was still a shrine outside St James Park with flags and scarfs from all the supporters. A few weeks later it was all arranged in the church which was only a stone's throw away from St James Park. I asked Steve Harper to do a speech, I also said a few words as did Glyn. It was only around that time that I went through all my old texts and realised just how many players I was updating on Pavel's condition over the Christmas period, I counted thirty-eight! When we organised the memorial at the church of course all those thirty-eight were there to say goodbye to Pavel. The only person who couldn't make it from Newcastle was Kevin Keegan because he was away.

The church was full to capacity with over 600 inside and there were at least another six hundred mourners outside of the church too. I have to say, although at that time I was at loggerheads with the club, the club was well represented. Steve McClaren was the manager and he was there as was Lee Charnley the chief executive with other representatives from the club. Everybody knows that I had my issues with the club but at that time I couldn't speak more highly of them. We flew over Pavel's family and sorted out where they were going to stay. The club then paid tribute to Pavel when we played Manchester United at home and the club gave me and Pavel's family a VIP box for the day. Pavel's brother Milan Srnicek was asked to go onto the pitch to thank the fans on his brother's behalf. Milan told the papers afterwards that only now did he understand why his brother loved Newcastle so much and it was another highly emotional day.

35

The Football Agent Game

Being a football agent was something I wouldn't have even thought of becoming if it wasn't for Pavel Srnicek. If I'm honest with you the only reason I carried on with it in 2016 was because I had promised I would make a go of it to Pavel. After the funeral Dennis had encouraged me too saying that I would do well, and it would only take a couple of players to get me on the map. Back in the day to be a proper football agent like someone such as Eric Hall you had to have various qualifications and pass certain exams, it just so happened that when I was looking into becoming a Football agent in 2016 it had become a lot easier. The F.A. had changed things so all you had to do then was pay a fee of £500 to register as a football agent and that was it! You didn't need exams what you needed was contacts which is what I had in my favour. There weren't many at the time that had a better contact list than me that's for sure so I thought I would be made for the job, but how wrong I was. As soon as I was registered and I had my foot in the door with the F.A. I text every single person that I knew in football i.e. Alan Shearer, Lee Clark, Steve Harper etc... Even people in the lower leagues of football to get the word out on the grapevine that I was now a registered football agent. I received a lot of feedback, some saying I was mad, wishing me good luck or just saying they would put the word around. I've got to be honest, I felt right out of my depth right at the start. I needed to find some players so I needed to start going out and watching more games. I was aware that my portfolio wouldn't look as appealing as all the other agents out there that had been in the business for years. My one saving grace was that I was an expert when it came to social media, sites like LinkedIn became my hunting ground for business. The first bite of my rod was a player called Scott Fenwick from Gateshead. I knew Scott when he was at Dunston because I had been on the committee. Scott had done well at Hartlepool and ended up at York and he contacted me. He told me he'd seen my posts and that he was actually looking for representation as he was at York City and was looking for a move. I told Scott to come over to mine and that we'd discuss it over a cup of coffee. After several discussions Scott told me he'd be more than happy to be the first player on my books so I should get a contract drawn up. As I'm getting the essential paperwork set up for Scott, I receive another message from a young player named Luke Lloyd who was only 17 years old and who played at Carlisle United on a 2-year apprenticeship and he wanted to know if I would be interested in working for him? Straight away I thought, 'great I'm on a run here.' I told Luke yes, I would but as he was only 17, I'd need to check it over with his parents and they'd have to accompany him to our meeting and he agreed. I set up the meeting in bar Revolution downstairs from my office.

The meeting went well and I chatted with Luke's mam and dad who were really nice people. Luke was a quiet kid and extremely pleasant. At that meeting I was shown some recordings of Luke playing and he certainly knew where the back of the net was as he was a striker like Scott Fenwick which was great for me because everybody needs goal scorers. Often half the way through the season when teams lose their centre-forwards through injury there's usually a rush at clubs for goal scorers.

I got contracts drawn up for them both from a solicitor I know. I signed Luke first back in Revolution and got the photograph as you do smiling and shaking hands. I met Scott the following day and did the same. Scott told me he liked the sun and had thought about playing abroad so I rang my mate in Gibraltar and tried to get an angle on it but nothing came off. It was only then I got another call from abroad and the deal was done. I was up and running and hoped the New Year would bring me a few more onto my books. Everything was going great and in early 2017 I received an email which looked quite official. When I opened the PDF up, I realised it was from the F.A. and it was a charge. I was thinking 'what the hell' I didn't understand because as far as I was concerned, I hadn't done anything wrong. It turns out I was being charged with signing a minor which was alarming because that word "Minor" made me feel like some kind of Jimmy Savile! When I looked over the email the penny dropped, what I'd done wrong was when I joined the F.A. I hadn't ticked a box which allowed me to sign minors. What I should have done was tick it and that would have meant I had to pay £60 more on top of the £500 fee for joining, because I hadn't ticked that box and I signed 17-year-old Luke Lloyd I'd broken the rules unbeknown to me. When I've tweeted the picture of me and Luke signing with me, somebody who had it in for me had reported me. It turned out that I didn't actually know the guy who had reported me but he clearly did not like competition. He had reported me and a high-profile agent for the same offence and then gloated about it on Facebook which was drawn to my attention.

It wasn't just me and the other local agent on charges that year, another one hundred and twenty-three agents in Britain were also facing charges for the same thing so it just goes to show it was an easy mistake to make. I was then summoned to go down to London to answer these charges. I didn't know what to do. This really wasn't my world and I had no idea how I was going to get out of this. In the end and after asking around I was given this number and it was the guy in The F.A. who was dealing with the case. It turns out this guy was an ex-police officer and he'd literally just started in this job. I found out that some of the one hundred and twenty-three were panicking bigtime because it was their main livelihood, luckily it wasn't mine. I had only got into this football agent lark because of Pavel and treat it more as a hobby than anything else. I know some of the other agents had been charged with six or seven charges regarding players all under the age of 18 and they'd be facing major consequences if found guilty. The worst thing about it all was this was never going to be solved quickly because The Football Association don't do things quickly. Everything with them is a long drawn out process.

If this whole thing wasn't bad enough, I then received a second email saying thanks for responding Mr Wraith but please pay attention to this other PDF because it's another charge. It was from the ex-police officer dealing with the case so he could have told me all about this second email on the phone. When I read the second email it spelt out that now the F.A. are looking into a second accusation against me because I was on the committee of Dunston FC at the same time I was an agent so I was like, 'what the hell?' It was only then that I'd realised I'd broken another rule so I was in quicksand as now I was potentially facing two F.A. charges. Even though Luke's parents stepped up in my defence saying that I hadn't done anything wrong and that Luke was now 18, I don't think it made a bit of difference.

They only saw me as breaking the rules to them and the fact that I was green as grass who'd not profited and even been out of pocket wasn't going to make a blind bit of difference. It felt like I was facing the firing squad at dawn, it wasn't my world. I didn't have anybody to turn to because it wasn't my industry and often, I would look to the sky and say, 'God Pavel you got me into this mess where are you when I need you'? Thankfully Malcolm James the chairman at Dunston was great when I explained it to him. He said if I needed to resign then they understood. When I went back to the F.A. I told them that, although I knew a lot of villains, I wasn't one of them. I just said "You can't have expected me to read the full F.A. 100-page booklet and recite point A of question 27" etc... I told The F.A. I'd walked away from Dunston FC and that I was just a football agent so they let that one slide when Dunston contacted The F.A. and explained Steve Wraith was no longer part of the club. Mal explained it was an oversight on their part by keeping my name on their website and the F.A. accepted it thankfully. Unfortunately, the first one with that awful word "Minor" was going to stick. I mentioned the name Jimmy Savile earlier and for five months that's what I felt like with that F.A. charge hanging over my head. I was worried that the next thing in this was going to be a newspaper headline of, 'Steve Wraith and Minor Affair' just for good measure! I remember being on holiday around the end of it at Centre Parcs, it was taking its toll and I was beginning to fret. I was more annoyed with myself for allowing myself to get in that situation in the first place. I contacted Mr ex Policeman from The F.A. and explained that it was starting to affect my mental health and that I couldn't sleep for thinking about it. I was beginning to become depressed and I asked if he could give me any guidance or light to when this was going to end? I told him the facts that I hadn't made £1 from the agent business and the only transfer I'd made I'd done it for free. He couldn't say anything to me because he had them bloody rules but he did tell me not to worry too much because my punishment wouldn't be too severe. He told me that because I pleaded guilty, I would have to stand in front of The F.A. at Wembley, but I didn't go. I couldn't bring myself to face the music and it was dealt with in my absence. I sent a letter in the post saying that I was guilty of negligence for failing to read it and being green. The outcome of it was a £500 fine for being an idiot. Today in 2020 it's still a sore one because I was fined through my own sheer stupidity. When it was all over it was such a big relief because I thought I was going to end up on Sky Sports

News being linked to some bloody "Minor" affair. I'd also heard of football agents being fined £20,000 so I'd started thinking I was at least going to be fined £10,000. At the end of it all I just remember looking to the sky and saying, "Right Pavel I gave it a bloody good go but never again".

After my brief flirtation with the football agent game I returned to Dunston UTS FC as part of the committee. It is a great little club and currently plays in the Northern Premier League.

If I'm honest over the last few years I have had happier days following them home and away than following Newcastle. I have seen them win the Northern League title, a couple of cups and been involved in the wonderful FA Cup run which saw us beat Chester City and took us onto the national stage with a televised game against Gateshead which saw a record breaking crowd of 2000 cram into our ground. I even got my hands on the FA Cup which they brought to the ground as part of a promotional tour. I have made some good friends at the club such as John Alexander, Tony Cleugh, Billy Irwin, Terry Armstrong and Gary and Danielle Watson. If you get a chance to go to a game one weekend at the UTS Stadium you won't regret it.

36

Rafa, Rafael....

I was sitting at home one day when I got a message on LinkedIn of all places from a guy with a short message which said, "Hello Steve I work for Rafa Benitez maybe we should grab a coffee sometime." Straight away I thought it was a wind up! As I was looking through the guy's profile there wasn't a great deal of information so I just thought wind up, yeah definitely a wind up. I did respond though with my number. He sent his, so I rang him. He sounded a canny fella so I arranged to meet him in town in Blakes on Grey Street. When the time came to meet this contact, I walked in Blakes and as I did, I saw this guy sitting there with a journalist I knew well. When I sat down with him, he told me that him and Rafa had heard a lot about me and that I came highly recommended. The agent then then said I was the man who they'd need to be speaking to when in Newcastle. He went on to say that Rafa was taking the job but he didn't know how long for. He said they may be here for only five months but it also could be five years so it would be nice to be in touch. The agent then said that if there was anything that him and Rafa could do for me then not to hesitate to ask. He went on to say that he viewed me as a means to build a healthy relationship with the supporters and if I could do that it would be beneficial both ways. I'm not sure if there's someone out there putting me in touch with these links from behind a bush in Liverpool, first Dalglish now Benitez. If you are reading this, I'd like to buy you a pint!

When Rafa's Newcastle managerial career started his team invited me into the director's box for the last game of his first season. I took my dad John and my brother Rob.

That day we beat Spurs 5-1 and we're all cheering like we'd just won the league even though we'd just been sent down. Typical Newcastle! We were invited down to meet Rafa in his office after the game. We had to walk through the empty stadium and down the tunnel to get there.

Rafa's office was just along from the teams changing room. Sky Sports News was on the TV screen and a hot buffet was laid out. "Whatever you do don't touch the wedges or Diet Coke but help yourself to anything else", was what we were told. At least we knew what Rafa's after match meal was! When Rafa came in he shook our hands and made us feel at ease. He talked football from start to finish. He just wanted to know our opinions of things and that blew me my Dad and Rob away. I mean here you've got a Champions League winner asking Steve Wraith from the Sunday League his opinions on football. We knew we were sitting in the presence of greatness and that our club was in very safe hands.

I kept in touch with Rafa's team over the summer and they were kind enough to invite me each home game. Sometimes, I would take my friends and family, other times I would take former players such as Supermac. I got to meet some incredible people too such as Rafa's family including his wife and brother, and some of Rafa's worldwide connections in football from clubs such as Real Madrid and Barcelona. If any of them stayed I would make sure they were looked after at hotels and restaurants and got some on guest lists at clubs if they fancied a later night. In Rafa's second season not only did we get promoted at the first attempt but we actually won the Championship on the last day of the season and It was great to be invited down to Rafa's office to celebrate with him and his backroom staff. I had a photo taken with Rafa and the trophy that night too which was very special.

When Rafa first arrived at the club he called Newcastle United 'a project.' He was talking about the long term, but it soon became apparent to him after signing a new contract that Ashley was seemingly not a man of his word. He constantly moved the financial goalposts making it impossible for Rafa to fulfil his ambitions at the club. The arrival of Amanda Staveley at the club for a match against Liverpool in 2017 looked like the only chance we had of Rafa staying beyond his contract. She had helped facilitate the takeover at Manchester City and was now hoping to do the same at our club. I was told about her interest and was told that she would be joining us for a match but did not know which game.

I was doing my usual pre-match talk with Supermac at The Dog & Parrot in Newcastle when one of my friends text me saying, have you seen the press? I went online and the headlines were, 'Amanda Staveley arrives in Newcastle!' I'm glad I was forewarned because when I turned up at the match with my dad and my brother Rob, Amanda was there with her husband. We were introduced and I sat between them for lunch. We talked about the club, the city, the history of both, and discussed how people felt about the current owner. We chatted on and off for an hour and then headed out into the directors' box. With the world's press set to focus on her I opted to sit away from her. The last thing I needed was Twitter going into meltdown and being asked 101 questions later that evening. This didn't stop a really sneaky photographer taking a photo of me next to Amanda.

The game against Liverpool was an entertaining one finishing 1-1. The atmosphere was electric with 'Wor Flags' doing another great display and Amanda and her husband Mehrdad loved every minute of it. After the game Amanda went to introduce herself to Lee Charnley to set the wheels in motion for a takeover.

When the time came for me to leave the ground I received a tweet from Mark Douglas the chief reporter for The Evening Chronicle and it read, "Steve Wraith's going to hate me for this tonight", then he posted the picture of me sitting in the vicinity of Amanda and her husband. He put on question marks and "What does Steve Wraith know about the takeover???" I switched my phone off and went for a few drinks with my mates before heading home.

The first takeover attempt came to nothing sadly, despite a lot of hard work and effort on Amanda Staveley's side and she was accused of being a time waster by Ashley in the media.

With no takeover in sight and Rafa's contract into its last year I knew we would be saying goodbye to Rafa sooner rather than later and so it proved. After keeping us in the Premier League his contract ran out and he was gone as quickly as he had arrived. Enter Steve Bruce.......

37

I get Knocked Down...
but I get up again

I gave this chapter a funny title but really it is no laughing matter. I have suffered some traumatic experiences in my 48 years. I was involved in an 80mph car crash in 1992 where the car flipped three times and landed on its roof on the other side of the central reservation. I walked away from the wreck with a tear in the shoulder of my suit jacket. Then there was the post office robbery in 1995 that I have mentioned. The third and most traumatic event was in 2006. I was thirty-four and to this day I still have no idea what it was all about. I'd been with around a dozen of the lads from my football team on a stag-do in Liverpool for three days. When we got back to Newcastle me and the lads went to the Hollyhill Social Club in Felling.

They used to sell LCL Pils in there for 66p a bottle which was like rocket fuel so we were all tanked up from this boozed-up weekend. None of the lads had any bother in Merseyside in the three days we were there but as soon as we got back home things took a turn for the worst.

When I came out of the club at around 11pm there was me, Ian Brown, Steven Spence and a couple of young kids, one being Danny Rowley. These youngsters were proper 'young uns' who'd only just turned eighteen and it was their first stag-do. As I was walking up towards my home with my group of lads I noticed two lads coming down the other way, now I'm not sure if something was said but all of a sudden, I heard a load of shouting and bawling which was coming from these two guys, I had no idea who they even were. Steven Spence then turns and says to us, "Ere listen lads I was gonna go for a pizza but after listening to all that I'm off" and off he went and Ian Brown did the same. This left me on my own with the two 'young uns' but the shouting is getting louder although incoherent. It was then I could make out, "You fucking bald cunt" and that's when I got the SP. By now these two eighteen-year olds were shitting themselves so I told the pair to get away quickly and I'm going to go up this street as I live around the corner. "Are you sure you'll be alright?" they both asked but to be truthful I wanted them out of the way, I wasn't thinking about me. I told the young lads to beat it sharpish but the best thing to do was split up so off they went and I was left to face the music. I then turned into Tarlton Crescent which was connected to my street when all of a sudden, I think, do I stop or do I run now I'm out of sight? I thought now the 'young uns' were out of sight I'm alright, that was until I could hear these lumbering heavy footsteps.

Now bearing in mind I'm pissed and I'd been out for three days solid and I'm no good to anybody I started to up my pace. I'm nearly home, safe and dry surely now so I thought well that was a close call but I'm about home. As I got to my street it was like an ice rink because the weather was awful with blizzards but I think again that I'm safe because I can't hear anybody behind me. Then in a split second and where they came from, I don't know but I felt a pull on my bag, then a clump on my head. By now I'm slipping all over like Bambi on ice but I manage to get across to the other side of the street and away from my assailants. As I was on the other side I hid behind a parked car and I thought I couldn't be seen, that was until one of them shouted, "THERE HE IS THERE I CAN SEE HIS FUCKING BAG"! I then ran to the bottom of my street into one of the houses back garden and I see their lights on and I bang on the back door but no answer. I continue to bang like you see in them horror movies but all off a sudden I get another bang to the back of the head which sent me down like a ton of bricks. The deer had been caught by the lions. What happened next was that I had two sets of feet reigning down on me. All I could do at that point was to curl up into a ball and take what was coming and in the end, I just pretended I was dead and that's all I could have done because there was two of them and I was steaming drunk. It had been impossible for me to fight back. When I got up my bag was gone. One of the things I remember when I was taking these blows was hearing one of my attackers saying, "He's fucking done, leave him". I laid there for maybe a couple of minutes aching and grunting when I got up, only again I heard footsteps and it's one of them bastards. One of them had come back to try and pull my wedding ring off but he never got it. I managed to hide my phone as well so he didn't get that. I then laid there for around ten minutes before I got up and staggered up the street. When I knocked on my door and Dawn saw me, she screamed.

I didn't know it yet but at that time I looked like The Elephant Man John Merrick. I had blood coming out of my ears, nose and mouth. I was covered in blood, bruises and dirt from head to toe. Dawn was completely hysterical because she was expecting our first child Rebecca at the time. She got me in the house and tried to clean me up the best she could in the shower. My mam came around frantic because she was a nurse and I was taken to The Queen Elizabeth Hospital. It wasn't until I saw my reflection in the mirror that I even realised how much of a hammering I'd taken.

In the hospital it was hard because I was praying to God I hadn't any lasting brain damage. I consider myself so bloody lucky that thankfully I got the all clear which is remarkable considering the number of heavy blows to my head. Twenty-four was the estimate. In the end, apart from the beating I'd received the only thing I lost was a bag of clothes which could be replaced. The next day all the lads in the football team were gutted because of what had happened. With Felling being such a small place there was certain people who knew who'd done this cowardly needless act. It didn't take me long to find out who the two people were behind the attack on me.

The first thing I did was go to The Bay Horse pub near the Atlantis gym with all my pals. Now I had no idea what these two big men looked like but when I went into the pub, I know that the two where in. I wonder what they thought when they saw me sitting there with all my pals as if nothing had ever happened! The police were obviously involved, the hospital had rung them because it was a very serious assault. I even had to go on an I.D. parade to pick them out but I never picked them out. What I will say is the type of lives those two people lived it was always going to come back on them and it did. It's because of this that I really believe in karma because the people responsible for attacking me that night did upset others around six months after that. Retribution was then carried out swiftly and these people were left in a severe state shall we say. I dare say they'd even think twice about doing that kind of thing to another person again. I know you readers might be thinking I had something to do with their downfalls but I can honestly say that wasn't the case. Both were dealing drugs around the Felling area and they tried to rip another party off to the tune of two grand. Those two people were dealt a serious lesson in life from the heavens above shall we say. I heard that they were bundled into cars and nature took its cause. What goes around comes around my friends.

38

Mental Health

Today in 2020 I feel like I've achieved everything I've wanted to on this earth. The only thing I've got to do is walk my daughters down the aisle at a wedding or civil ceremony and perhaps have a grandchild or two. Those are the last two tick boxes in Steve Wraith's life to complete. As long as me and my family are fit and healthy in body and mind then anything else is a bonus. Many years ago, I set off on my goal to become an actor and I've done that but along the way I've achieved so much more. Today at forty-eight I'd like to think there's life in the old dog yet. I'd also like to think that there's more chapters and exciting times to be revealed along the way. I don't think anybody can be truly happy because we've all got things which will upset us, set us back or make us sad. It's how we deal with those things when they arrive. You have to know yourself truly and I personally didn't think I knew who I was until I got into my late twenties. Up until then I was still finding myself and that's because I've been a late developer like I was in school. Being late at things isn't always a bad thing because it's given me time to learn from others first. Anybody who gets up on a morning and thinks they know everything is a fool.

The one thing about me is I'll always listen to criticism as much as pleasantries if that makes sense because you can learn from both in equal measures. I truly believe that I have always been a nice person. With me being in the media spotlight I'm quite self-critical. A lot of people may look at me and think I've always been a picture of solidity but what people don't know is Steve Wraith has his moments when he's not like that. I would say the signs are there for everyone and we can all have some form of mental breakdown. I'm an emotional person and I cry quite a bit and I don't think that's a bad thing. It helps relieve stress. I am the same as everybody else. If I'm left alone with my own thoughts then I can get into that mode of becoming depressed, luckily, I have trusted friends who I can talk to and again I think that is so important. They do say it's good to talk.

One thing I did take particularly badly though was the death of Chris Heron from my Sunday football team. Chris used to score 60 to 70 goals every season the guy was really some player. Chris had had some kind of domestic then he ran onto the Metro line and he was killed instantly. He was only 21. My whole team was devastated. That was my biggest test not only as a Sunday league football manager but as a human being. The outpouring of grief was something I hadn't really had to deal with before. I had twenty plus squad members all feeling the same as me. Some didn't want to play football again it had affected them that badly. I had to deal with the media and helped the family through that ordeal. It was a terrible time, but together as a team we got together and rallied around Chris's family. We wore our Felling tops for his funeral and gave him a great send off. Over the next decade we got together and played a remembrance game each year called the Heron Cup. We are getting too old these days to run around but believe me he is never forgotten.

39

Biggest Influences and Heroes in My Life

Although he died when I was 10, I would say the biggest influence on my life was my Grandad George Davison Green. He was everything a Grandad should be and more. He was always laughing and joking and playing tricks. He was into football and liked a pint. He had fought for his country in the second world war, been a headmaster at a school and a referee and linesman in the old first division. He was married, a father to three girls and a Freemason. He crammed a lot into his life and lived life to the full. Fast forward to 2020. I'm married two girls, a Freemason, a school governor and have been involved in football in some shape or form for nearly 30 years. There is no doubt I have followed in the great man's footsteps and I know he is looking down on me with a big smile on his face.

From a boxing point of view, I'd have to say Mike Tyson has always been my hero in that world. I don't believe for one minute that he committed rape despite being convicted. That conviction tarnishes Tyson's reputation with a lot of people. Although I had a spark of interest in boxing it was Mike who gave me the real love for boxing which I still have to this day. Seeing his rise from the back streets of Brooklyn with his mentor Cus D'Amato to becoming the youngest ever world heavyweight champion in such a short space of time was truly remarkable. Tyson in the early days with Teddy Atlas was just a monster, a total machine and anyone who was a boxing fan in that era would get up at stupid o'clock just to watch a thirty-five second fight usually. There's an old saying which goes, never meet your hero's but I went on to work with Mike three times and I enjoyed every moment.

In the football world I've met all the Newcastle legends from 'Super Mac' to 'Wor Jackie' but my ultimate footballing hero is Alan Shearer. Alan is the ultimate ambassador for the North East. He is not only Newcastle United's record goal scorer but he still tops the Premiership goalscoring charts. He had an amazing career and I'm lucky that he's always had faith in me. Alan doesn't do many 'Evening Withs' but he has worked with me on numerous occasions. I was able to give something back to him by organising a charity football game for his charity 'The Alan Shearer Foundation'. Our target was to raise £50,000. I'm happy to say we raised £54,000 and it's something I'm really proud of handing over that cheque to Alan Shearer. That was such a big moment for me. Although Alan's a ridiculously busy guy he's never said no to anything I've ever asked him if it's for charity or just wishing people well. Alan will help anybody out if he can and he's a very genuine guy.

Musical hero has to be Paul Weller. The Jam essentially were the music soundtrack of my youth. They were my first band and I was gutted when they split up. I hated the Style Council but when Paul came back and launched his solo career through the 90s, he got me hooked again. The Stanley Road album is one of the greatest albums of all time. If I was allowed to have a top three then Morrissey would come second to Paul Weller only because I got into Moz late. I never really appreciated him dancing around with flowers in his back pocket until well after he finished with The Smiths and I was in my late twenties. Like with a lot of bands I didn't really appreciate The Smiths until they were gone. My number three would have to be John Lydon aka Johnny Rotten from The Sex Pistols. The Sex Pistols were man-made by Malcom McLaren but were a voice of a generation and I consider myself lucky that I've seen them live three times. When I was in my first year at college, I even dyed my hair green and red and started wearing second-hand clothes from charity shops. I would constantly have 'Never Mind the Bollocks' on my Walkman.

I've never looked up to any villains so I draw the line at calling them heroes. The Krays were a big influence on my life as has been well documented in other books and documentaries. Freddie Foreman has been a good friend and always been there for me to speak to when I've needed advice and he's always given me his honest opinion. Fred knows what kind of person I really am and his word goes a long way when people have been out to cause me trouble. I only hope that I've been able to repay Fred by being there for him in recent years. I've never been in the same industry as Fred but we have so much in common that we've been able to support each other. He chose his path and has lived with the consequences and played by the rules. I respect him for that...

40

What Happens at The Lodge...
Stays at the Lodge!

When I was a teenager, I used to go to Heworth Golf Club with my Dad and Grandad on a Tuesday afternoon to a Rotary Club meeting. Local businessmen would congregate for a lunchtime pint and some food and there would be a guest speaker. We had professional golfers, football referee's and even football managers. I remember Jim Smith who at the time was the Newcastle manager coming in to do a talk. Rotary gave me a good understanding of the charity sector.

I'd never heard about the Freemasons I was completely ignorant as to what it was. The only thing I knew about it was watching an episode of Bergerac and they all wore weird outfits whilst sacrificing sheep. The way it was portrayed on that episode of Bergerac it was all like the illuminati so it wasn't something I was going to ever consider. It wasn't until around 2008 when a fella who I knew called Chris who was a fellow Newcastle fan approached me and said, "Have you ever thought about joining the masons Steve"? I said I hadn't given it any thought. Chris then gave me a leaflet and told me to have a look at it and to give him a shout if I ever fancied it because he would be able to get me in. I've got to be honest this leaflet was on my bedside table for a few weeks and all I could think of was Jim Bergerac so I didn't bother. My mindset was I didn't have the time to join any kind of Charles Manson cult-like fiasco and I just ignored it.

In 2012 I received another message, this time from a man named Neil King. Neil was someone I'd knocked around with in my early teens plus I knew him from when I had the Post Office. Neil just messaged me out of the blue on Facebook (this is where social media is great) which said, "To be one you have to know one". I messaged Neil asking "What on earth does that mean" and he just said, "Aah it's the Freemasons and I'm in em". Again, I was just thinking it was that bloody Jim Bergerac nonsense. Neil then told me he was in the Gateshead Lodge and did I fancy being in, I told him to be honest I don't think it appealed to me but I didn't tell him it was because of an episode of Bergerac. Neil then started really selling it to me and telling me how great it was and I was just straight with him and I asked him what benefits would it give me and do you have to pay to join this mad cult? Again, Neil kept banging on saying just how he knew it would be right up my street and that it was certainly not a cult. I told Neil I'd look into it and go along for one meeting.

At first, I was invited along as a social guest and at the end of that very first meeting everybody got up to have a singsong. Well I'm not going to lie, I was sat there thinking, what the bloody hells this because I was watching a room full of blokes all singing. Once I got over the initial embarrassment of that I figured I was an actor anyway who'd been taught to sing and dance so it wasn't that bad and maybe I could live with it after all. That night, although I found it a little strange, I left with an impression that hadn't put me off going back for some reason. The next stage was to then go for an interview which I passed. From that day in 2012 it's something that I've never regretted. There is a difference between rotary and freemasonry. That difference is you do a ceremony. However, I can't say anything about that ritual. If there's anybody out there that wants to know what that ceremony is you can just simply Google 'ceremonies in freemasonry'. Some of that will make sense and some of it won't make sense but there's nothing strange about it I can assure you.

The average age of a lot of the members in the lodges I visit is 65 to 70 and a lot of our members are dying off. The most worrying thing is I can't see a lot of these young people on street corners joining the masonry in years to come. It is going to take masons my age to recruit and keep the tradition alive. If you're serious about living the masonic life then the one thing you must be is disciplined which I am. In my lodge we meet nine times a year and it's a huge part of my life. Freemasonry has changed me massively for the better and I focus 100% on my responsibilities. It really has become my religion and it's my way of reaching out to God. I certainly believe in a divine spirit and that's a big part of being a Freemason. To be a proper Freemason then you really need to stand tall and be an upstanding member of society and I've definitely changed a lot of my ways to be just that.

41

What Motivates Me?

My number one motivation in life is simple and that's to put food on the table for my family.

I want to be a success in life and in everything that I do. Looking back on my life so far, I guess I have shown that the key to being a success in any field is hard work. For example, I didn't succeed in the acting game when I was younger but I went back to it in my thirties and achieved my goal. On the doors I was polite, professional and didn't take liberties and as a result I found myself head doorman at many of the premises I worked at. I got involved in the event game and worked my way up from small events to running a company and promoting bigger and better events. Two years into school I couldn't read or write properly, now I own a publishing company and have written 17 books, and even in Freemasonry I have worked hard in my first seven years to become Worshipful Master of my Lodge. The message to you the reader is simple. You can be as good as you want to be. If you want to sit on your backside scrolling through Facebook on the settee, smoking weed or playing on computers then you're not going to achieve anything yourself. Don't be blinded by what anyone else is doing, focus on yourself slowly and everything else will fall into place.

I left school with three GCSEs but I didn't let that hamper my progress and I went out there and made my own luck. I'm not saying it's ok to blow your chance at school, but the most important education is being brought up correctly and putting yourself across professionally in anything you do.

Always remember your manners in life they cost you nothing. I was taught all the correct things to do in life by my parents and grand-parents and I've never forgotten them.

These days I know I have to work hard every single day to maintain the level of consistency that I present in my many fields. My plan for the future? I'd like to make it further in the acting world. Having two agents now is only going to help in my quest in getting to the next level. Not only have you got to work hard as an actor but you've got to be realistic and realise what you're up against. I mean I'm up against the Tom Hardy's of this world! In the meantime, I'll keep my several business projects ticking over nicely until I get to that platform. I would say my main focus in life is making sure that my two daughters get through the next decade of school, college and then university and they're set up nicely in life. I've got to be honest, with my girls being so young it does worry me because today it's not a nice world we live in. I've no doubt over the next twenty years there's going to be more bumps in the road connected to my journey but there's also going to be lots of positive things to come too.

I'm still going to keep myself involved in the professional boxing, music events and Newcastle United Legends nights which I am sure will please a lot of you reading this. I'm hoping to have time to write more books in the future too. I'm currently working on 'Operation Sayers' which will be out October 2020 and the final Eric Mason book will also see the light of day in the next year or so. I am also an ambassador for two top clothing brands 'Crossed Paths' which was set up by my friend Emma Louise, and 'Jab Signature' owned by my mate Jon Owen.

My dad once said to me when I was a kid that I'd be very lucky to go through life with five real friends. It something I've never forgotten. In my early teenage years, I knocked around with a lad named Matthew Gregory and I never ever thought me and him would grow apart but we both just moved on and our lives went in different directions. It happens. I had a great period living in Felling and being around my football team which I managed. Those lads are like family to me. I'm still in contact with most of them and I see some on a match day. I would say I've probably got as many female friends as I have males. I often meet up with them for a coffee or lunch to put the world to right. Dave Beaney, Neil Jackson, Sarah Jayne Iceton, Andy Thompson and Danny Coggins are all people who are close to me these days and I value their friendship and opinions.

I have to give a special mention to Albert Sayers who is now in his 70s and just retired from working the barrow on Northumberland Street which he has done most of his life. I've got to know him really well over the last decade. He has been a good consigliere to speak to on any issues I might have had and I will always be grateful for his advice and friendship. The same has to be said of Freddie Foreman in London.

My closest friend in life is Christian Simpson. Christian and I have both been there for each other in good times and bad. We may not see each other for six months but when we do it's like we have just left each other. We all need a friend like that....

42

The Changing Man

Looking back over my life writing this book with Jamie Boyle I have learnt a lot about myself. I have reinvented myself on more than one occasion. I don't think that's a bad thing.

I have learnt from my mistakes and tried to better myself. I've certainly never pretended to be something I'm not. I'm what Paul Weller would call the 'Changing Man'. I've gone full circle from actor, to Sub-postmaster, to doorman, to promoter, to writer and back to actor and it has been one hell of a journey.

The one constant in my life other than my friends and family has been Newcastle United. A faithful friend who is always there who you love and cherish. They give you the biggest high but can also dish out the lowest of lows but you love them unconditionally. In the past it has been like being in love with an abusive partner. They have slapped us in the face season after season yet we have fixed up our makeup and gone back for more.

I don't feel as a Newcastle United fan that we have a divine right to be in the Champions League every season but wouldn't it be nice for us all to see Newcastle United win something at least once in our lifetime? At the time of writing this book it's been over fifty years since Newcastle won a domestic or European trophy. It would be great if before I was laid to rest in my black and white striped coffin, to bloody win something, even the League Cup! Do I think it can be achieved under the current regime? DEFINITELY NOT! So.... when I'm dead and buried on my headstone in the graveyard it will read, 'Here lies Steve Wraith, if

Newcastle ever win something can you please knock hard and let me know'.

My life has been every boy's dream and I wouldn't change anything for the world.....

"Success is not final, failure is not fatal, it is the courage to continue that counts"

Winston Churchill

Also available….

The Sayers:
'Tried and Tested at the Highest Level'

ISBN: 978-1-9114820-5-5

Coming from a huge close-knit family of street traders long before it was legalised, Stephen Sayers spent his early years on the barrows, witnessing constant brushes with the law. Aunties and uncles were frequently incarcerated and a hatred and distrust of authority swelled within the younger members of the family. The scene was set. Standing alongside his brothers and cousins in vicious street fights and feuds with rival gangs, they've been linked to multi-million pound armed robberies, extortion, unsolved gangland murders and protection rackets. Those links made them a formidable force in the criminal underworld. Stephen gives us a first-hand account of growing up as a Sayers and living up to the reputation the name carries. He didn't just carve out a criminal career, he wrote it in blood on the streets. If you've heard the rumours... if you believe them... the Sayers run Newcastle. Check out: *www.thesayers.co.uk*